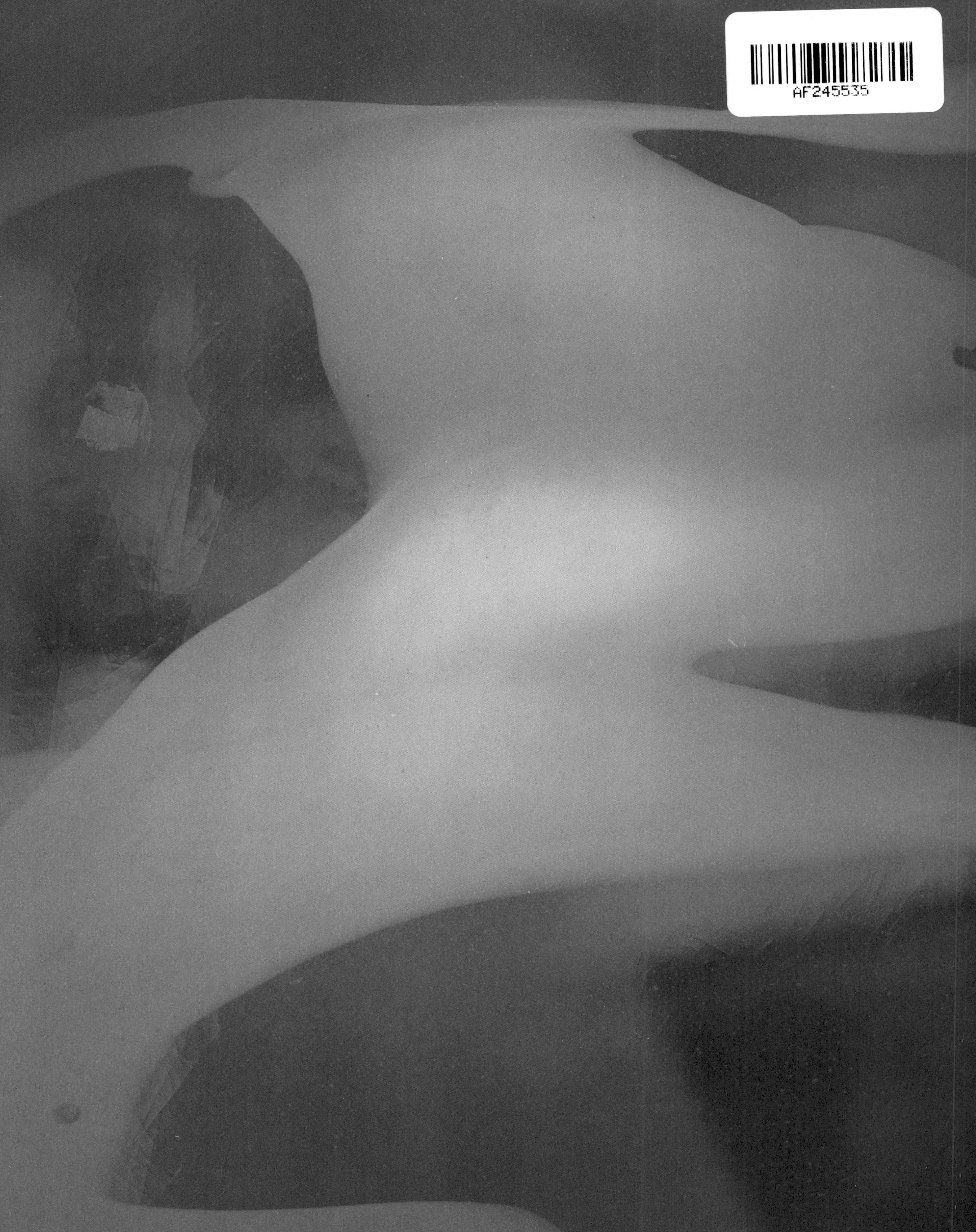

AF245535

BRIAN CLARKE

PROJECTS

TONY SHAFRAZI GALLERY

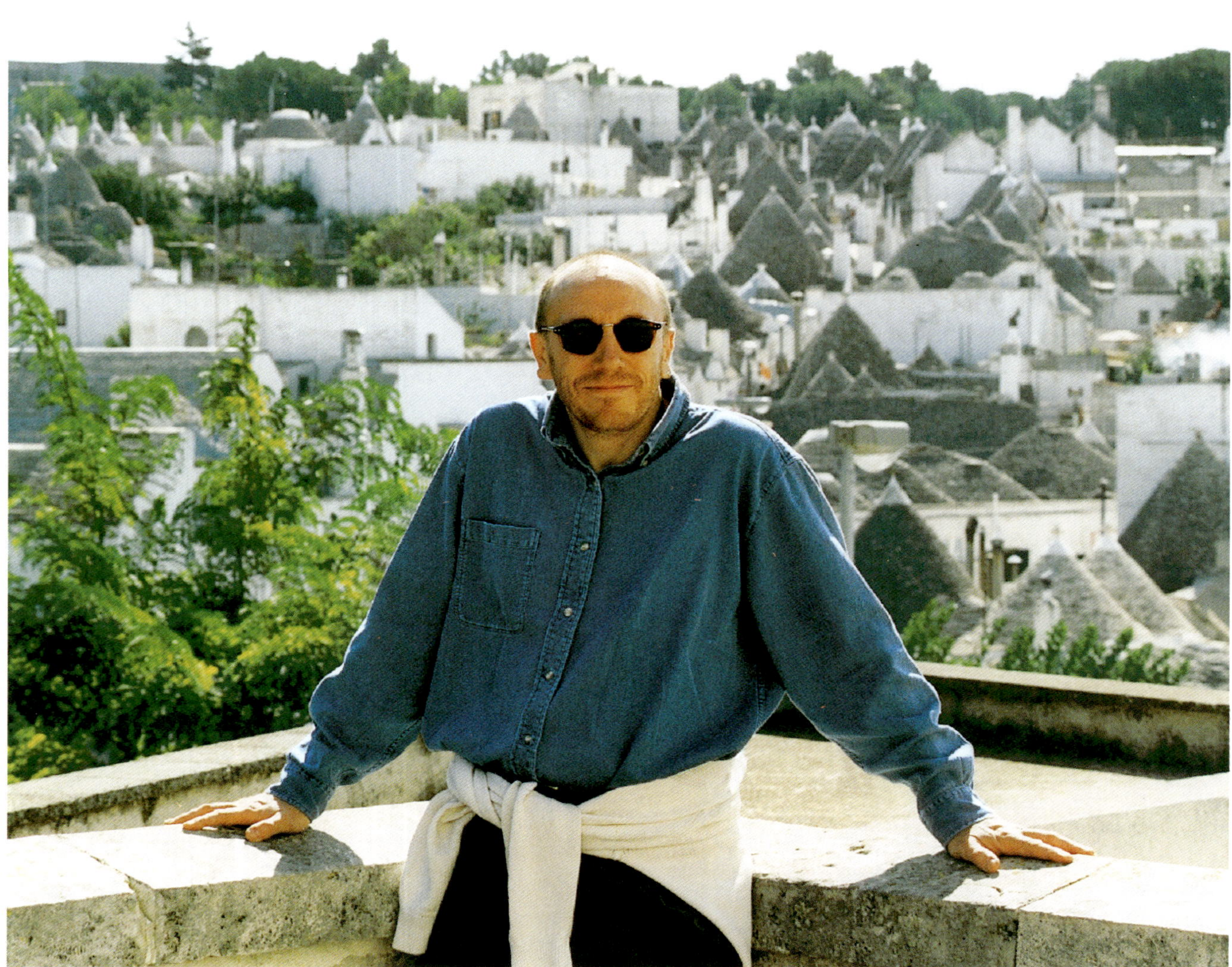

Brian Clarke in Alberobello, Italy, 1997

Rather like the random incidents that recur in Brian Clarke's work, there was an element of chance that led me to his studio in London twenty years ago. I was immediately drawn to his paintings by their combination of vibrant colors, their interplay of order versus randomness, and their rectilinear grids with contrasting free forms. It was a private viewing and I remember a conversation with Clarke about the music of a then progressive German group called Kraftwerk.   He drew analogies between their electronic works and his own compositions in acrylic and canvas. Although I never rationalized it at the time, I must have sensed the architectural qualities of his work and the next day I phoned him to buy one of the paintings; not an easy task because I was very spoilt for choice. The selected canvas still occupies a treasured place at home.

About ten years later, the same painting was loaned out and I remember seeing it, out of its familiar context, in a major show of Brian Clarke's work in Darmstadt.   Looking at it through fresh eyes was to rediscover anew the qualities which I had so intuitively sensed in the years before; an awareness that was heightened by the later works which surrounded it and which explored in more depth the same artistic preconceptions.

Brian Clarke's installation in the Shafrazi Gallery is a similar opportunity to take stock of his progress – to see it through the fresh eyes of today and the wisdom of a degree of hindsight.   It sums up his more recent preoccupations in a single bold gesture — a simple wall which carves across the space of the gallery. This sounds like a minimalist response until one reads the subtle nuances of color, reflection, transparency and motion described by the changing surfaces of the glazed wall.

It is clear that this is the same person pursuing with a remarkable integrity the same dominant themes from the past. This unbroken lineage is reassuring at a time when many artists have changed cultural horses over a similar period. The architectural structure of the paintings has moved out of the canvas and the luminosity of acrylic has been transposed into glass. But not just stained glass in the traditional sense — we see the fusion of art and technology in the manner in which Clarke works with industry to create even more glowing combinations of glass and color — both applied and integrated into the membrane itself. Clarke is a contemporary pioneer in this field, and his direct involvement in the production of this medium is responsible for the molten fluidity that he has achieved.

Over time I can see how the architecturally inspired paintings have given way to experimentation in his preferred medium of stained glass. If Brian Clarke were writing this, I am sure that he would reverse the emphasis and declare that he had always harbored a love of stained glass and architecture. But in reality, it does not matter which comes first. It is Clarke's multifaceted ability to work in such diverse mediums —

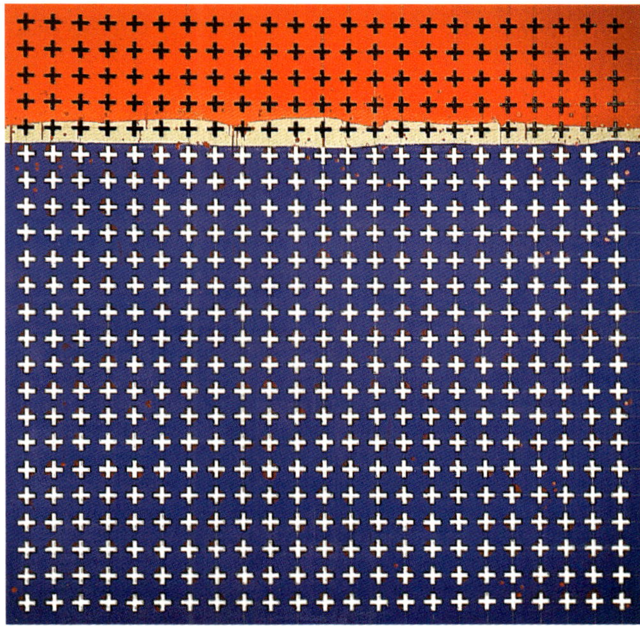

Last Few Moments, 1979, acrylic on canvas, 72"x72"

each feeding the other — that is one of his strengths. I know that he does not draw distinctions between the abstraction of an individual canvas and the contextuality of an architectural intervention.

This is rare, because for most artists and critics there has always been a division between gallery art and art in architecture. In any discussion with Clarke on the subject, it becomes clear that the pictures could not happen without his immersion in architecture, and similarly his work with buildings is dependent on his paintings — the two are totally interactive.

Clarke is one of those very few artists who understands the spatial world of architecture — the core issues of space and light. His path can be a lonely and difficult one to tread in an age of specialization. It is meaningful that he bridges the worlds of artist and teacher as a Professor in the School of Architecture at the Bartlett University College, London.

It is his sympathetic grasp of architecture coupled with an ability to challenge the spiritual dimension that explains why twenty years after our first meeting I find myself writing this introduction. Over this period we have collaborated on different projects where Clarke has demonstrated his ability to bind the architecture of my studio with his conception of space and color through the mediums of glass, textiles or canvas.

During those intervening years, Brian Clarke has demonstrated an ability to range far and wide — not only geographically but also culturally. It is a special talent that can respond with affection and sensitivity to a tiny Alpine Abbey and with bravura to the flamboyant celebration of commerce and art in a Latin American shopping mall. It is also significant that he can lavish as much love on a rug or tiny inlay of mosaic as on those vast ceilings with their urban scale; the artistic equivalent of a jump from the hearth to the boulevard.

Given the range of his achievements, Clarke still retains an adolescent-like spirit of curiosity and spontaneity. The work in the Shafrazi Gallery gives a flavor of those qualities, combined with a sophisticated command of technique. Whether intentional or not, there is a spring-like quality to an exhibition with an opening in June. The fleur-de-lys motif recurs in Clarke's sketchbooks, but here they are also a tribute to the late Linda McCartney, with whom he collaborated, bringing together her love of photography and his of glass.

There is no substitute for the first-hand experience of Clarke's installations, each with its own sense of place. But in the absence of that privilege, this book and the exhibition which provokes it are important records of his wide-ranging interests and the diversity and energy of his artistic responses.

Brian Clarke has spent a lifetime developing an architectural language. Not surprisingly, his most creative interventions have resulted from an early integration in the design process rather than making a later contribution — no matter how heroic the installations. In the transition from the isolation of a studio to the stage of world architecture, Clarke, like the architects themselves, needs the patronage of clients who are concerned with the spiritual as well as the material quality of construction. Given that level of backing and the chance of creating at a larger scale, there is no question that his best works are yet to come. When that happens it will be an enjoyable task to chart their evolution back to this present body of his works.

I was born in the North of England, in Lancashire. My father was a coal miner and my mother a mill worker. By the time I was twelve years old I had forged a romantic relationship with its landscape and an insatiable interest in its architecture. The great brick-built cotton mills with their exotic Egyptian names (reflecting the origins of cotton) were the focus of my youthful architectural fantasy. The small local art gallery with its Lowry paintings, Hockney etchings and Arthur Dooley crucifix were my first introduction to art.   A school day-trip to York Minster introduced me to medieval England and the pulse of history.   The warm, carved stone of the decorated Gothic vaulting, the pools of ruby light from the glass across the dark oak misericords and the Gregorian chant of the boys' choir combined to produce an experience unlike anything I had ever known. It was a glimpse into an alternative reality.

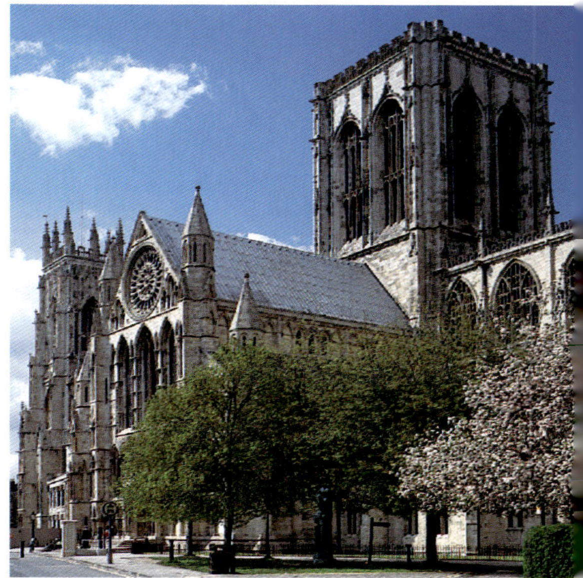
York Minister, England

Engraved clearly on my memory, that day-trip still recalls the first conscious experience I had of the combined power of architecture, art and music to touch the human soul. No artistic experience before or since has left so indelible an impression on my personality. I was nine years old. By the time I was twelve I was a full time art student, the last intake of a nineteenth century system established by Ruskin and his followers to educate the children of the working class in the arts.   Training at Oldham Art School was based on the Arts and Crafts movement and involved calligraphy, perspective and heraldry. By the time I was fourteen I could draw adequately from life and had developed a lifelong love of the crafts and in particular their application to architecture.

The Beatles and Pop Art formed the background to my daily life, changing the world and changing me. At age fifteen, following my Father's work we moved to Burnley, and there at the local art school I discovered, thanks to my drawing teacher Donald Matthews, the radical and transforming nature of art. At this time too I discovered stained glass. I suppose what really thrilled me about it was its application to building and the unique way it is rendered visible by the transmission of light through its substance.

Alfred Waterhouse's Manchester Town Hall (1868) thrilled me with the glory of the "new" Gothic and I began to notice stained glass in civic and ecclesiastical buildings. I don't think that I consciously considered the incorporation of the medium into modern or contemporary architecture until later; at this time I was captivated by the detail and beauty of the material. I began to picture myself in a tradition of artist stained glass designers that boasted amongst its number: William Morris, Burne-Jones, Matisse, Chagall and Léger. Their great achievements in the medium were

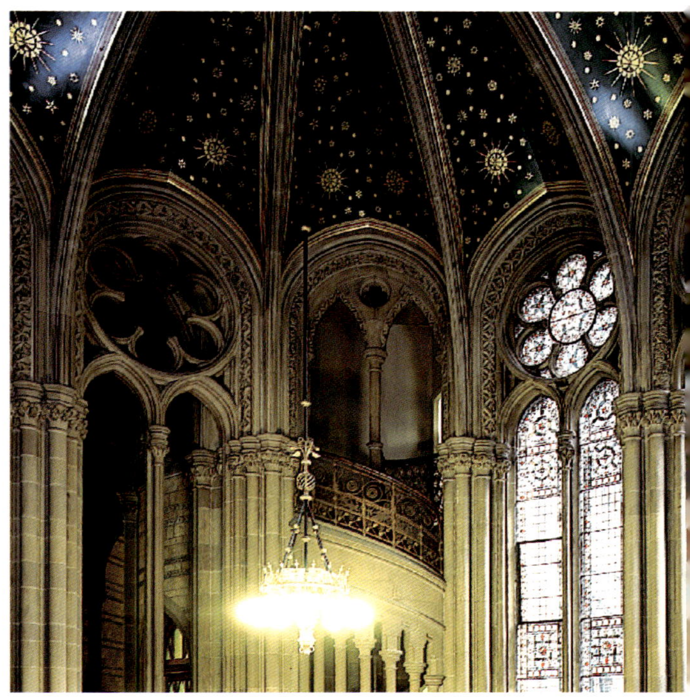
Manchester Town Hall (1868)

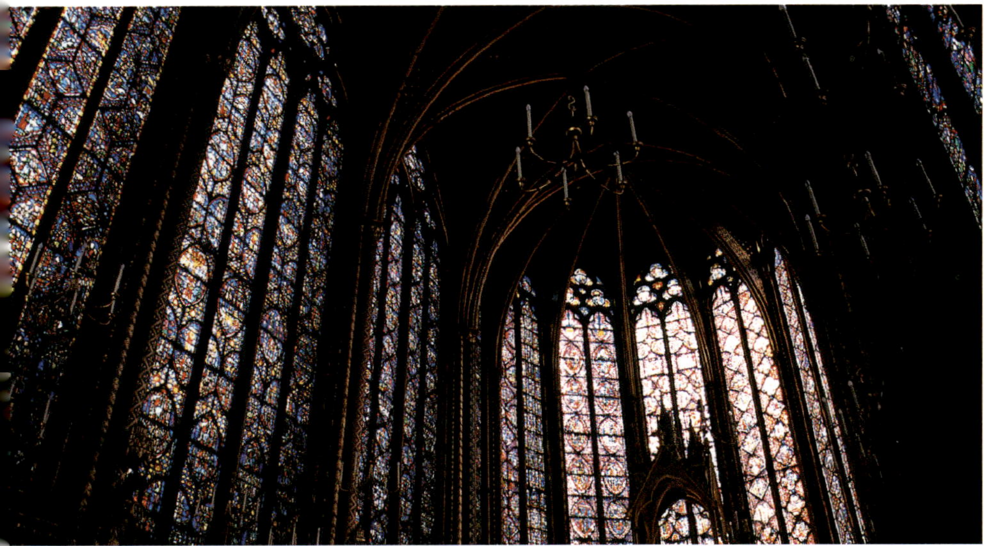

La Sainte Chapelle, Paris, France

all housed in churches and I saw my own future fixed in the same arena. At this time I had no clear idea how I might combine my dual obsessions of painting and architecture, but I was very clear that this combination was going to characterize at least my immediate future. Living near Manchester gave me easy access to great architecture of many periods and to some art (mainly nineteenth century) from the Anglo-Saxon at Whalley and Cartmel to the Gothic at York, from the breathtaking Pugin interiors of Scarisbrick Hall to the proto-modernist Oriel Chambers by Peter Ellis in Liverpool. At sixteen I went to my third art school, in Bideford, Devon. It was there that I was able to learn how stained glass was made. The poetry of W. B. Yeats, the paintings of Millais and the architecture of G. E. Street all helped form my artistic character during this period and by the time I had finished the period in Devon I was completely committed to a vague but passionate belief in the idea of combining art with buildings. It was a year or two later, in 1972, travelling on a Churchill Fellowship that I was able to go to Europe and the USA to study art in architecture. It was during this fellowship that I saw the extraordinary achievements in postwar Germany of artists Thorn-Prikker, Meistermann and Schreiter. Their contributions to architectonic art and in particular to stained glass are probably unparalleled in our time. It was also during this traveling fellowship that I first encountered the Fleurs-de-Lys of La Sainte Chapelle in Paris. La Saint Chapelle remains for me today one of the most sublime examples of the complete marriage of art and architecture. The harmonic integration of stone, glass and frescoes rises in La Sainte Chapelle to the pinnacle of Gothic achievement.

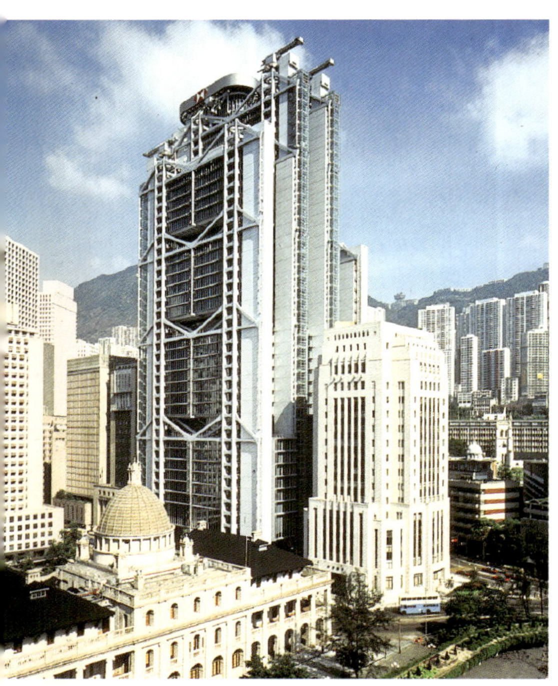

Sir Norman Foster's Hong Kong and Shanghai Bank Headquarters

A succession of commissions in churches followed, giving me an opportunity to develop my language in a variety of buildings and architectural styles. The key projects of this period are Habergham, Longridge, Thornton & Blackburn, but it wasn't until the Olympus European Headquarters Building in Hamburg that I feel I really began to explore the potential of stained glass (in this case combined with paintings) in contemporary architecture. By this time my attention was being dramatically drawn to the group or school of architects coming out of England: Norman Foster, Richard Rogers, James Stirling and Peter Cook. In the late seventies and early eighties the real "action" was in architecture. Radical thinking and the development of new visual languages and forms were coming at this time not from the artists but the architects. The real melting pot of artistic change moved during this period from the studio of the artist (ever more abstruse and dislocated from his communicative role) to the office of the architect. Popular music, too, in the late seventies underwent a profound shock to its system. Punk Rock re-established, for the first time since the sixties, the role of music as a vehicle for cultural change. It was the explosive creative force of Punk Rock that helped me galvanize my own position and use it to attack what I saw as the miserable malaise into which both music and visual art had fallen. Though unlikely bedfellows, the Sex Pistols and Norman Foster were equally responsible for charting my own rather unlikely course.

Though the road to large-scale collaborations in architecture was far from smooth, suffice it to say that from this point on commissions began to come. The first, the great Mosque of Riyadh International Airport, gave me the opportunity to develop the most complex ideas relating to the juxtaposition of opaque, opal and transparent glass. This gigantic project involved the

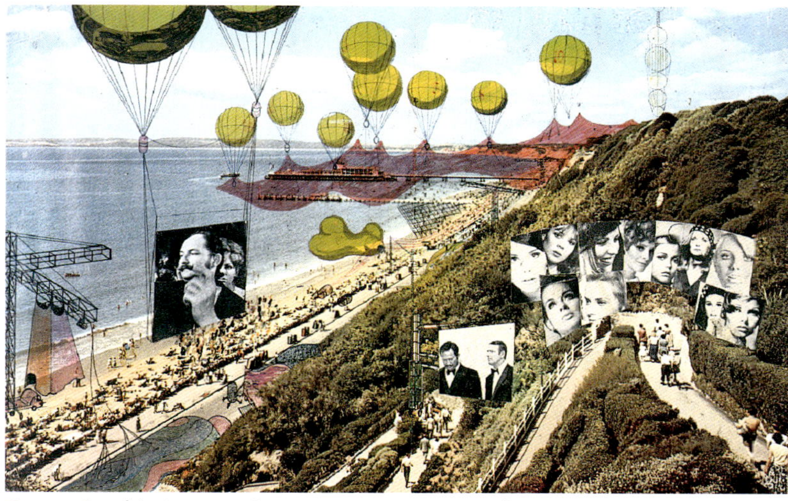

Peter Cook's Instant City Visits Bournemouth

services of four stained glass factories and over 150 craftsmen and really provided a baptism of fire for me into the so-called "large scale project."   A baptism not only of an artistic and architectonic nature but administrative and organizational, of working in close concord with a large team of specialists, consultants and craftsmen. Without these elements functioning efficiently in a big project, everything else will crumble.

After Riyadh and later Hamburg, the two pivotal projects that projected the work onto a different stage altogether were both in association with architect Derek Latham and were the Cavendish Arcade in Buxton and the Victoria Quarter in Leeds. Both these schemes provided opportunities to experiment in the manipulation of interior light on a large scale and the integration on both cases of first class 19th century architecture with my own work. The polychromatic glazed brickwork in the two elevations of Frank Matcham's splendid Edwardian "Victoria Quarter" were particularly difficult and rewarding to work with. The Lake Sagami Country Club with Arata Isozaki, "E.A.M." in Kassel, Germany, with architects Thomas Bieling and Meinhard von Gerkan provided opportunities to develop ideas early enough in the design of the building to avoid the legion of problems usually associated with being called in too late in the design process.

In the last five years my work has taken a very focused direction toward what I like to imagine is ultimately the complete integration of art and building.

I spend more time painting today than at any time in the past and am also designing more stained glass than at any time before. I have no time for anything but work because at present I feel that the two disciplines are coming so close together that I enthusiastically anticipate a new unexpected offspring to be born out of the marriage. Somewhere, mysteriously between art and

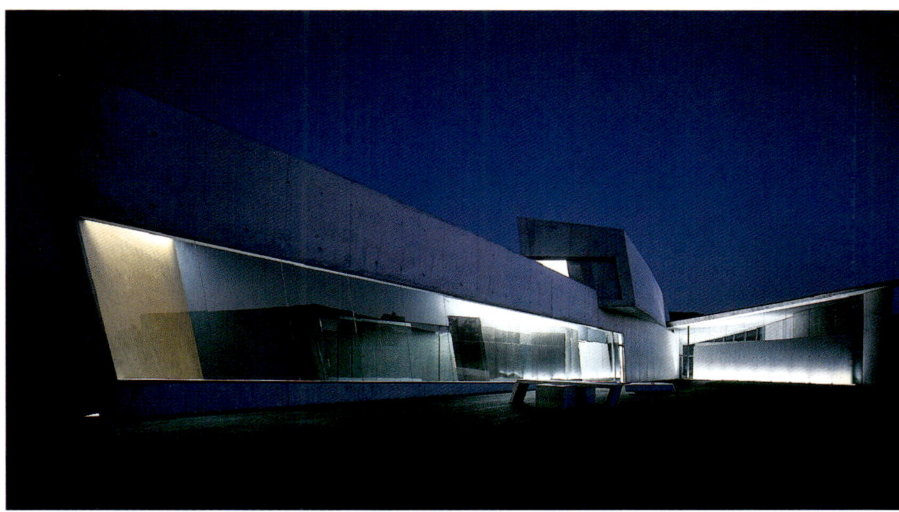

Zaha Hadid's Vitra Design Museum, Weil am Rhein, Germany

architecture lies a reservoir of thrilling and untapped experience. I see it coming to flower for me in the new organic modernism of Future Systems, in the glowing, pulsating spaces of Norman Foster and the courageous flashes of the future glimpsed in the buildings of Zaha Hadid. Wherever it takes me, I know it's an architectural journey and probably not the route any of us — especially me — expect.

Art has, until recent times, been cradled in architecture. The idea of portable autonomous art unrelated to buildings is essentially modern. The historical climax of the bonding of art, craft and architecture (in Western culture) is the Gothic cathedral. Modernism and the secularization of society has now freed art from liturgical bondage and set it upon a course that can radically transform our urban fabric.

There is no time left to waste on rhetoric or exaggeration, on self publicity or artistic hyperbole. Art really does have a pivotal role to play in our increasingly urban lives and I unequivocally see that role bonded optimistically to buildings. Art and architecture belong together, focused on a single goal that renders redundant the notion of "architect and art stars," and celebrate the role of the song not the singer.

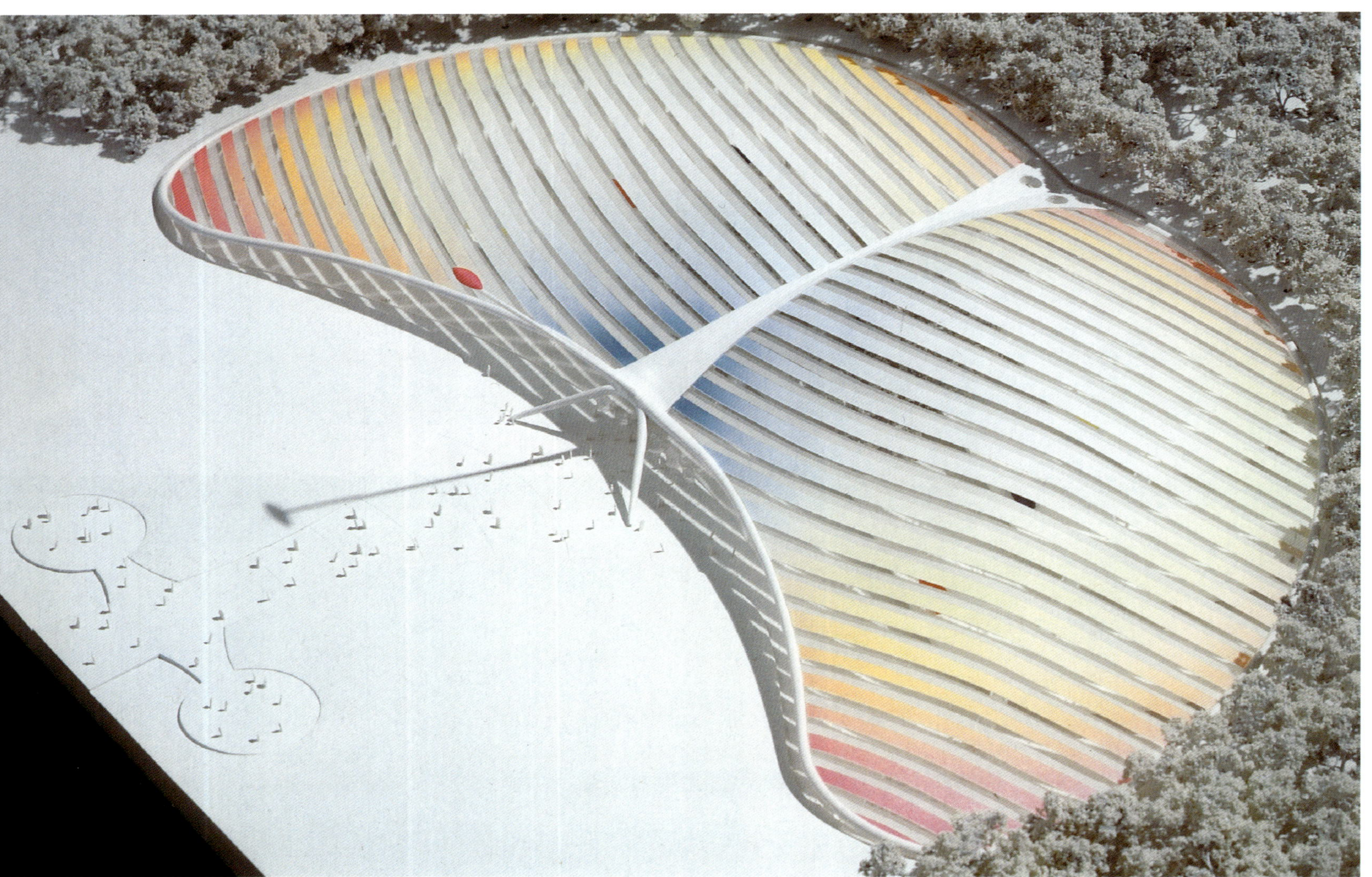

Model showing Future System's Earth Center, Doncaster, England (1994)

Light and its meaning have preoccupied artists throughout time. The substance of glass has often been the vehicle for their studies—as a symbol, a tool, or the embodiment of luminosity. The transformation of sand and ashes into a lustrous material has also positioned glassmaking within the realm of alchemy, while the physical and optical qualities of glass make it ripe for metaphorical allusions and supernatural associations. In the Middle Ages, it was believed that the colored light streaming from stained glass could enhance the spirituality of the humanity it battled. The glass "curtain wall" was first made possible through Gothic engineering of columns and buttresses. Nineteenth-century theoreticians and archi.architects promoted the beauty and functionality of glass as a building material, and it remains the material of choice today.

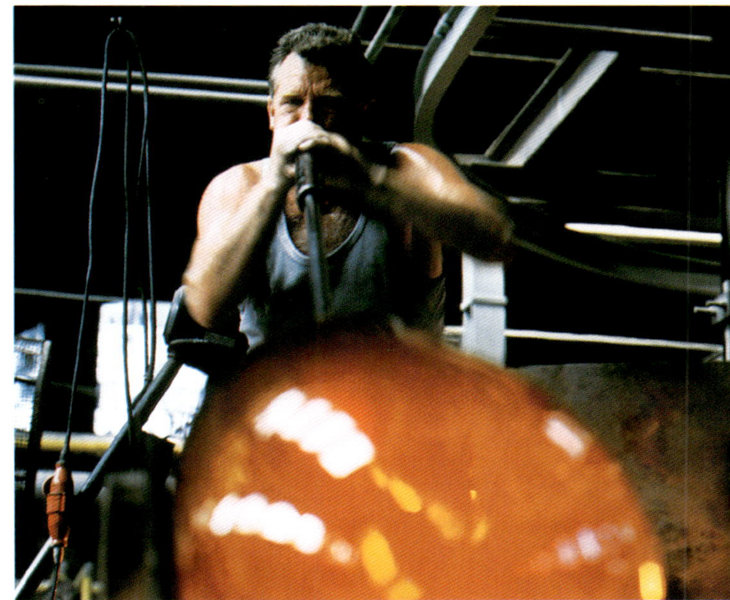

Glass blowing in Germany

As part of the modernization of the medium of stained glass which was initiated at the end of the 19th century, artists in post - World War II Germany and France chose to view glass as a canvas—in the traditional architectural context and, to a lesser degree, as autonomous panels. The structural lines that hold the pieces of glass together and support the massive weight have traditionally been incorporated, to varying degrees, in the composition. The German artists, in particular, increased the prominence of the lines as design elements for abstract and painterly works. Their works were conceived and developed with architects to be integral parts of buildings rather than decorative afterthoughts.

Brian Clarke is one of a handful of individuals who understand the vast potential of stained glass as a medium for the contemporary artist. While his designs are stylistically related to his paintings, Clarke realizes the futility of simply translating a design from one material to the other without considering the unique qualities of each. Glass — any bit of glass — makes a powerful aesthetic statement well before the intervention of the artist. It bends and distorts light, and thus reality. Its hues are abnormaly bright because light is transmitted through rather than solely reflected off, the surface. An artist working with glass must be able to gracefully walk the fine line between exploiting its properties and being overpowered by them. The sensitivity of Brian Clarke to these precariously balanced factors has helped to make stained glass, executed on a grand scale, once again relevant to the urban environment and to contemporary art.

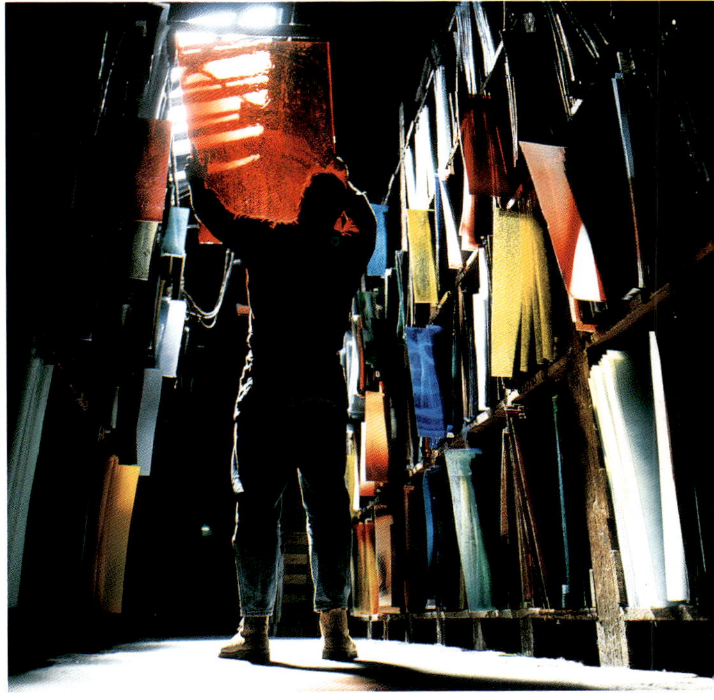

*Mouth blown, hand made sheets of colored glass
in storage at Clarke's German manufacturers*

Susanne K. Frantz
Curator of 20th Century Glass
The Corning Museum of Glass

CENTER NORTESHOPPING
RIO DE JANEIRO, BRAZIL

1995 - 1996

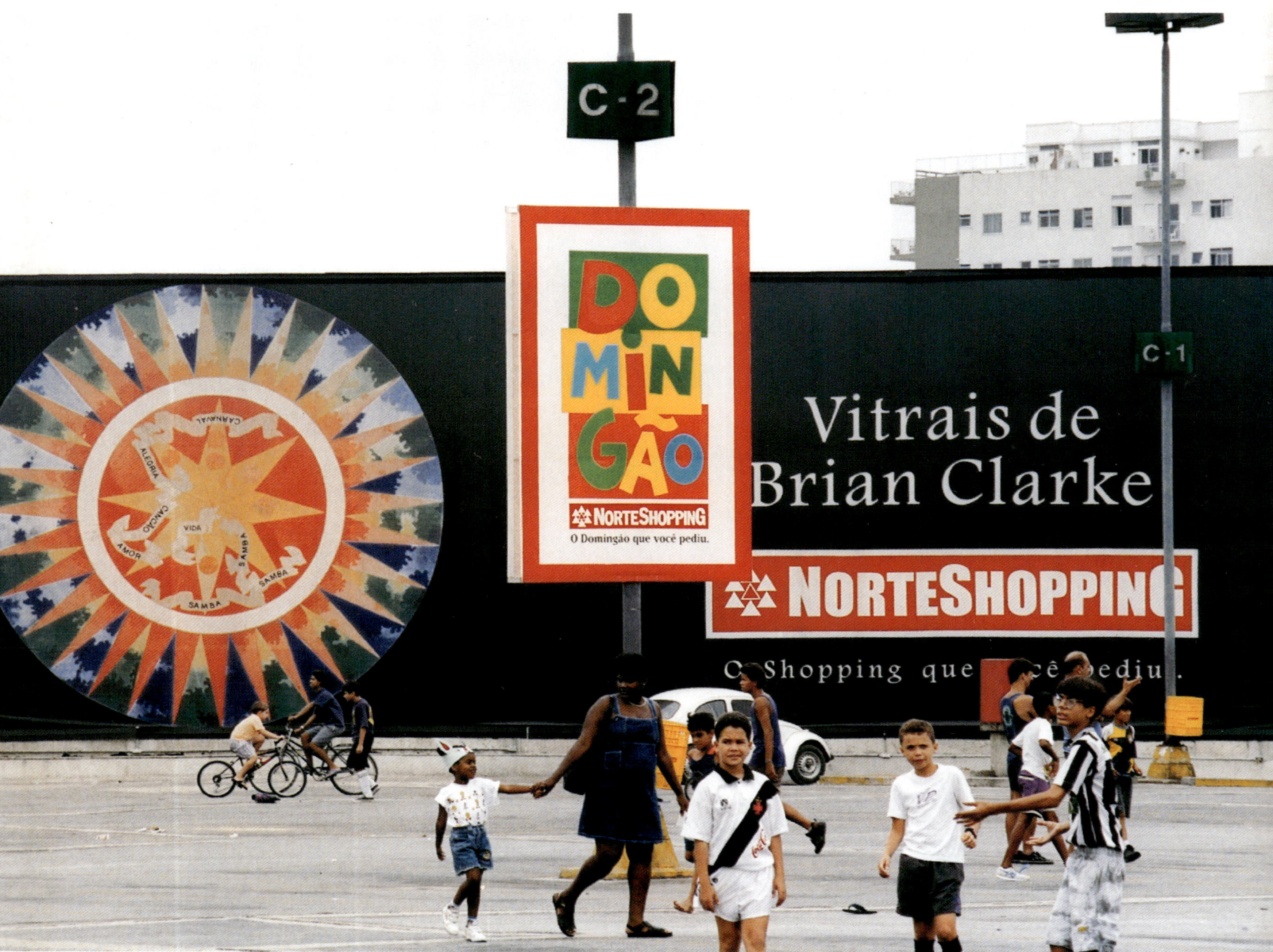

Architects: Designcorp, Toronto, Canada
Luis Carlos de Azevedo, Brazil

Stained glass rooflights and mosaic.
11,356 sq ft (stained glass)
1,571 sq ft (mosaic)

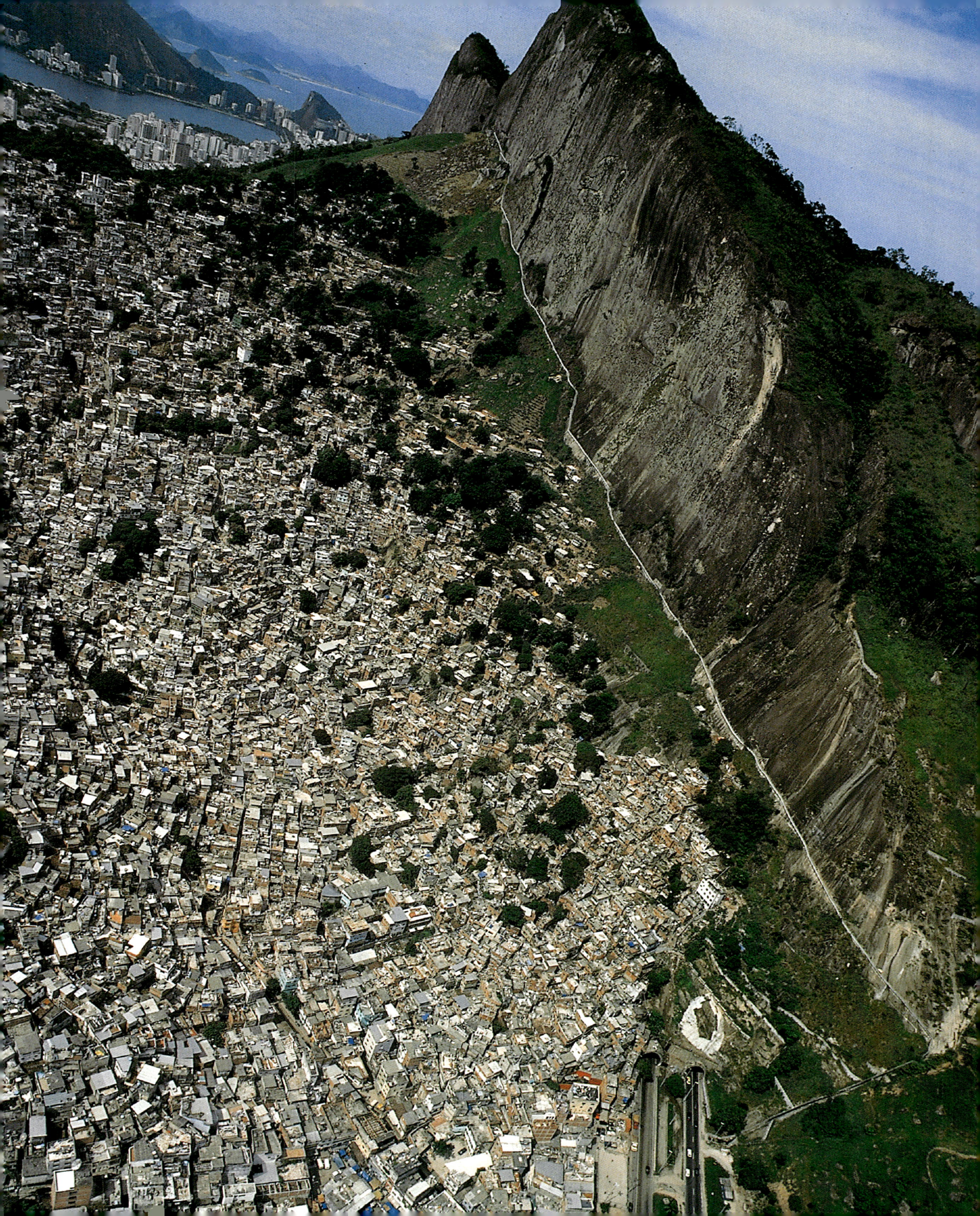

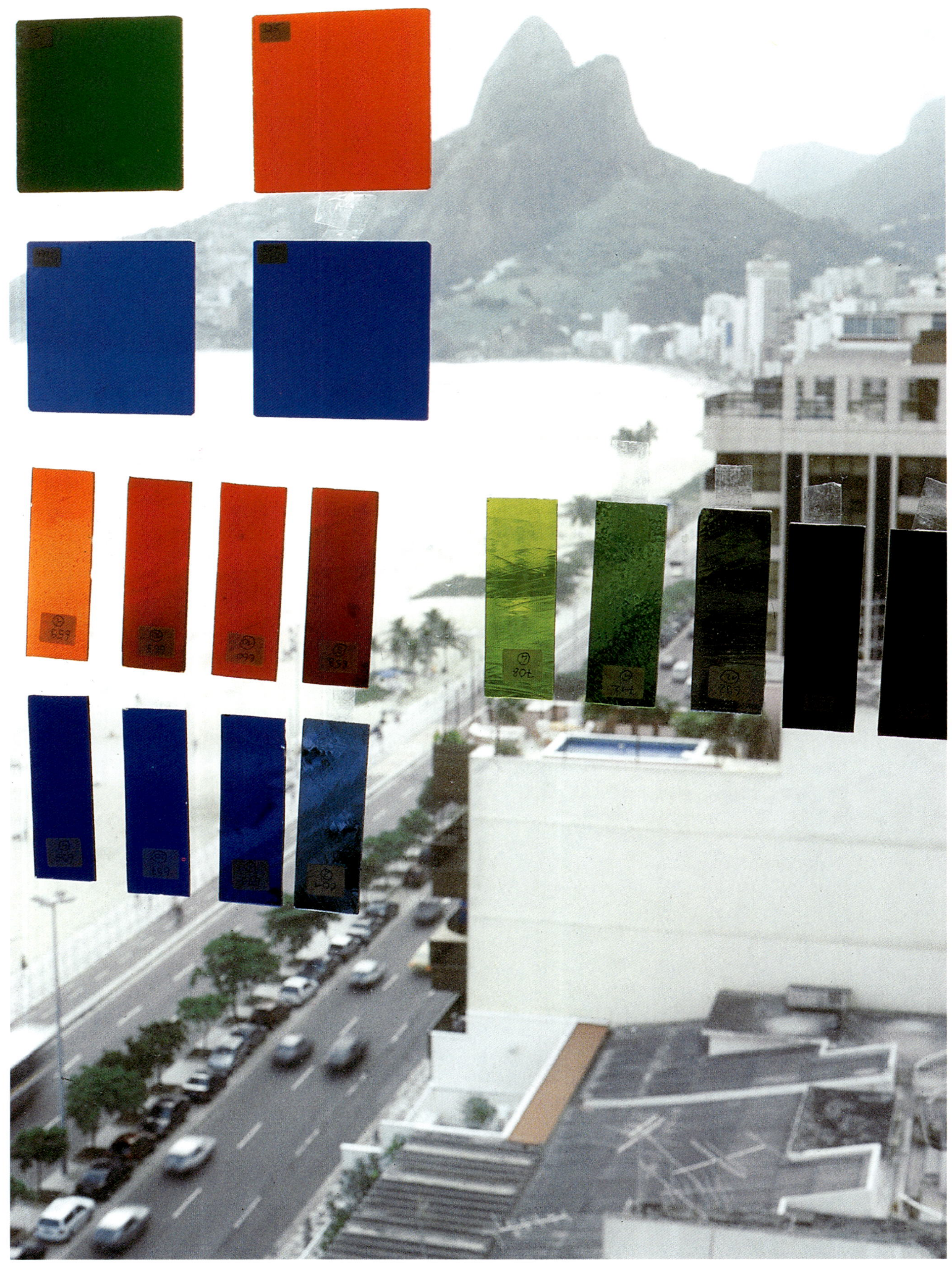

Colored glass samples taped to hotel window in Ipanema, Rio de Janeiro

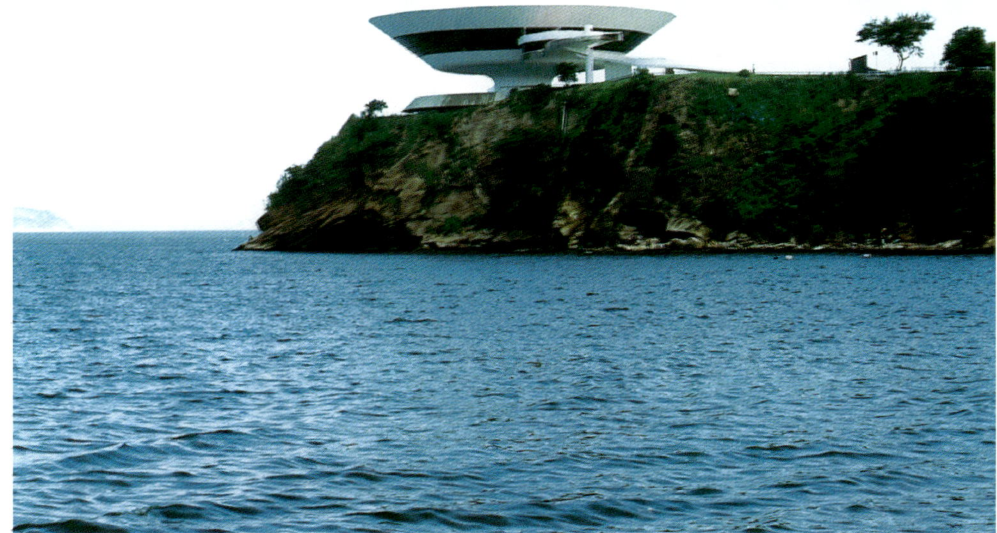

Oscar Niemeyer
Museum of Contemporary Art
Niteroi

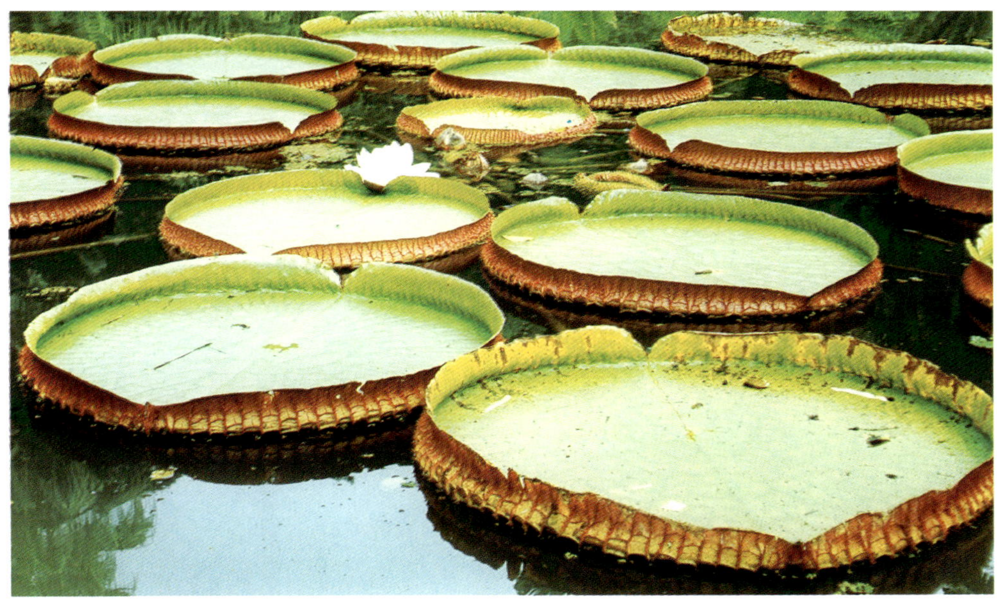

Giant Water Lilies
Botanical Gardens
Rio de Janeiro

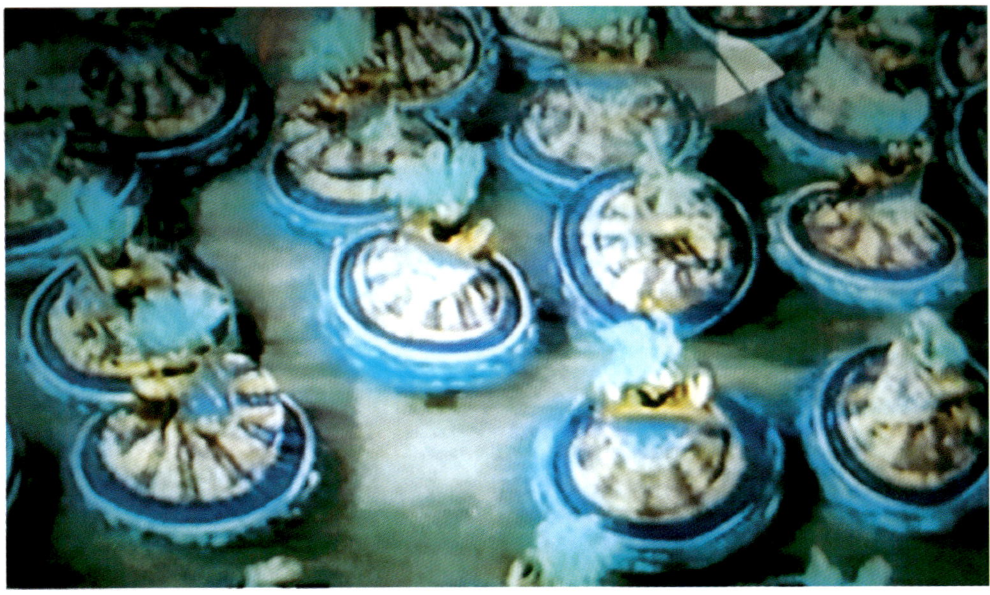

Samba Dancers
Rio Carnival

These forms inspired the circular elements of the NorteShopping composition

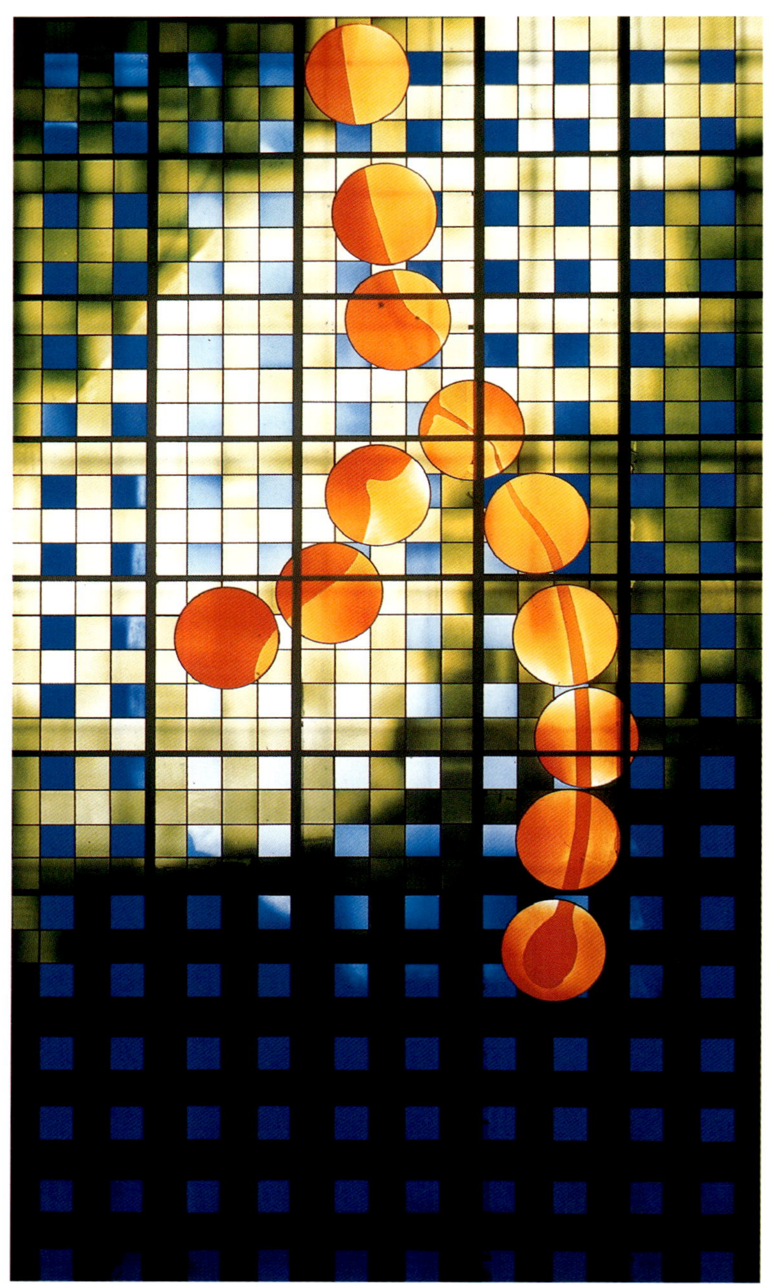
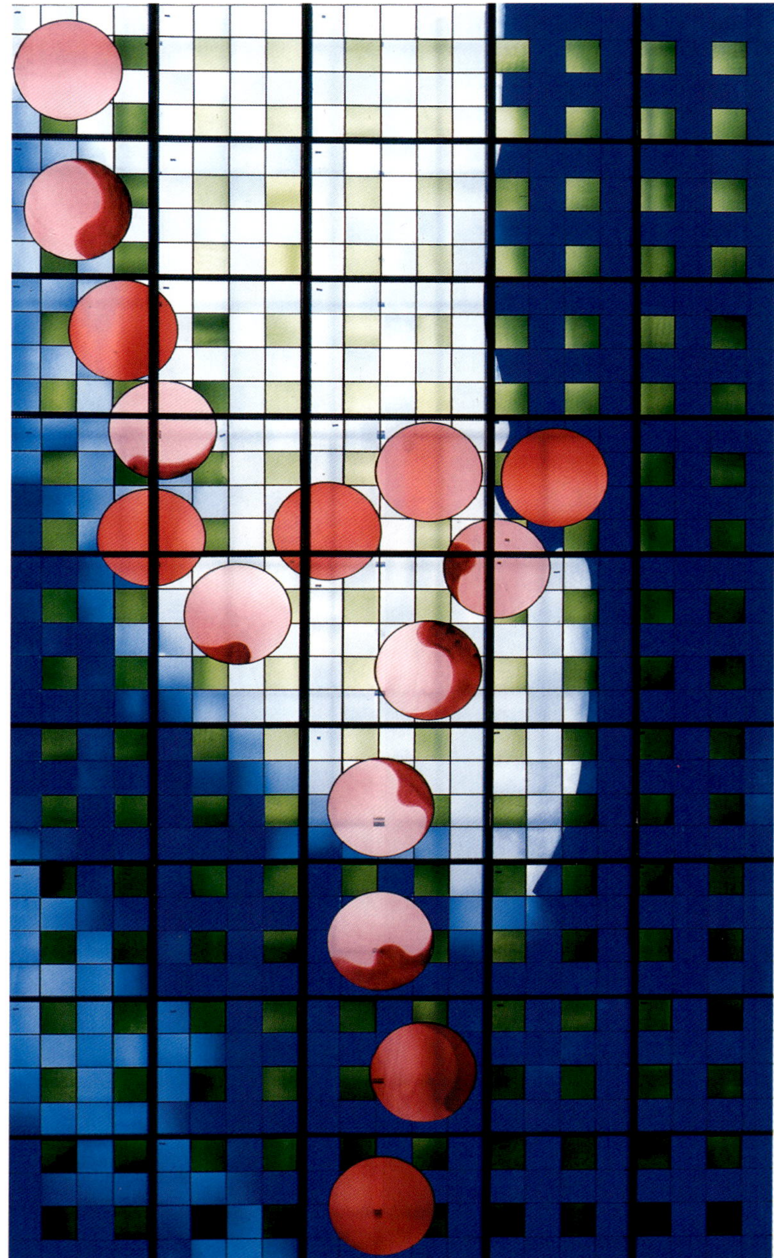

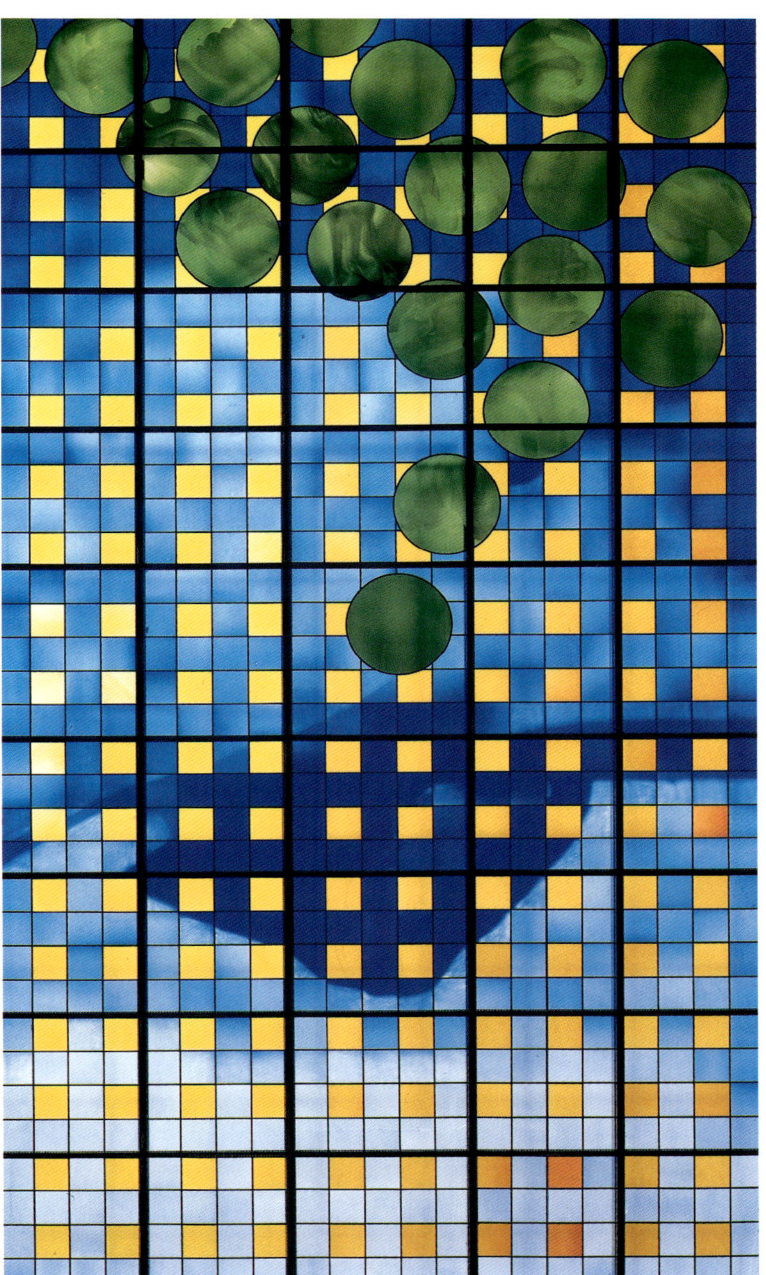

On my first trip to Rio I fell in love with the country, the city and the people. The glittering lights of the favelas cascading down the mountains by night are like giant rallies of exotic fireflies. The light in Rio is powerful and radiant but with a pink softness that robs it of the aggressive force of other suns.

The leaves of the forest trees are massive and daunting, the birds and animals are noisy and brightly colored, the beaches are endless and the people, of all colors, shapes and sizes are the sexiest on earth. I have a love affair with Brazil.

NorteShopping, one of Brazil's largest and busiest shopping centers serves a mixed community of cariocas including two large favelas. It's an area famous for its Samba Schools and for its music and dance. Cartolla, one of the great Samba musicians lived close by. Carnival is synonymous with Rio and the stained glass and mosaics here at Norte reflect that. It seemed to be all circles to me here for awhile, from the giant lily pads of the Amazon to the swirling chiffon of the "bandieros" carnival dancers, to Niemeyers Museum at Niteroi. Quite naturally the circle edged its way into my composition and gradually a language unique to Norte developed. I love visiting this project, meeting the people who work in and use the space, and simply watching the movement of transmitted color tracing its progress across the walls as the passage of sunlight changes with the hours of the day.

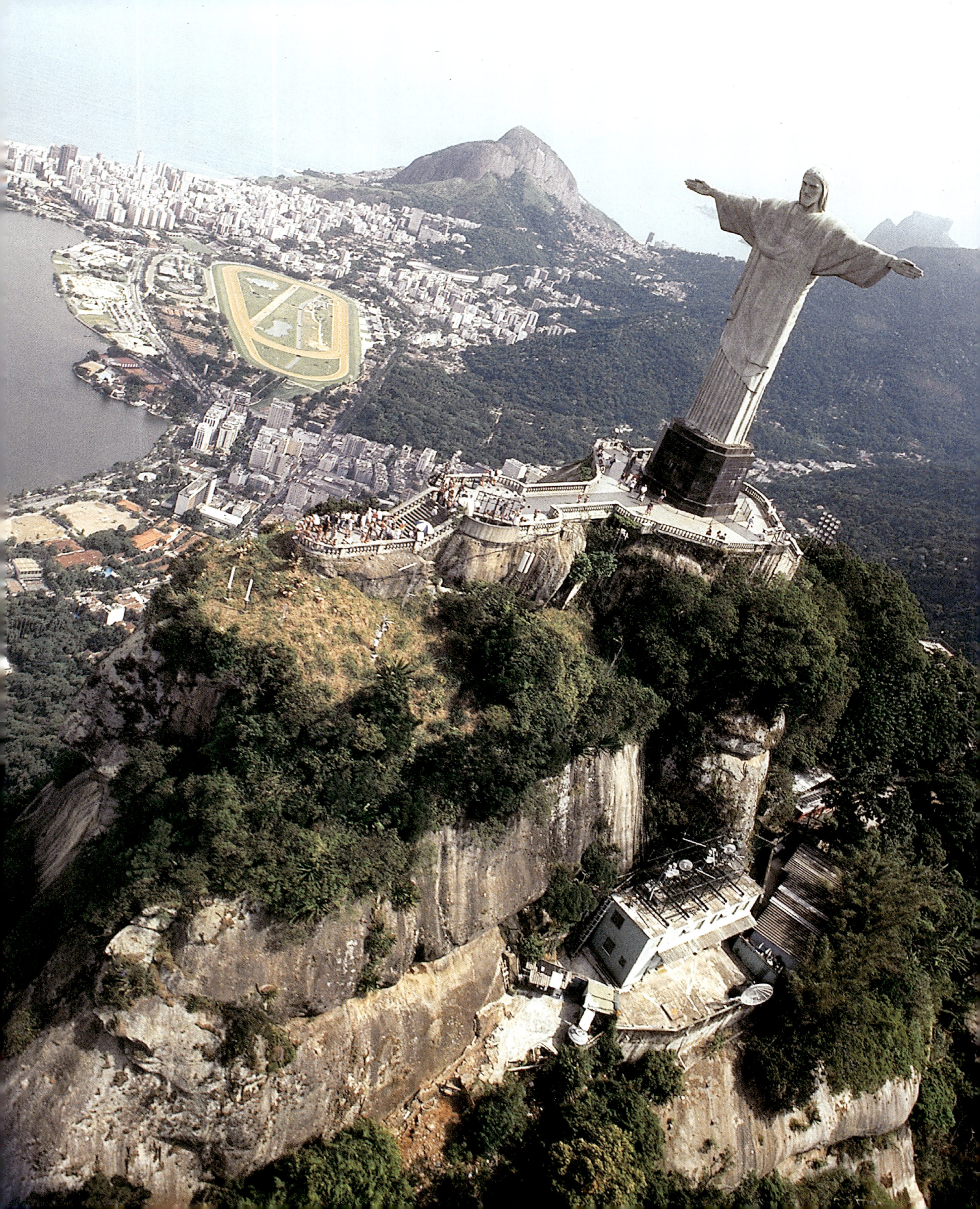

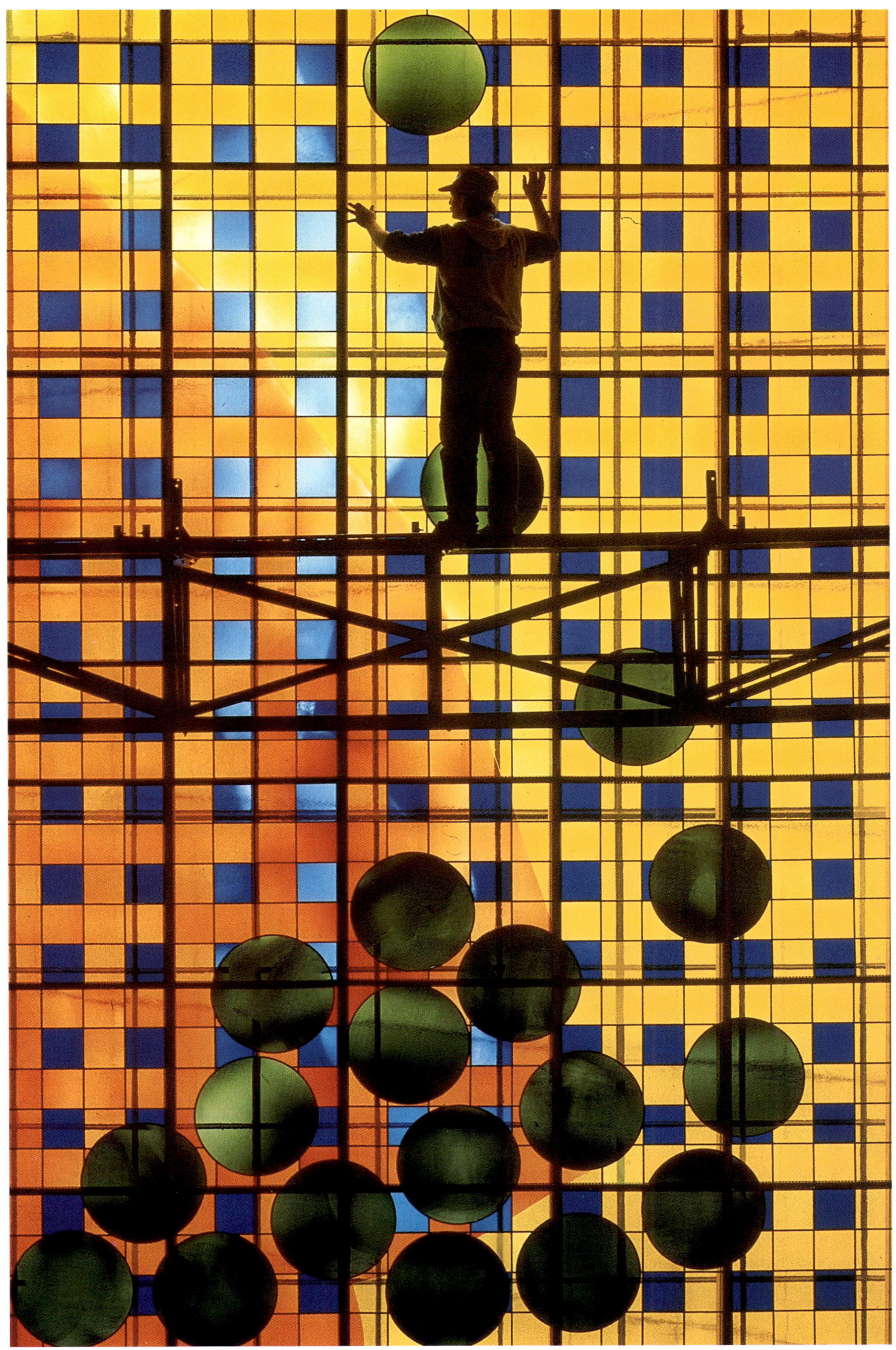

One of the Mall skylights at the glass factory

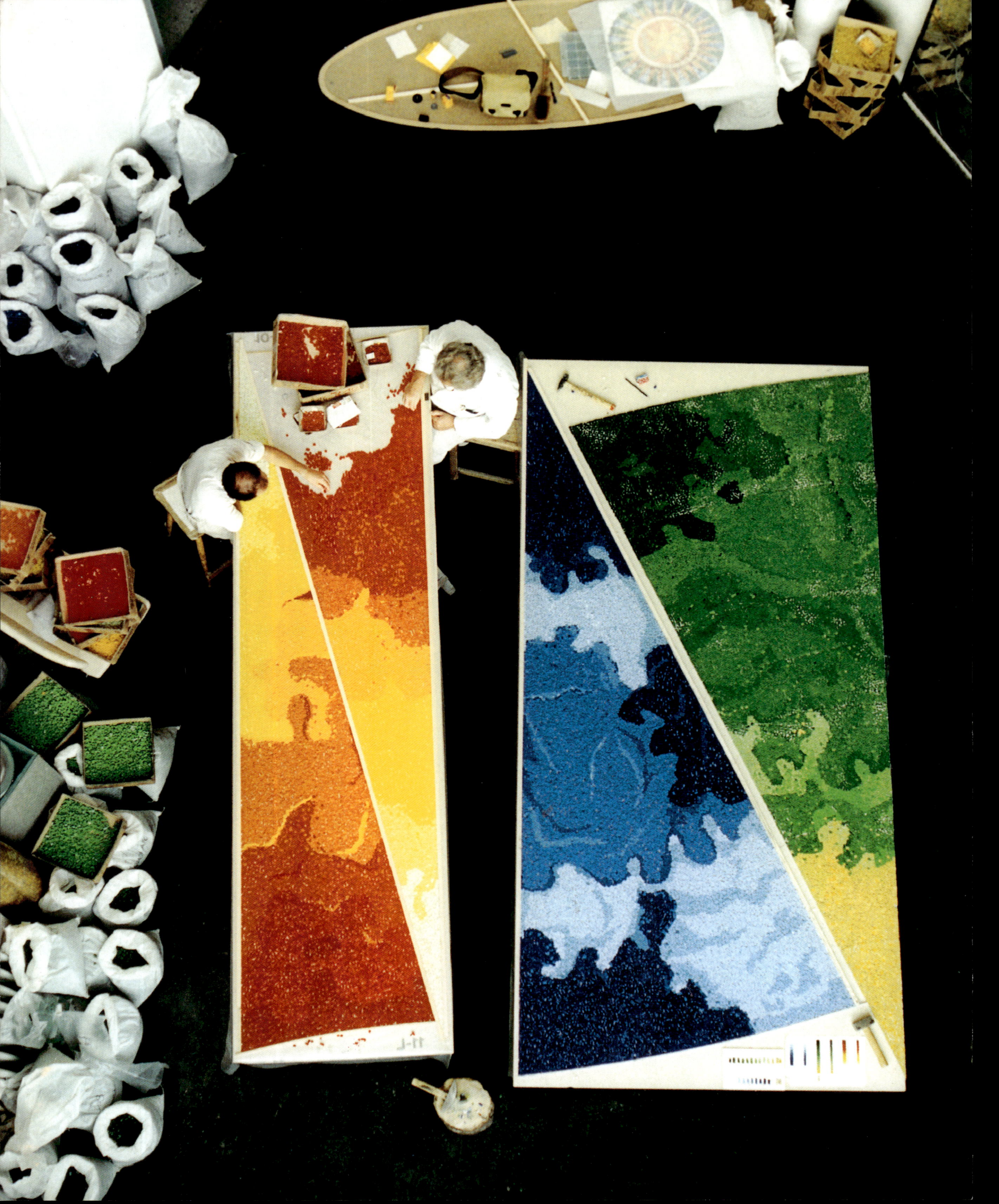

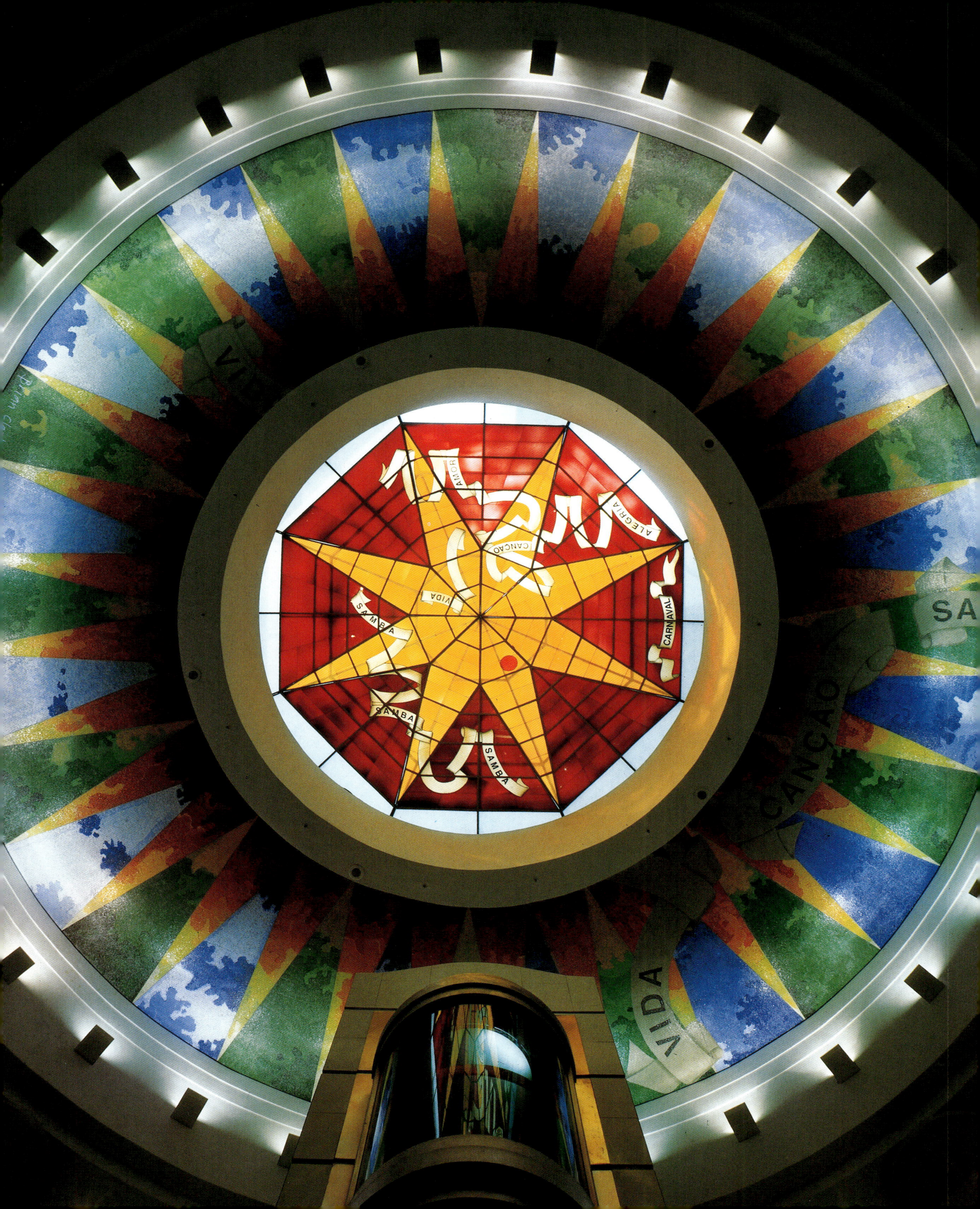

VIDA
SAMBA
CANÇAO
CARNAVAL
ALEGRIA
AMOR
CANÇAO
VIDA

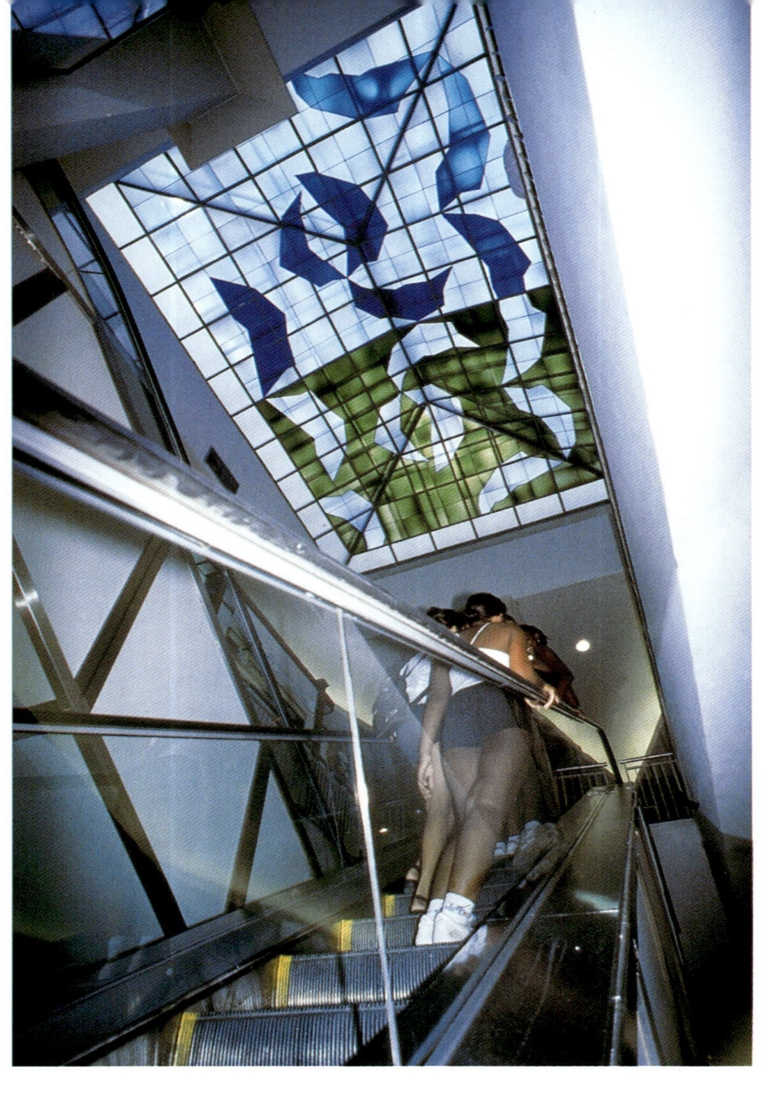
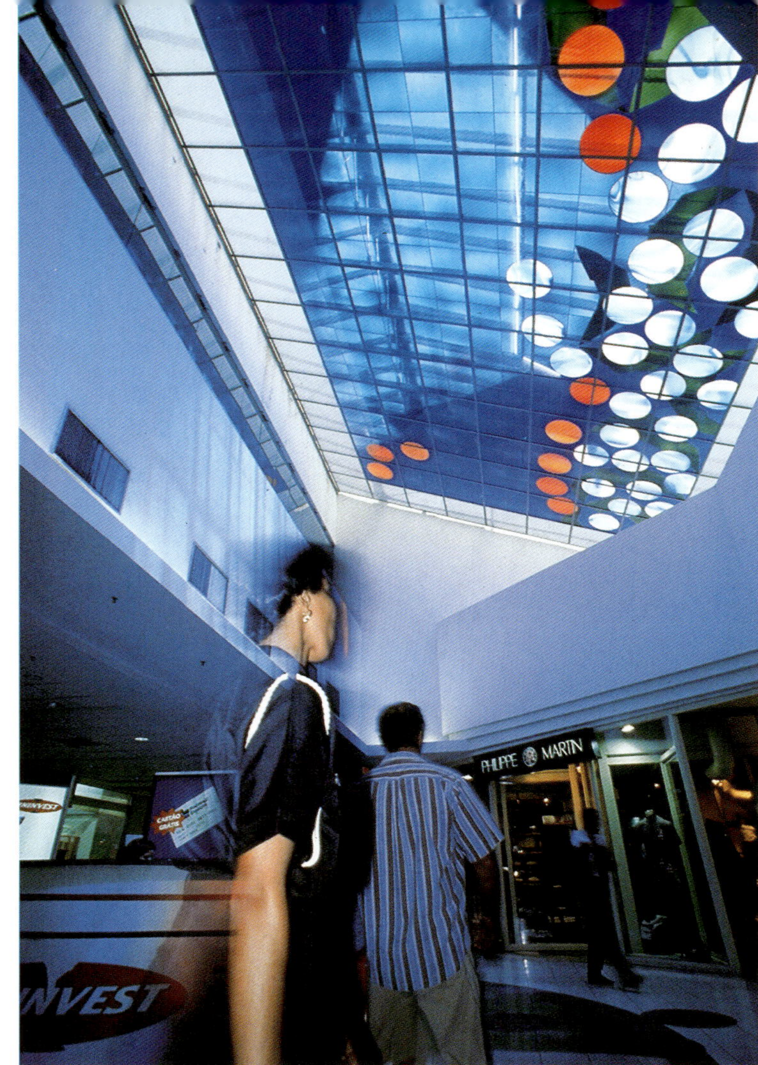
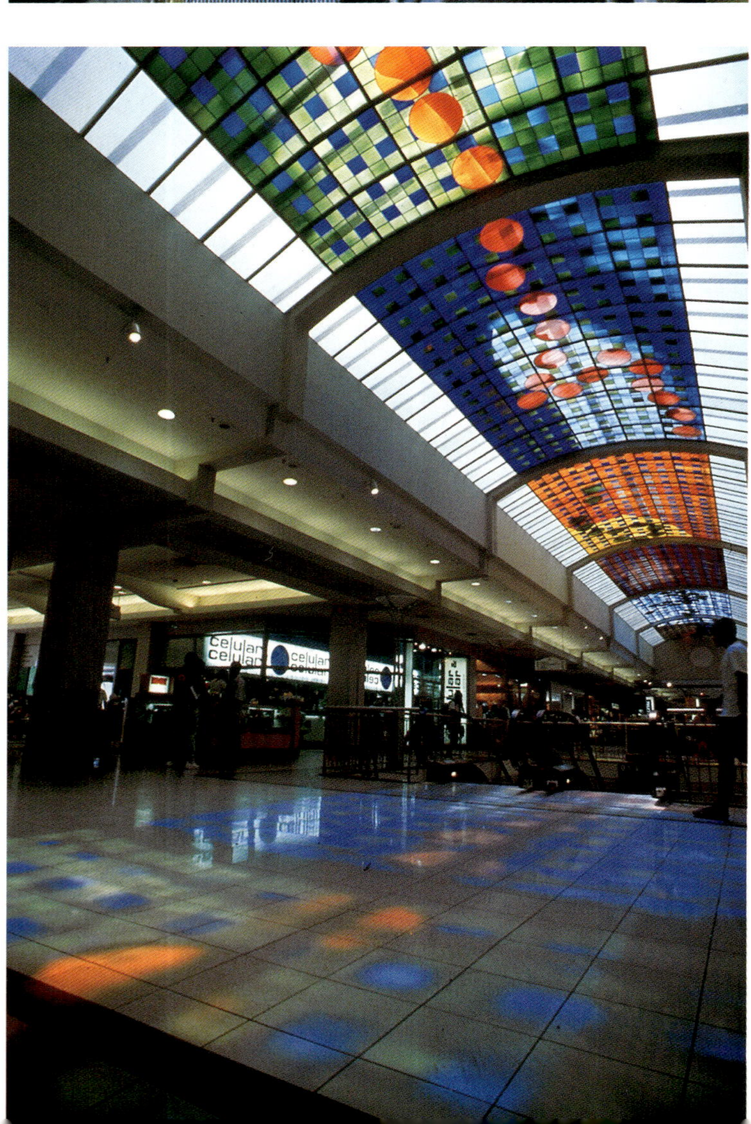
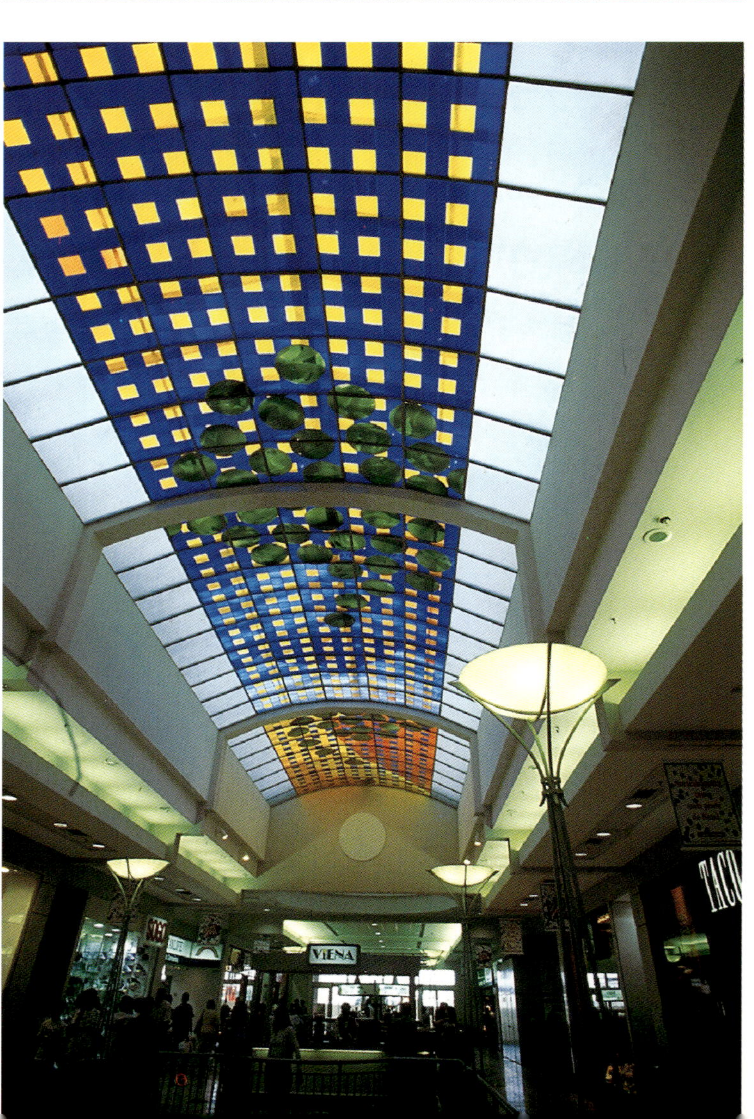

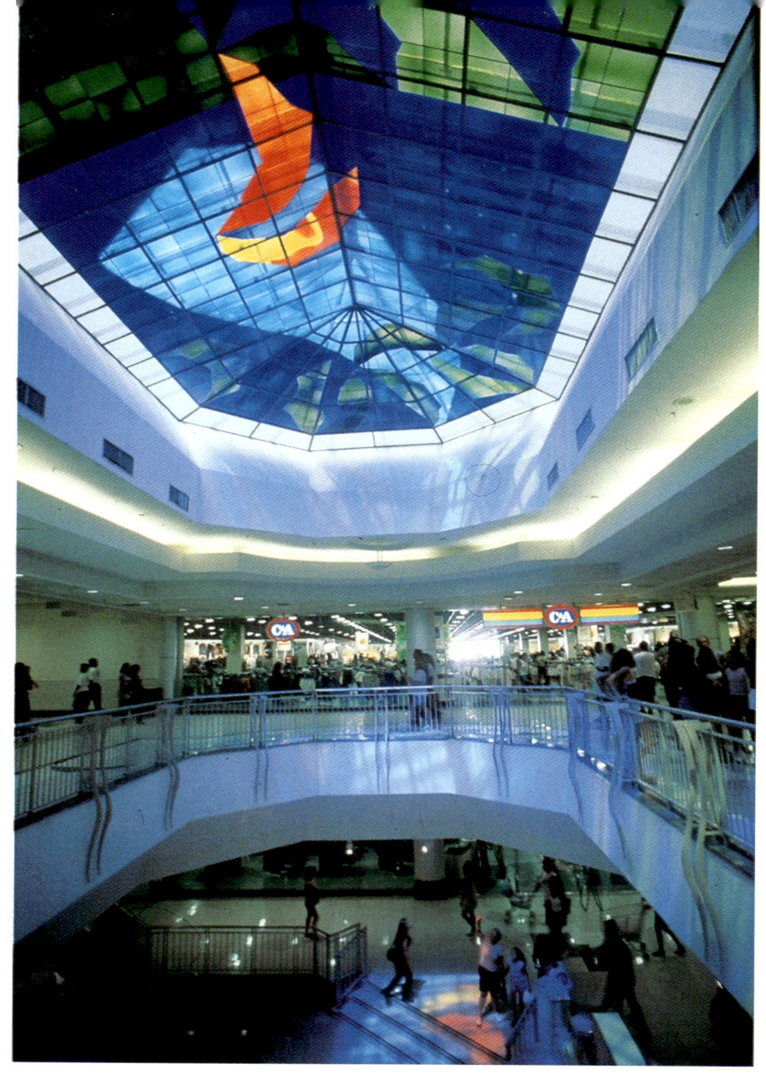

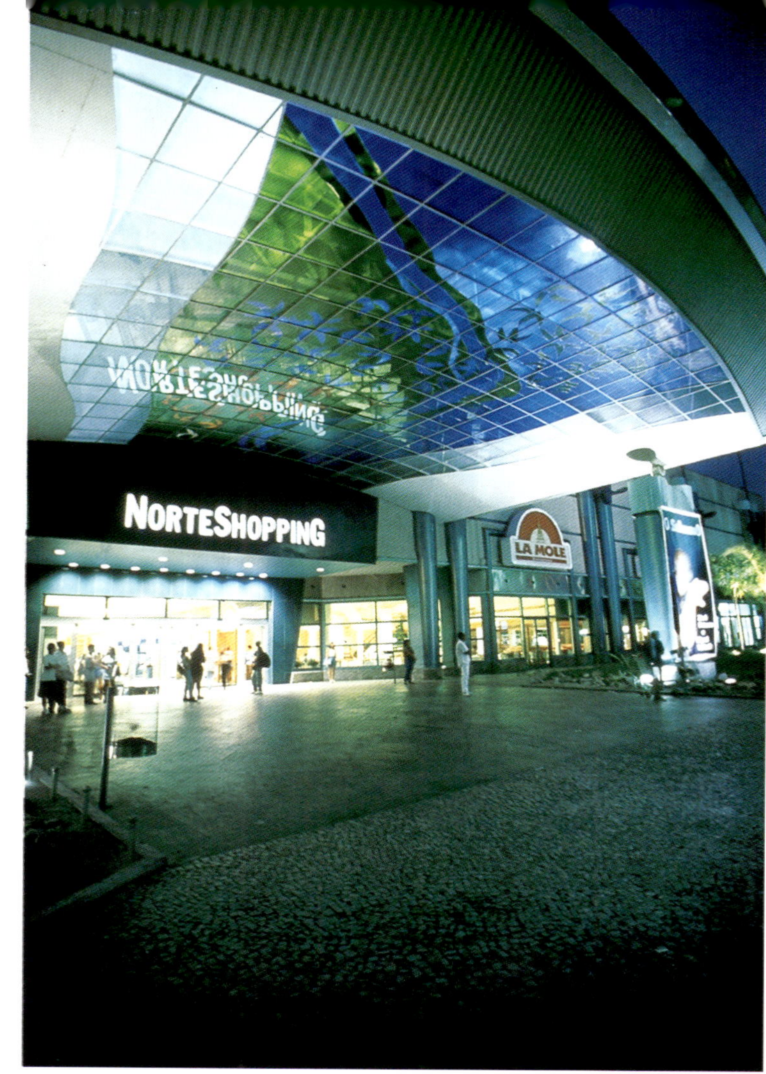
NorteShopping
LA MOLE

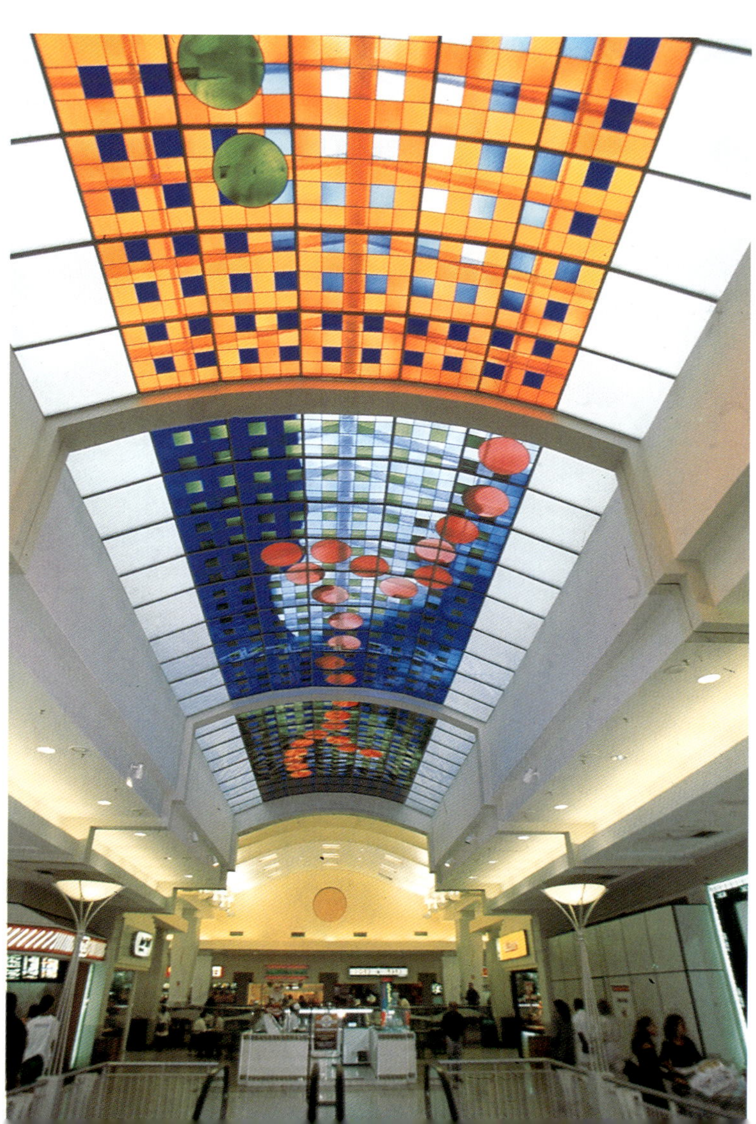

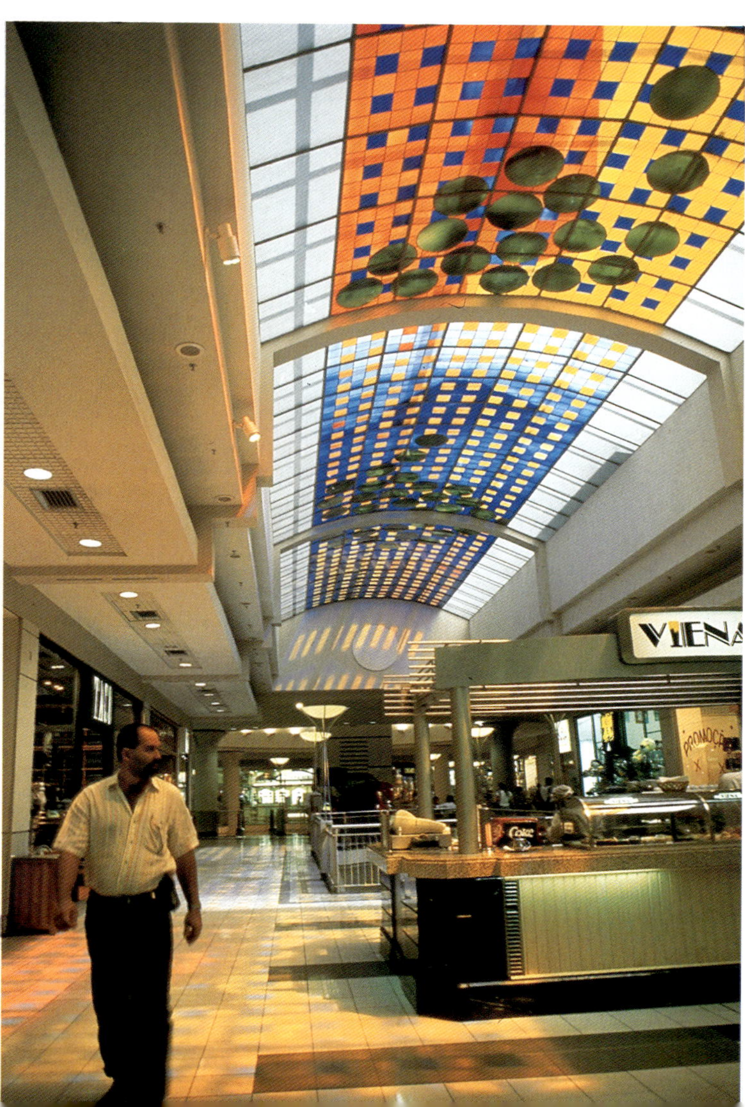
VIENA

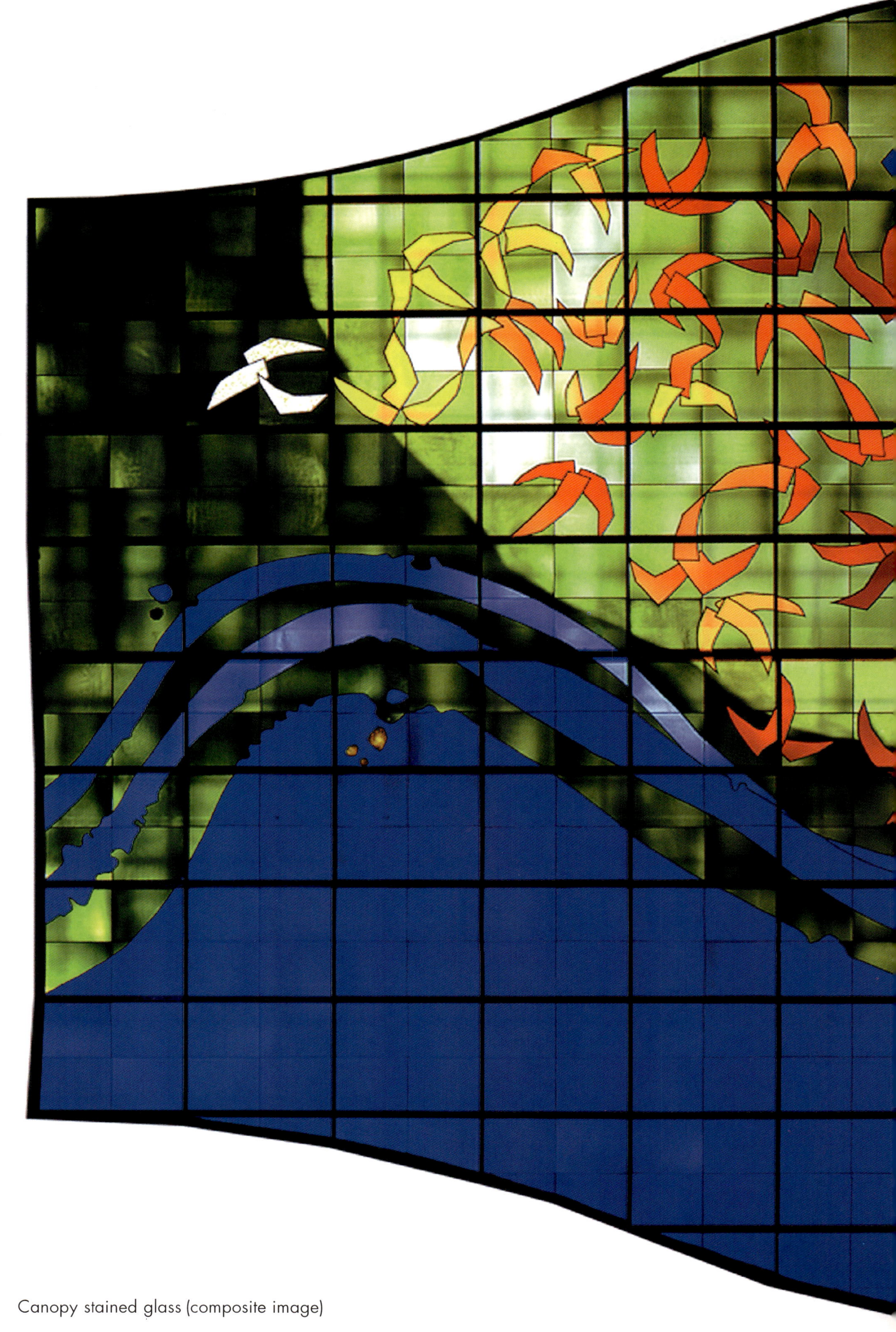

Canopy stained glass (composite image)

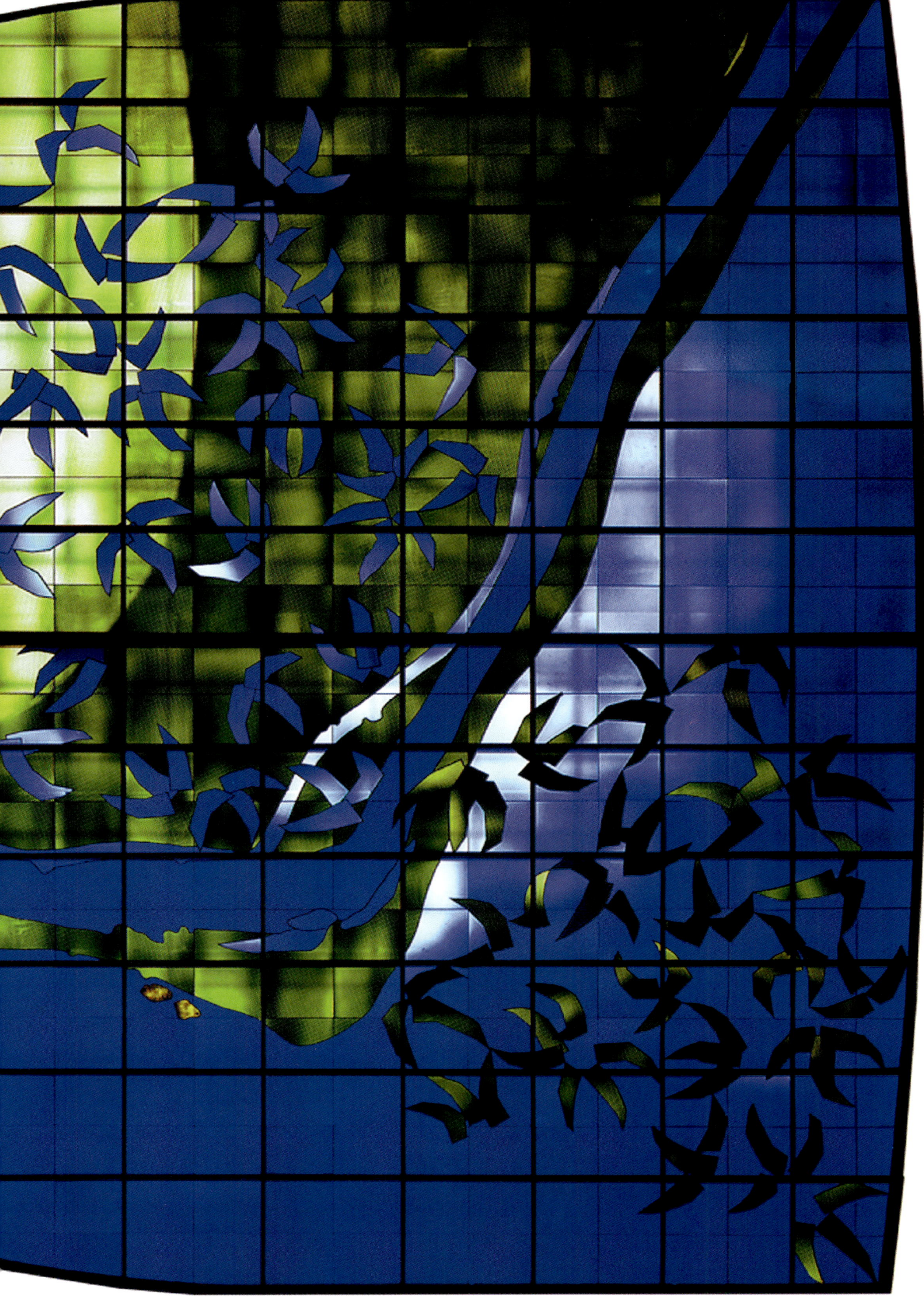

ABBAYE DE LA FILLE-DIEU
ROMONT, SWITZERLAND

1996

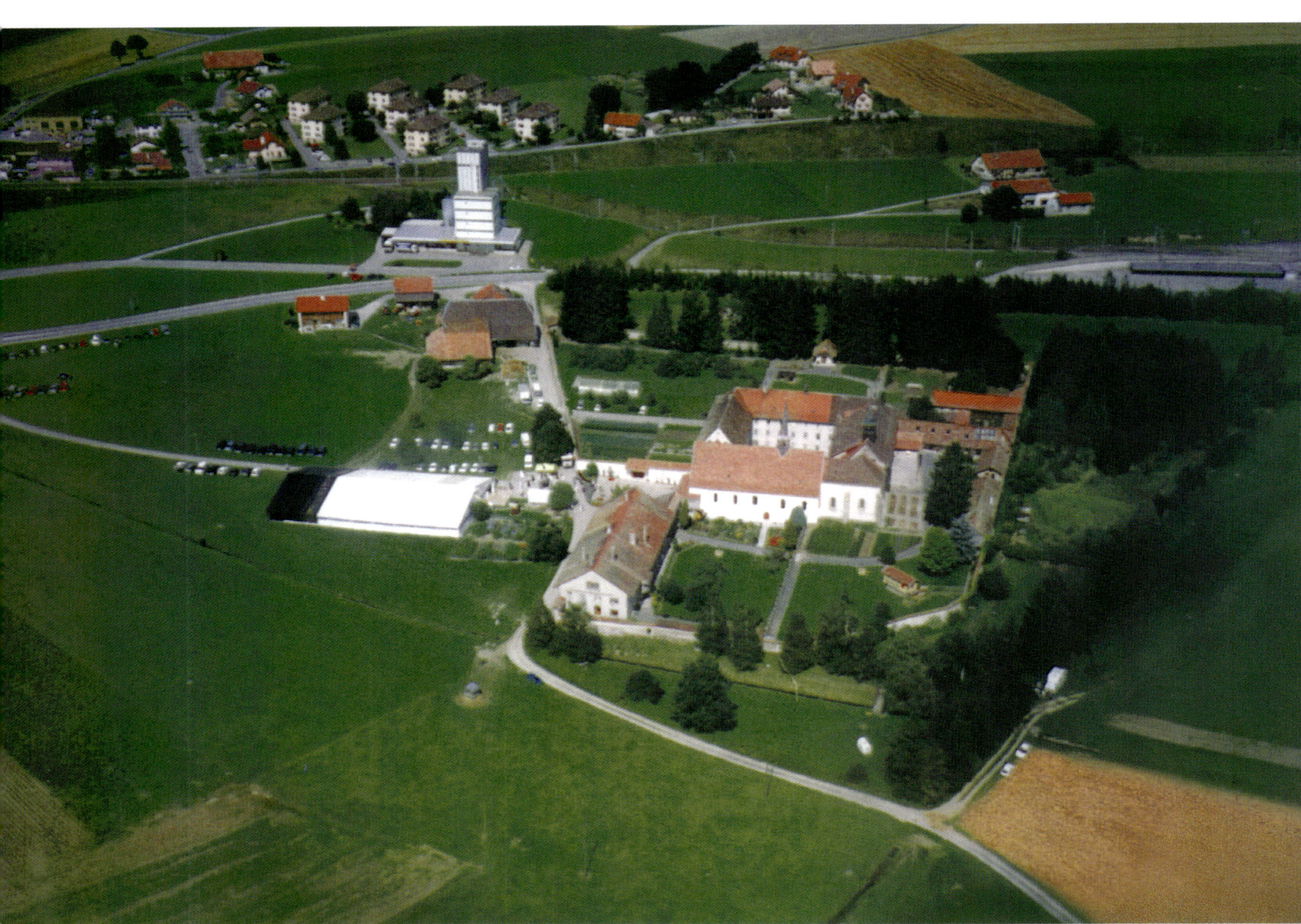

Architects: Margot, Mikulas, Page

Stained glass windows
300 sq ft (total)

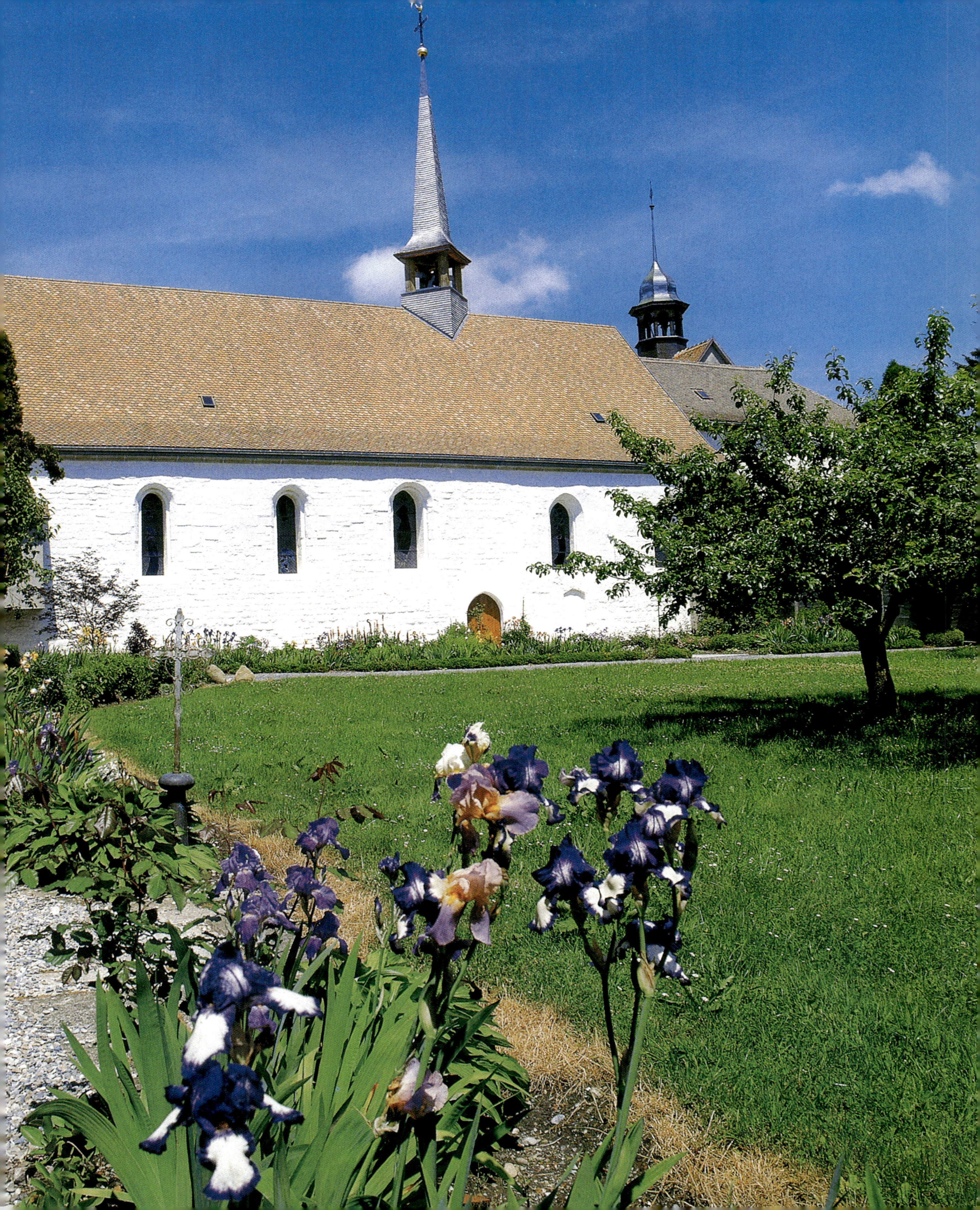

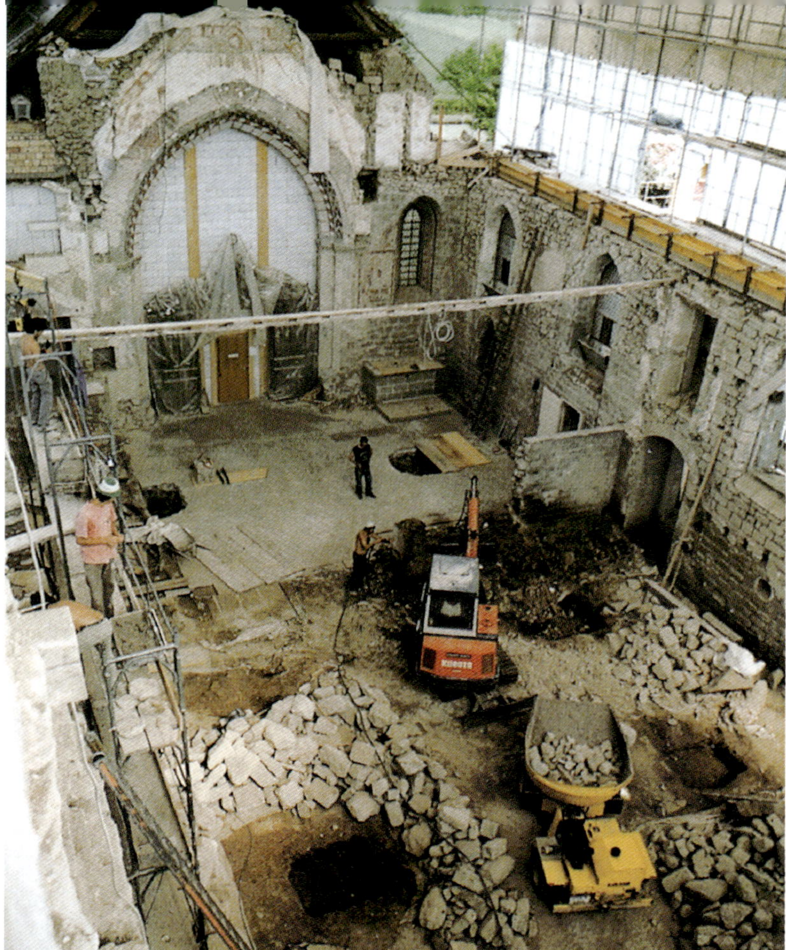

The nave of the church during restoration

The Cistercian Order nuns have occupied the Abbaye de la Fille-Dieu for over seven hundred years. It is cupped in the valley overlooked by the local castle, now the Swiss Museum of Stained Glass. Though heavily restored, the building retains substantial evidence of its complex and layered history. Fragmentary frescoes from the 12th century decorate the nave and choir with figurative and ornamental scenes. The fenestration is primitive and irregular with Romanesque and Gothic arches. Carved and worked wood is everywhere.

The windows take a simple orthogonal heraldic grid interrupted by organic foliage and avian forms. I thought frequently of the medieval and later hatchments so common to English churches of the same period. The windows are so small and deeply incised into the thick stone walls they shimmer like precious stones. The external movement of leaves and clouds cause shadow forms to play across the surface of the glass. This direct link between interior and exterior appeals to me very much. The north wall windows (as those of the eastern choir) are rich in color and density, where the volume of natural direct sunlight provides sufficient illumination for quite bold decisions. The south wall, however, backs on to an internal monastic cloister sheltered from the light. Here a more delicate monochromatic range of blues has to be used and this was coated with a thin matte of white enamel to help "sponge up" the little light that is available.

Working in this kind of architectural environment demands an entirely different approach to, for example, an urban commercial building or modern institutional architecture. The need for integration and concord is more important and a huge historical responsibility adds a juicy fervor to the design process. If an artist doesn't respect the architectural integrity and purpose (function) of the building, then his work will not wholly harmonize with it. The purpose of this building is anti-material, counter-worldly; if an artist isn't prepared to embrace this function he has no place being here.

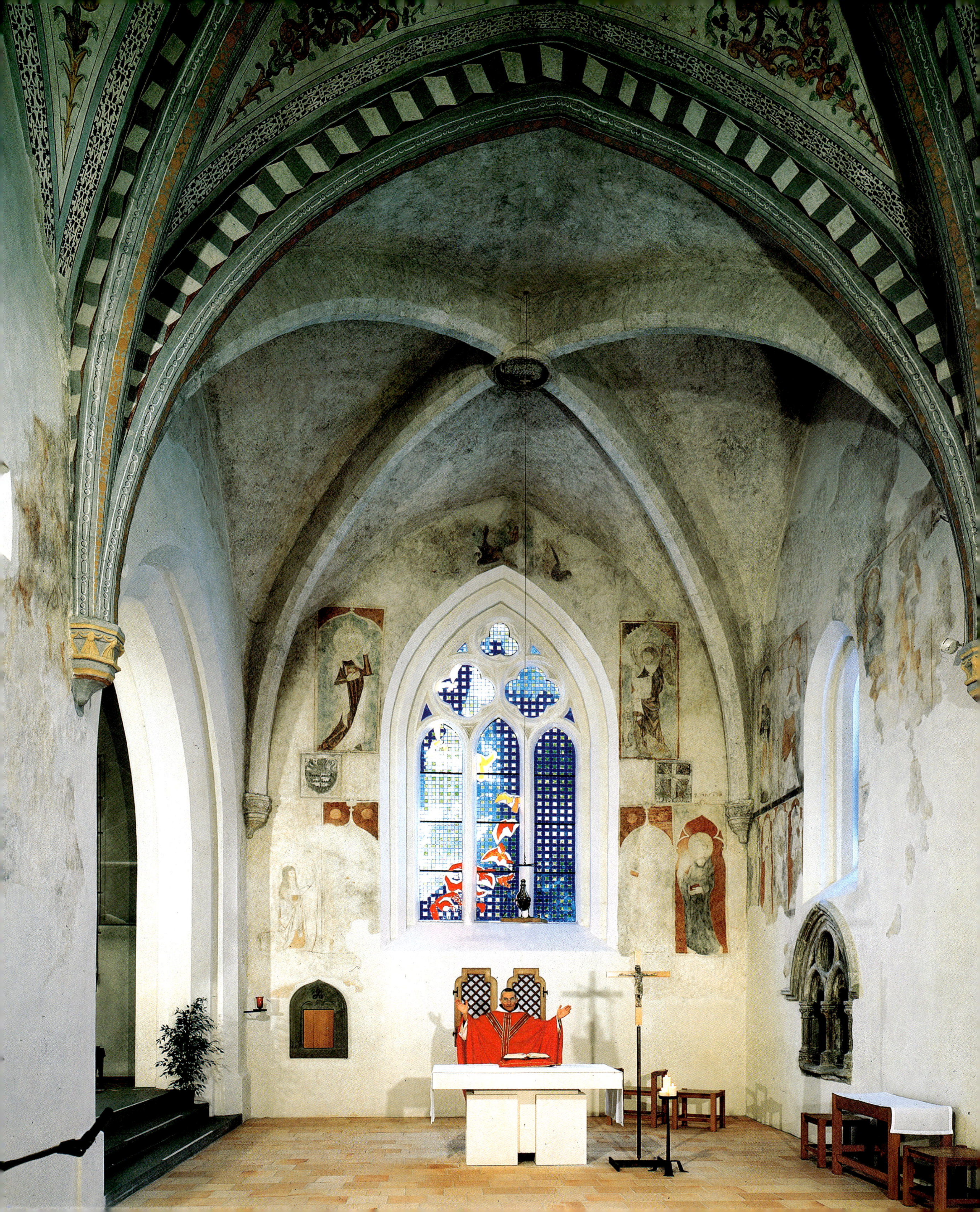

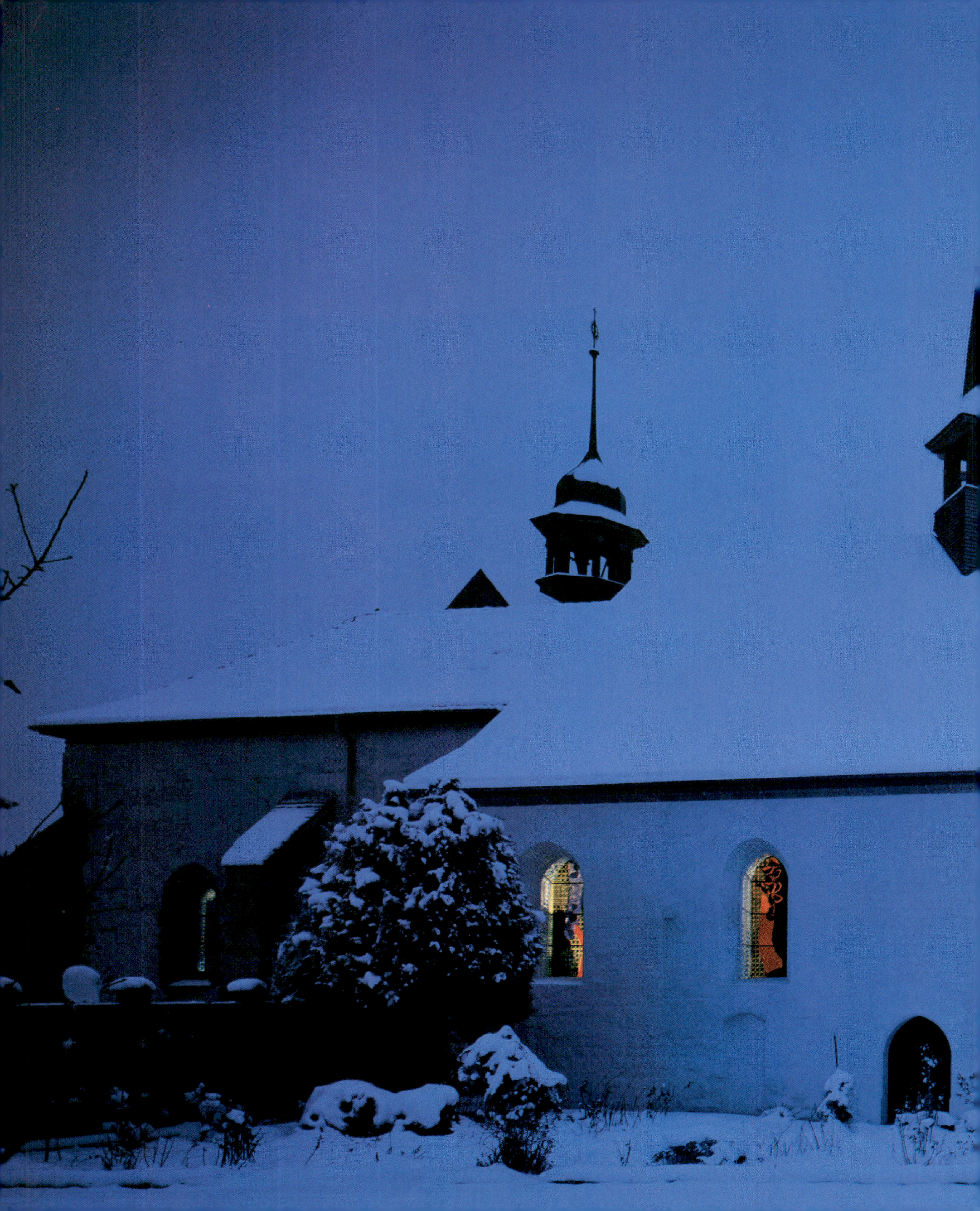

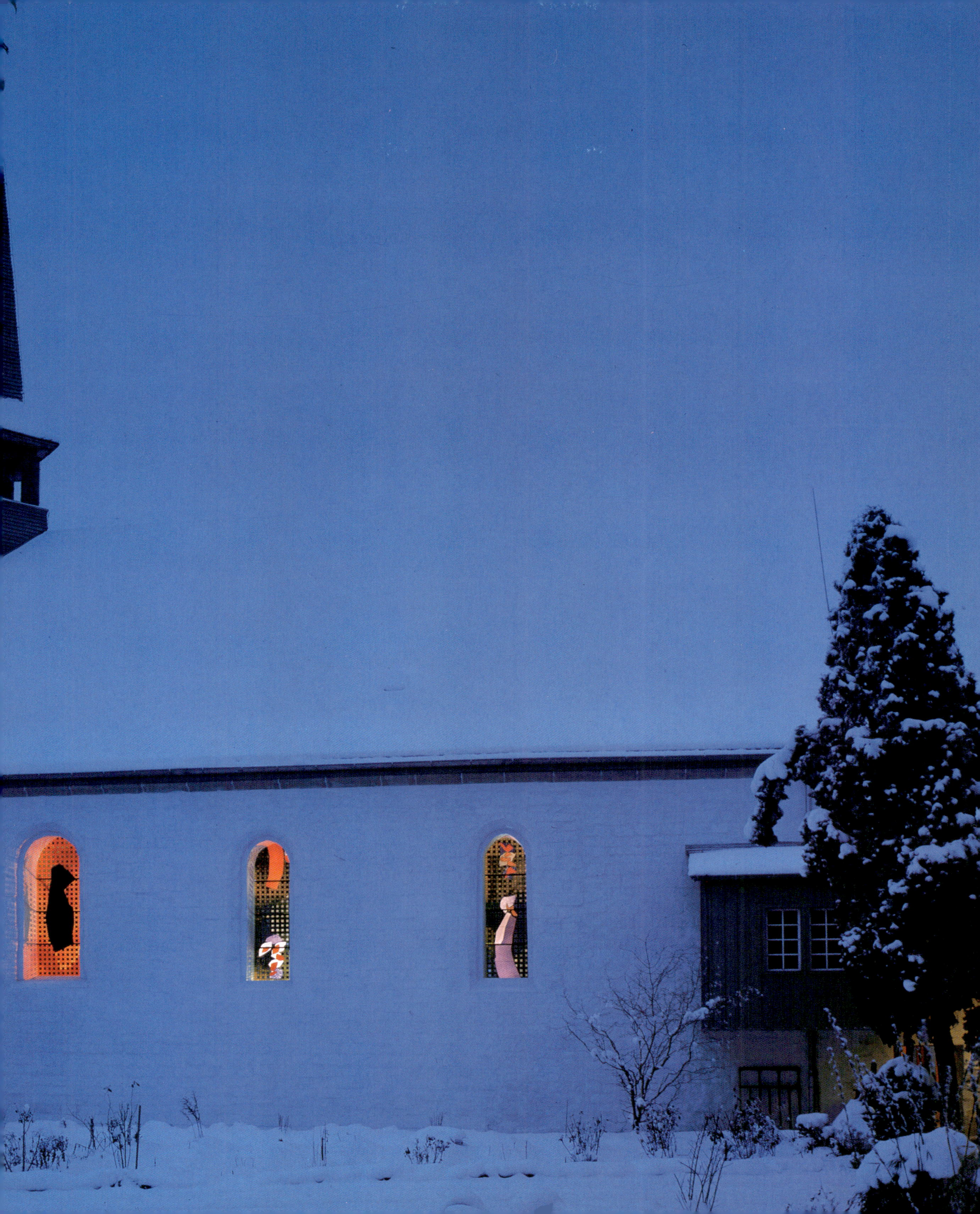

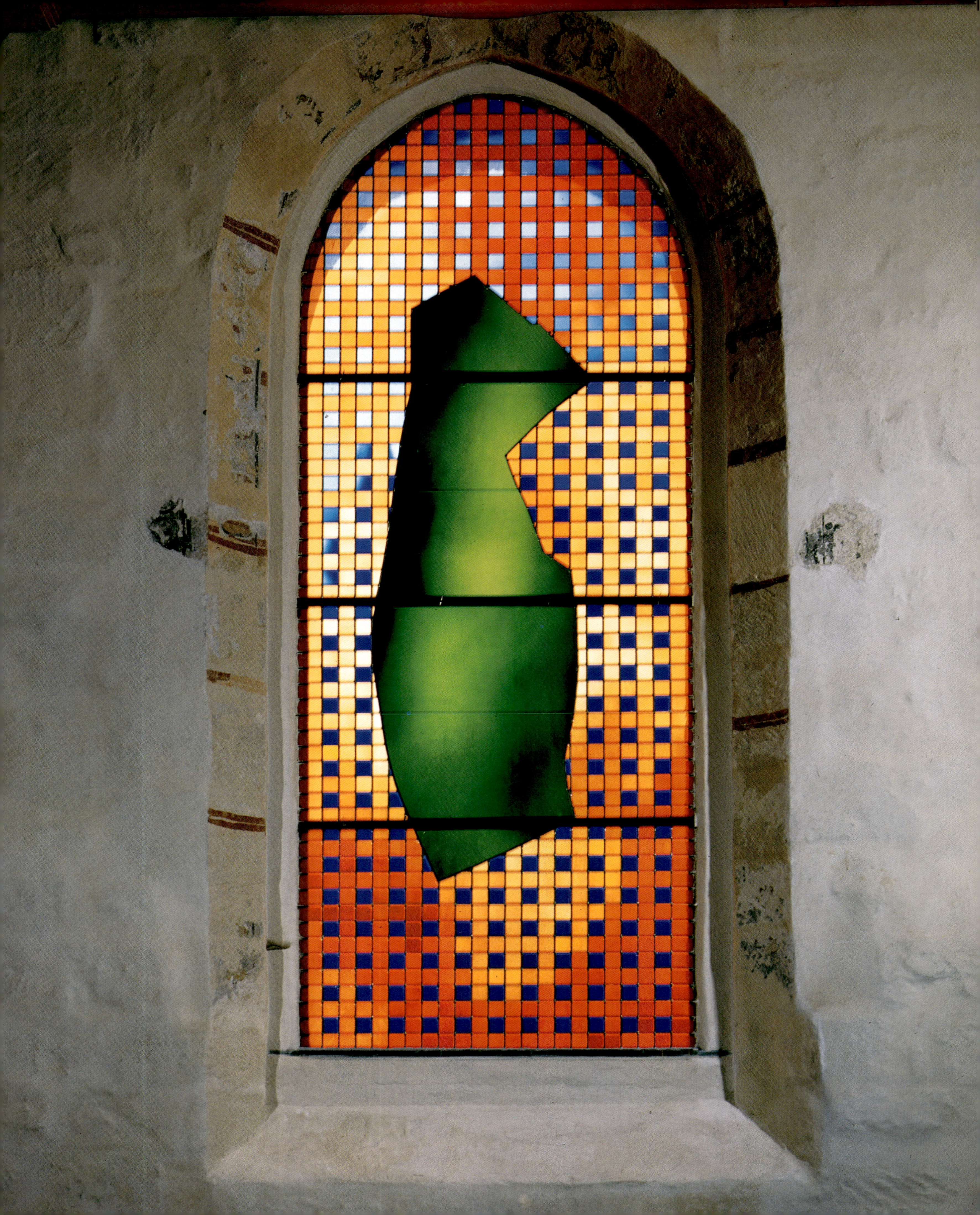

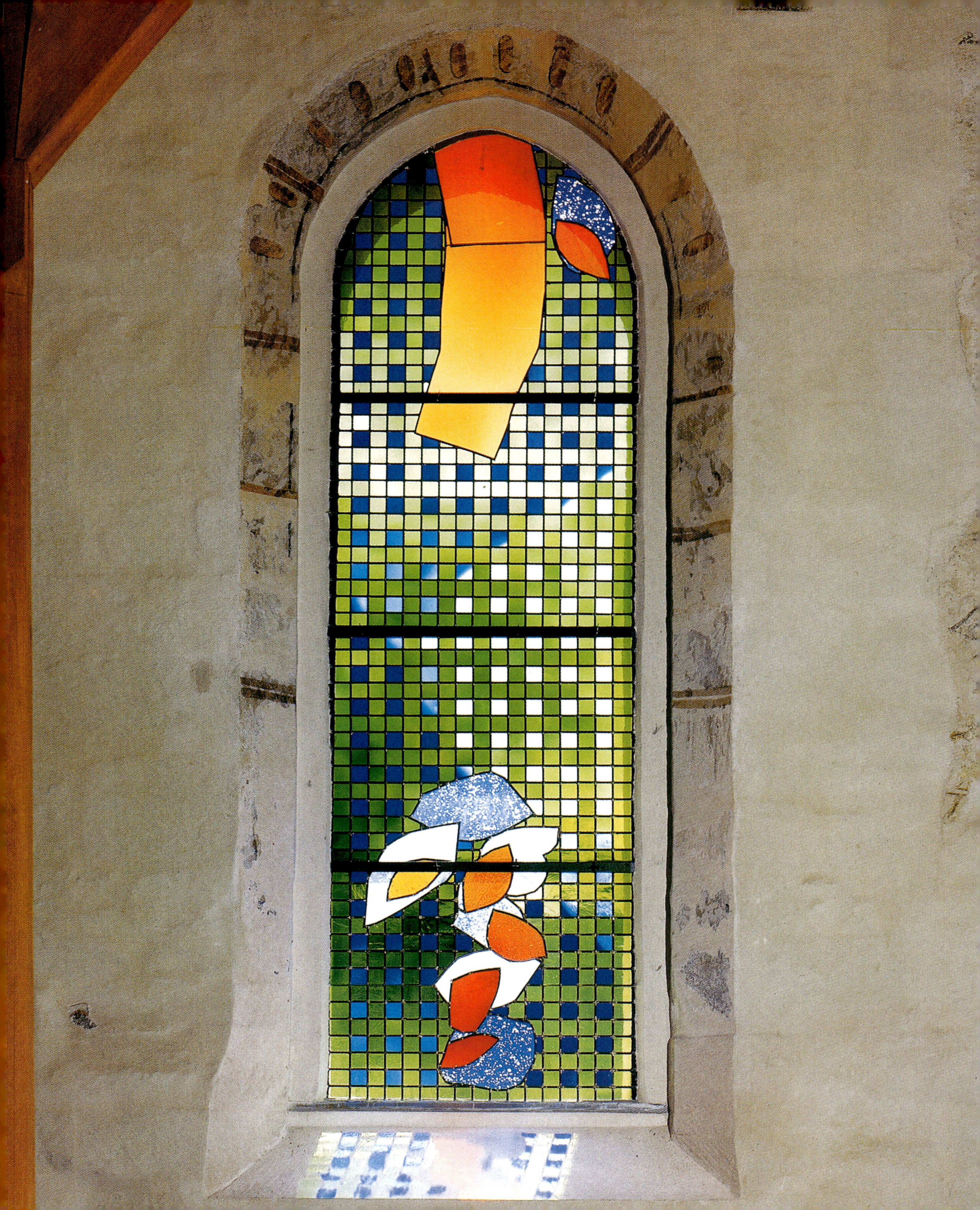

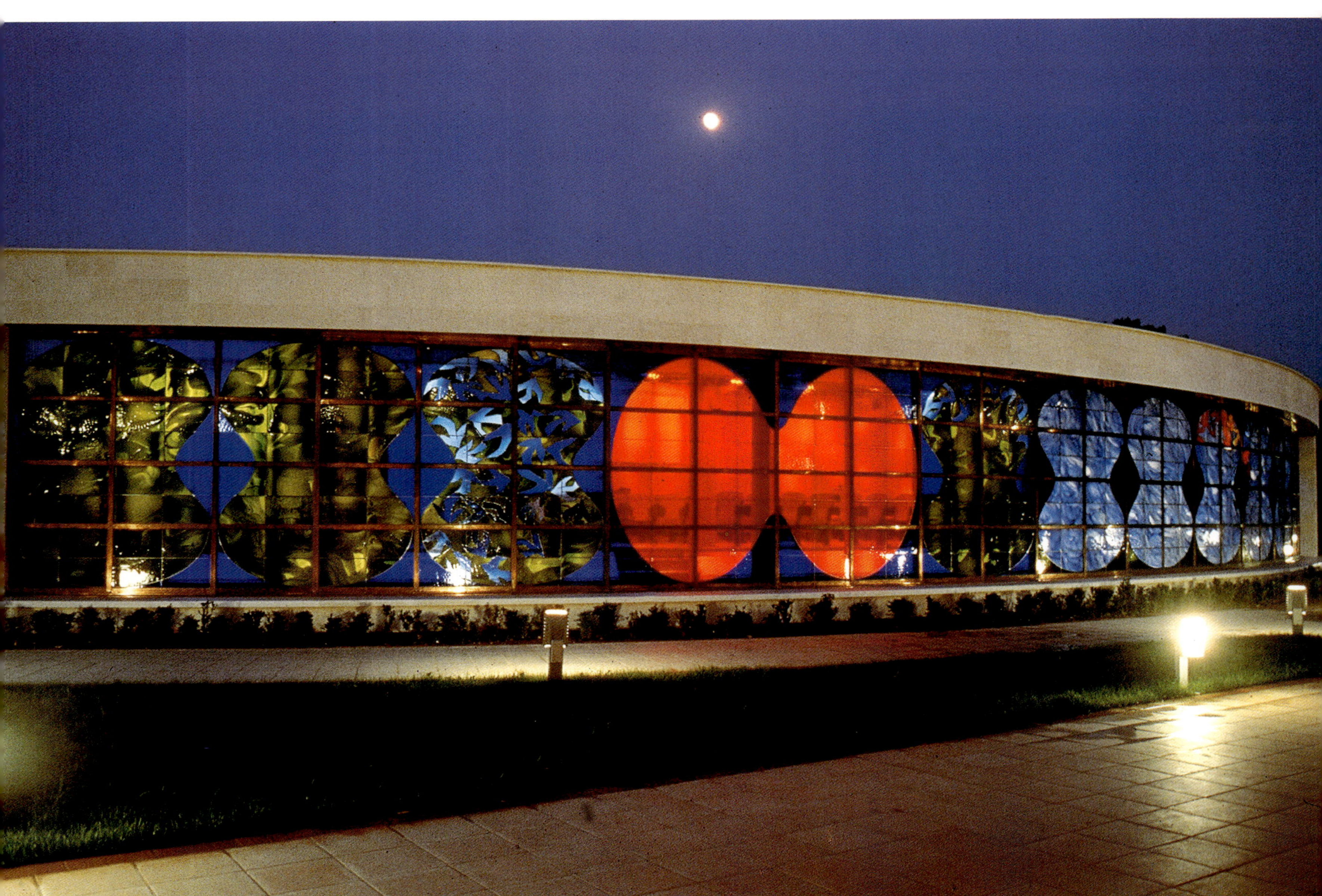

Architects: Angelo Rocco Dongiovanni and Emilio Ambasz
Client: Gruppo Putignano

Stained glass
1,076 sq ft

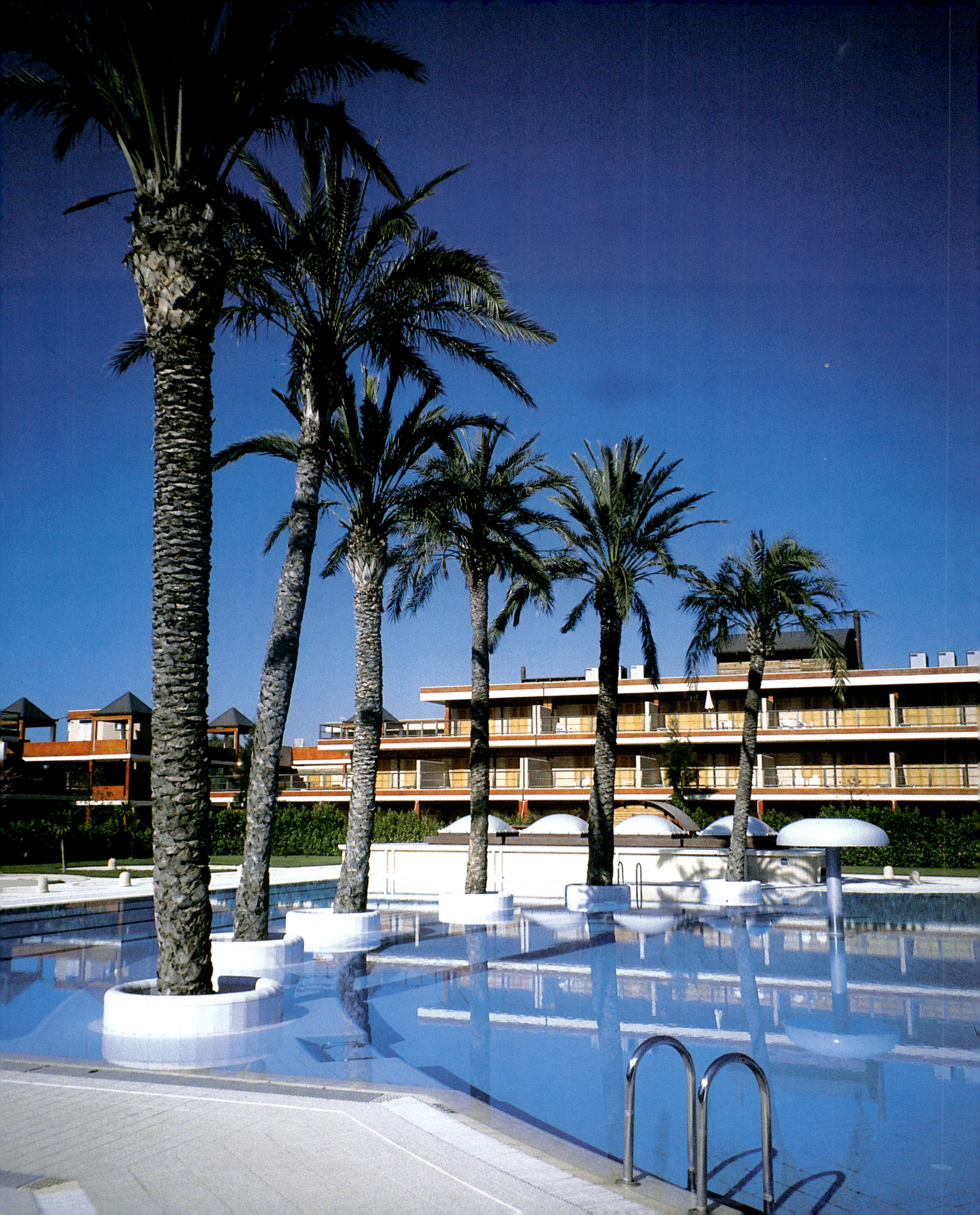

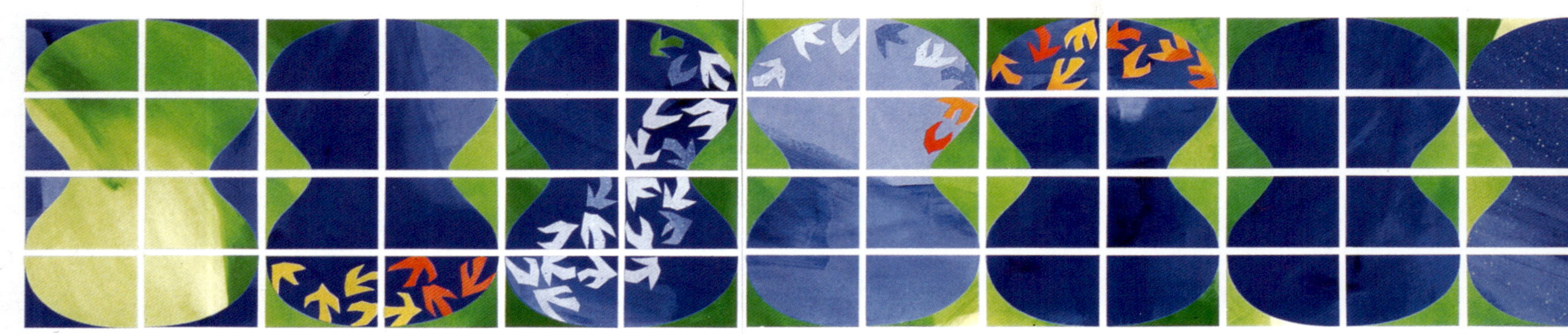

Design

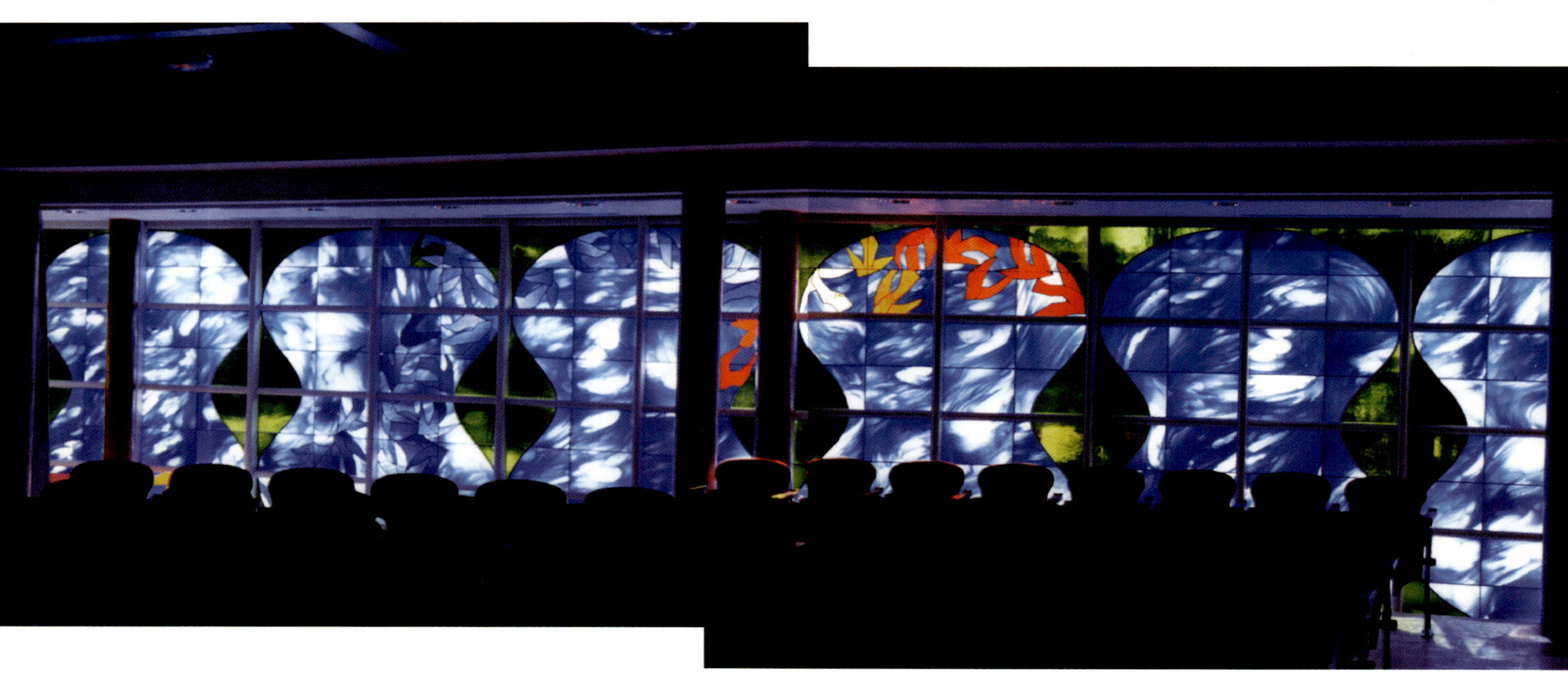

Snapshot montage showing interior view of stained glass

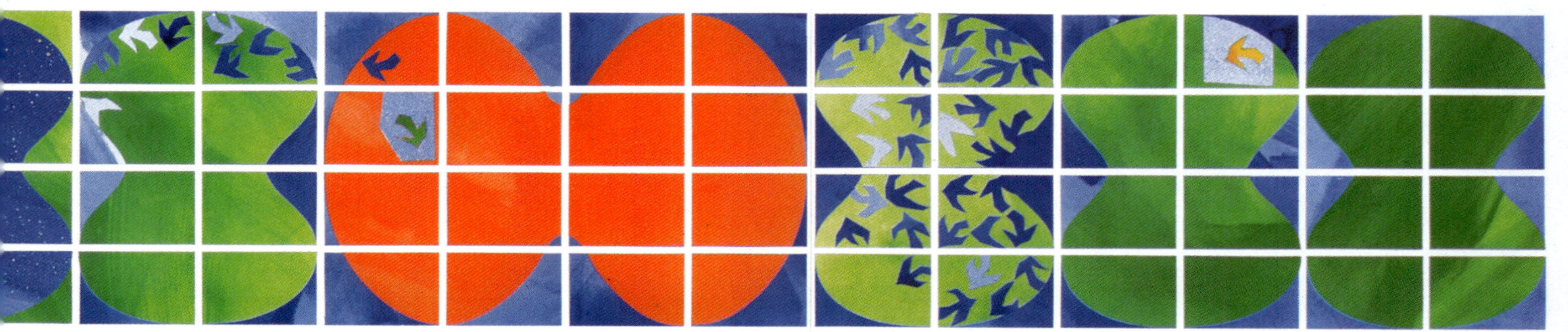

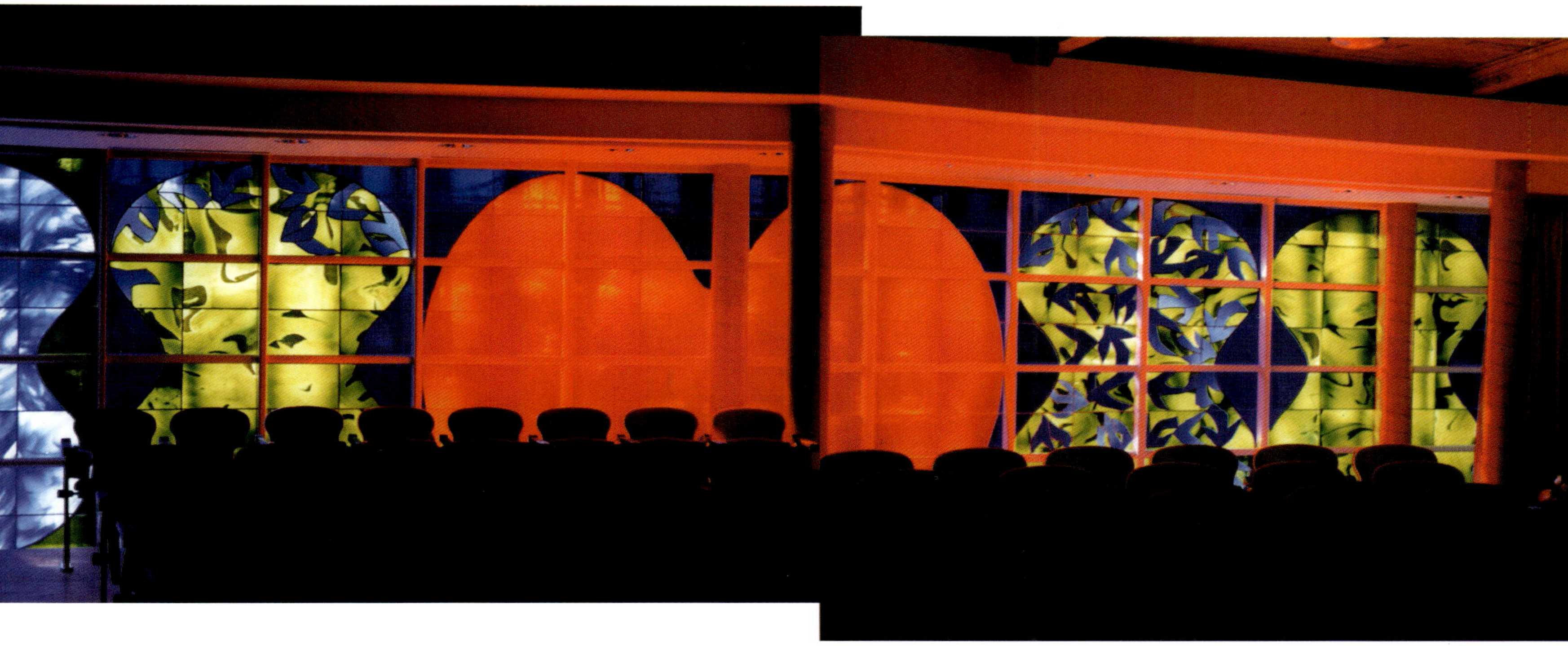

Finding "Villaggio Valentino" is an adventure that begins when in transit through Milan or Rome and via Bari takes you through the meandering lanes of Puglia, past ancient Trulies and churches until you reach this new resort. The conference center / theater forms part of the overall infrastructure of this resort and acts by night as a theatrical backdrop to the restaurant's open terrace. This is the first time I felt the real pull of huge organic forms and it was this wall that inspired the idea for the "Glass Wall."

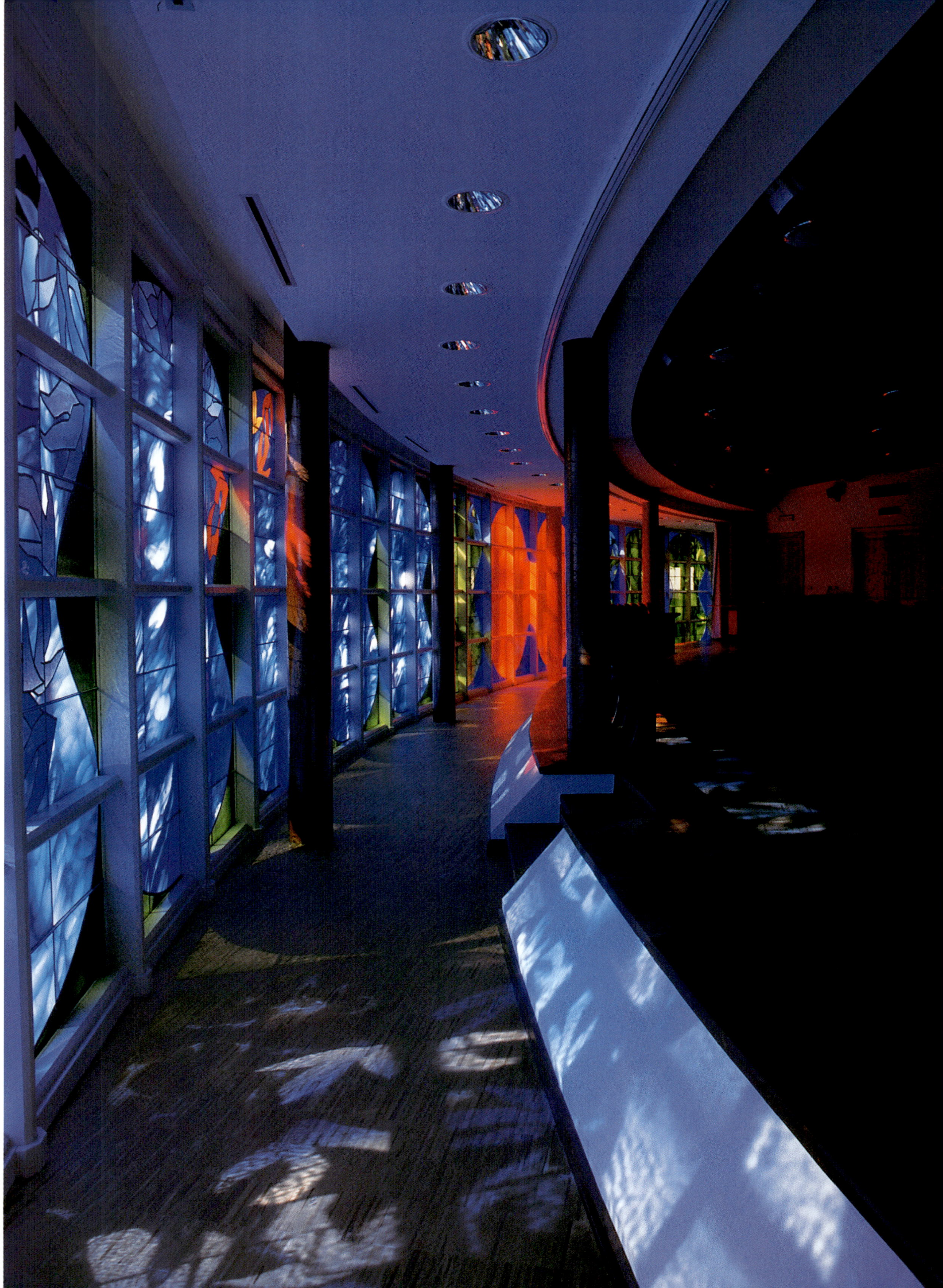

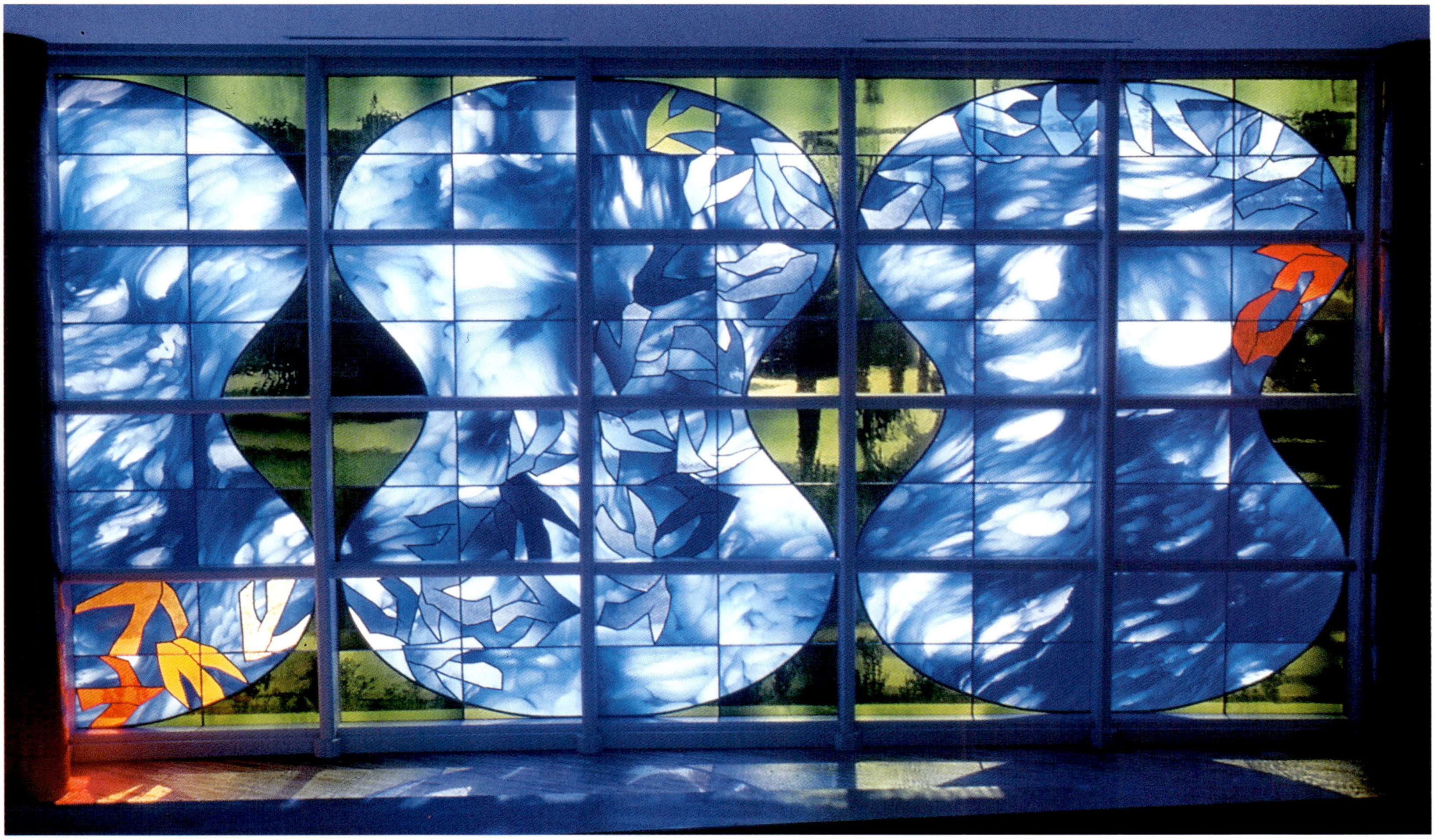

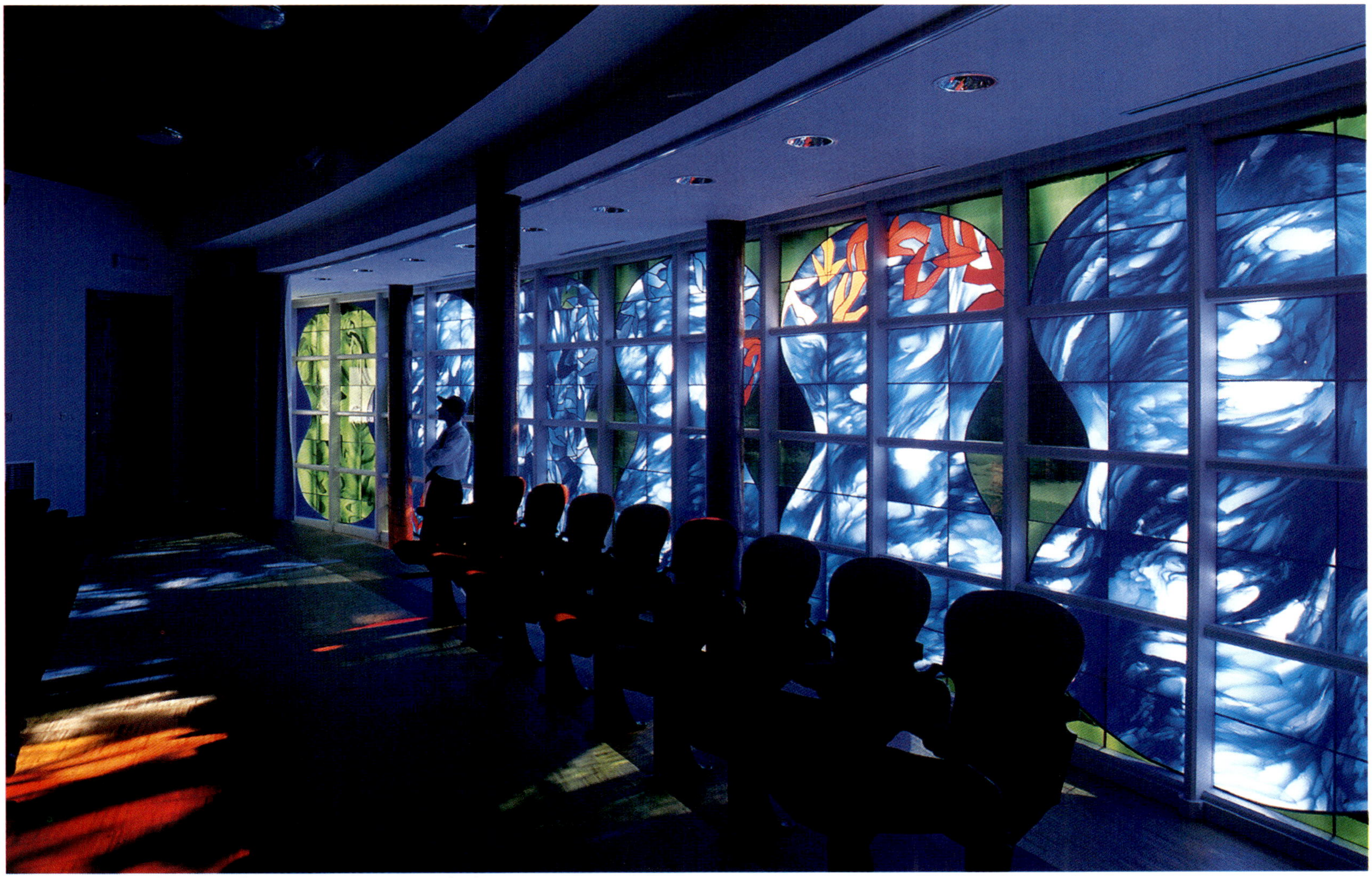

Interior views of the conference center stained glass

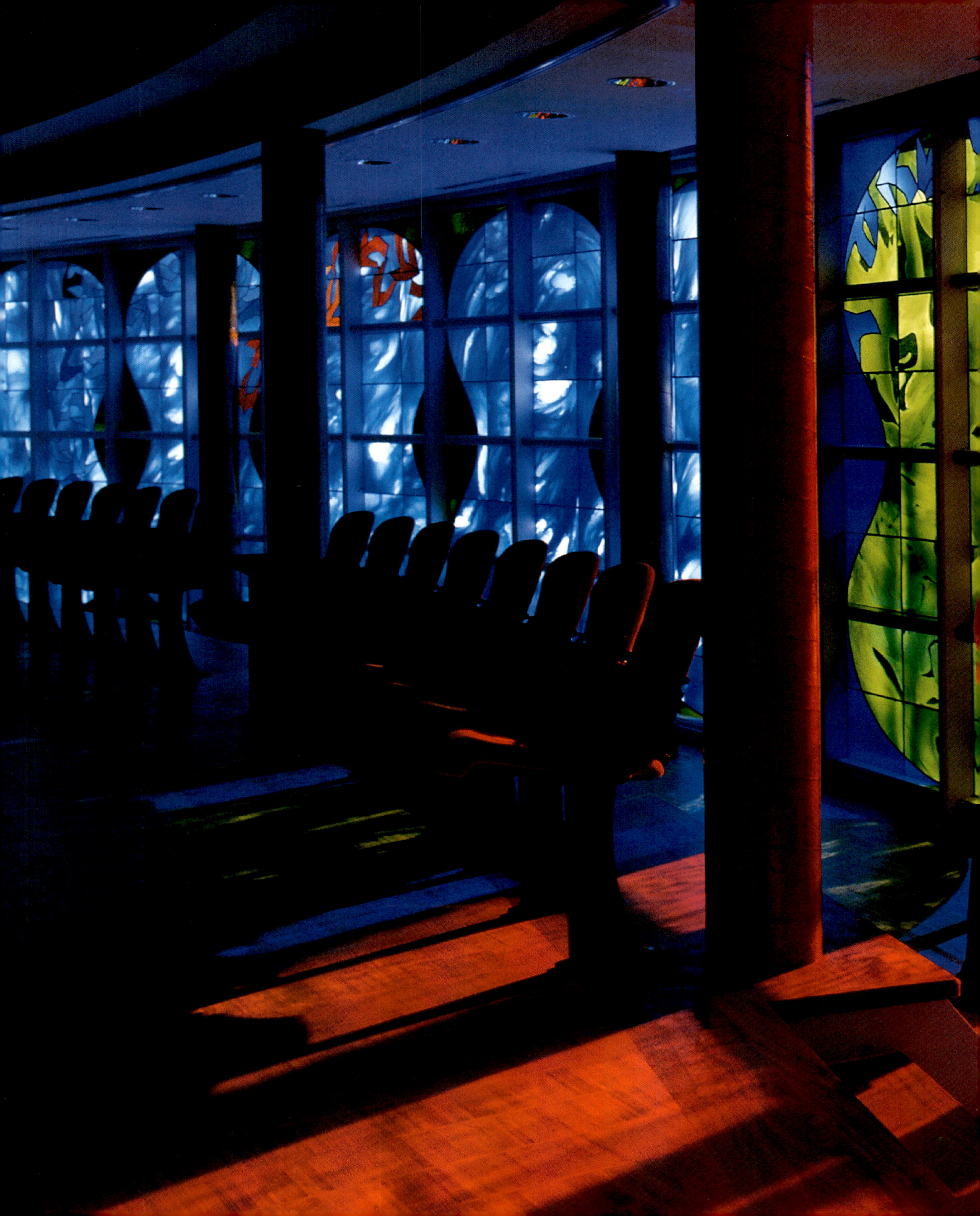

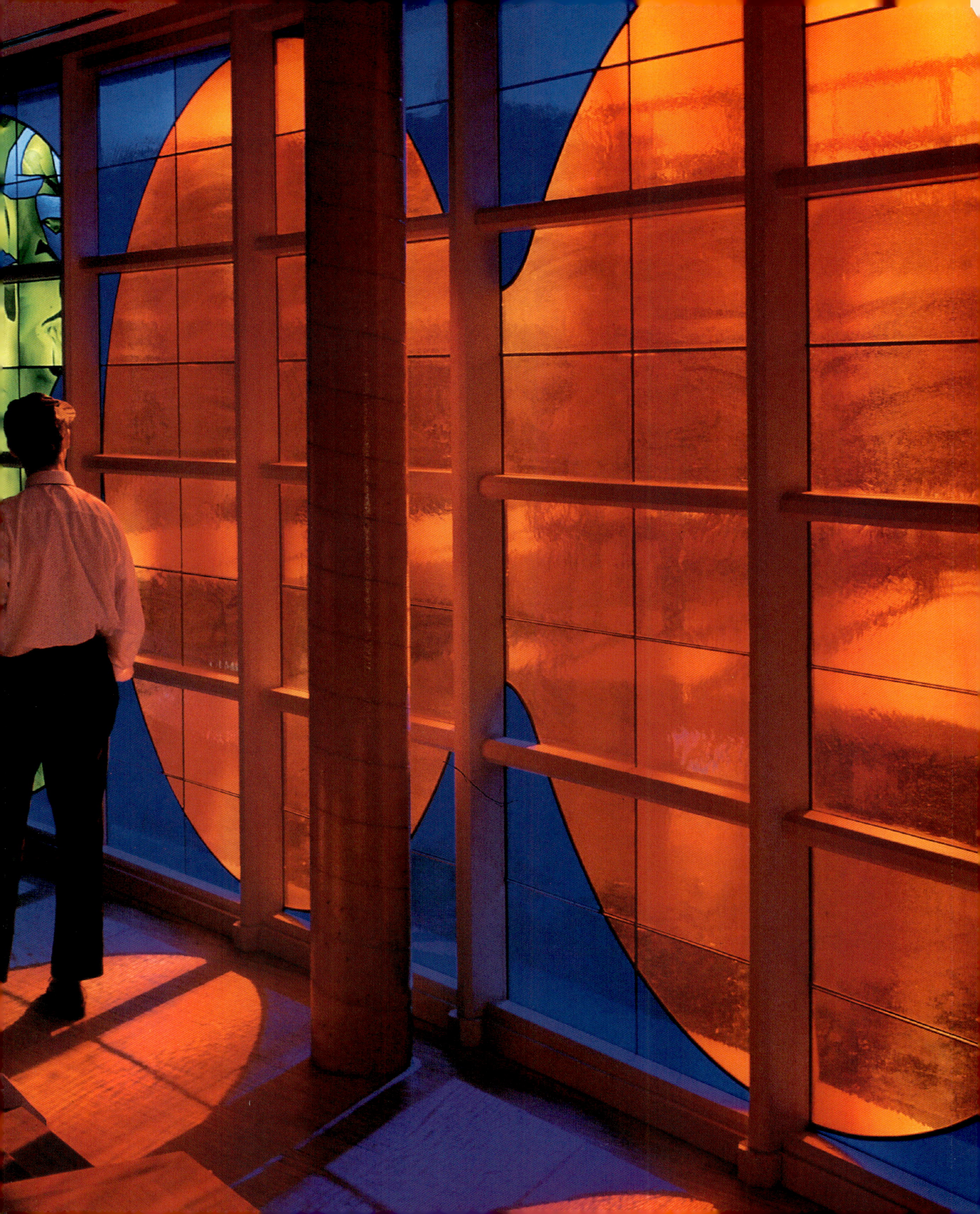

PFIZER WORLD HEADQUARTERS
NEW YORK, NEW YORK, USA
1996 - 1997

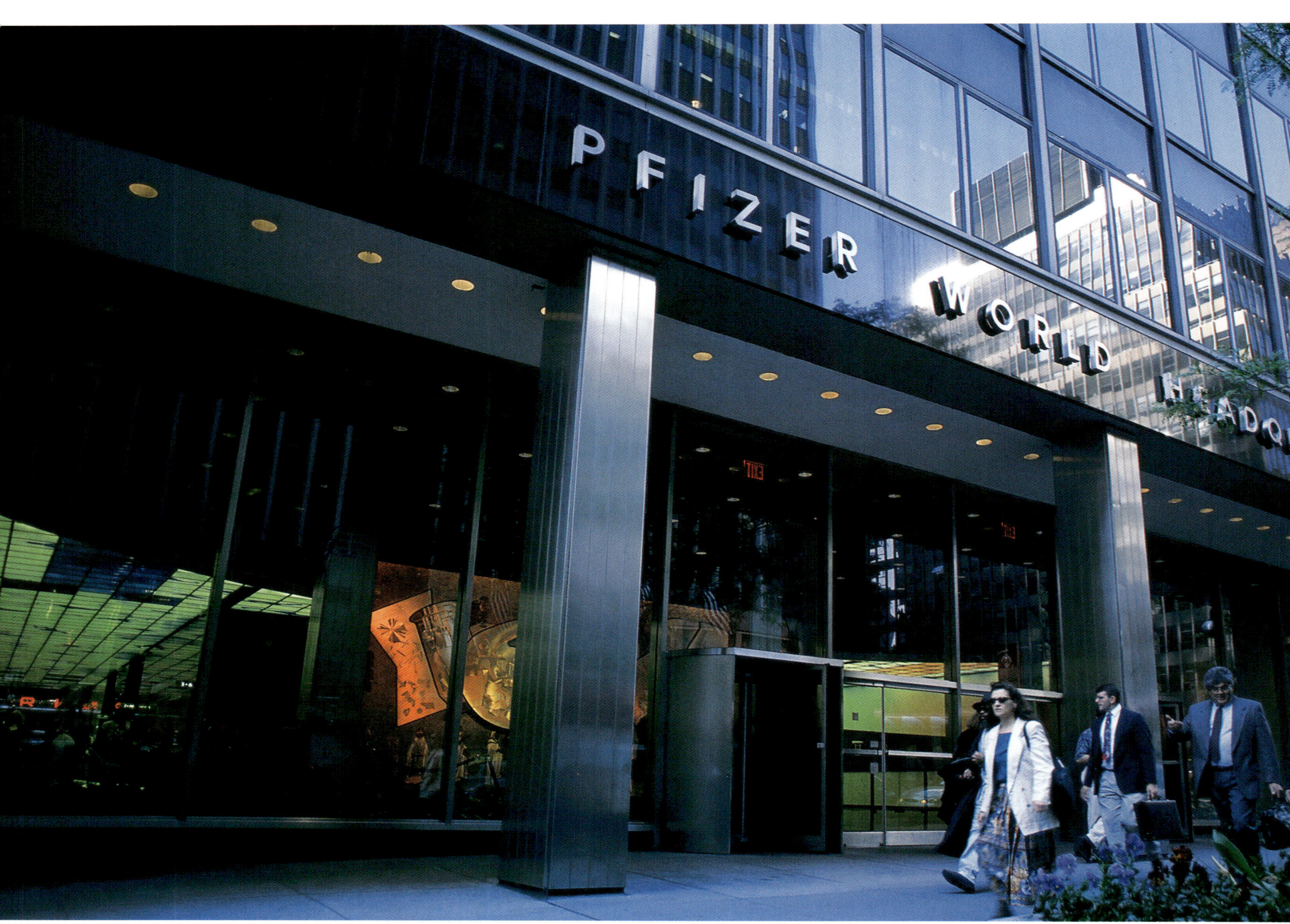

Architect: Hixon Design Consultants

Stained glass and mosaic ceiling
4,833 sq ft (total)

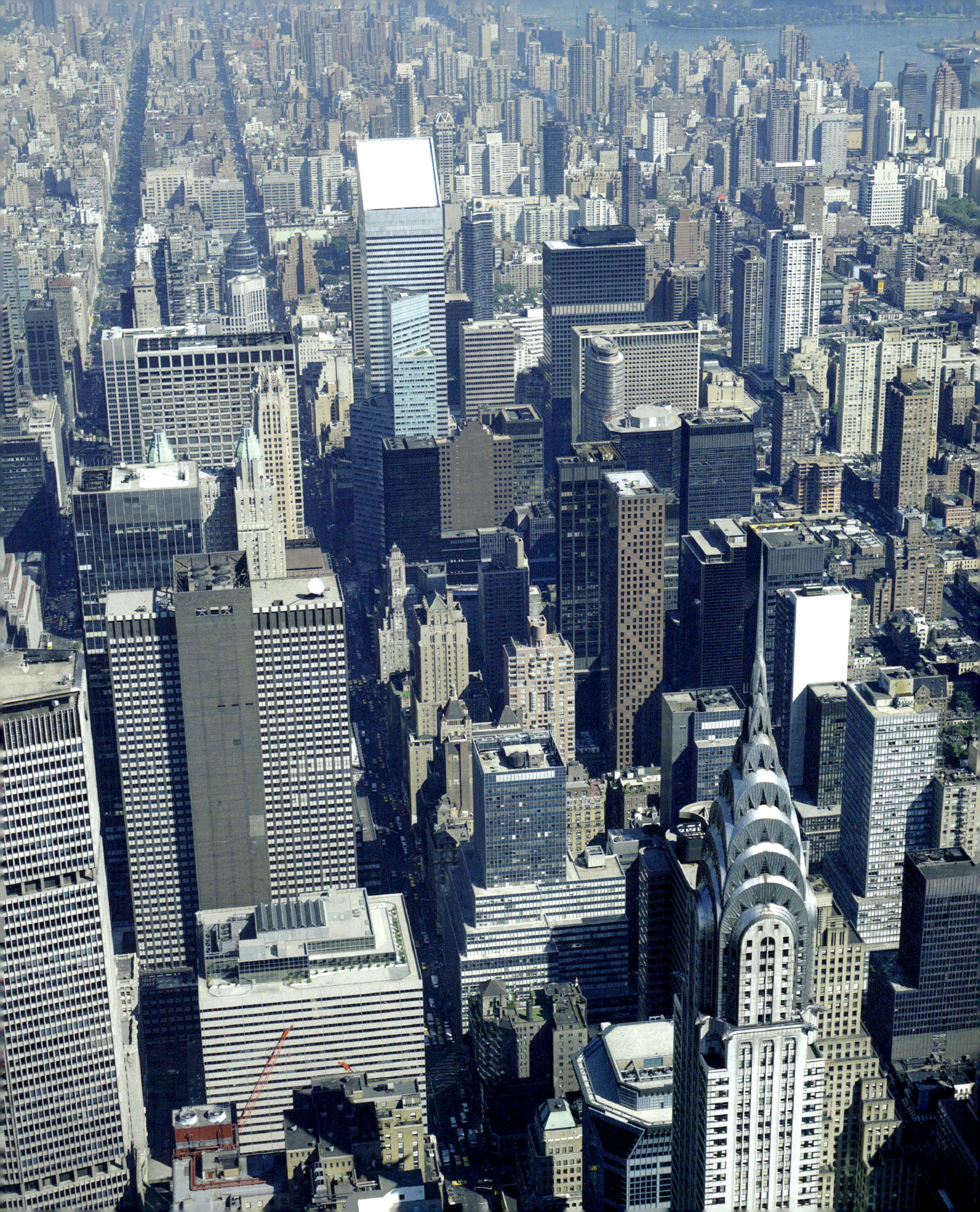

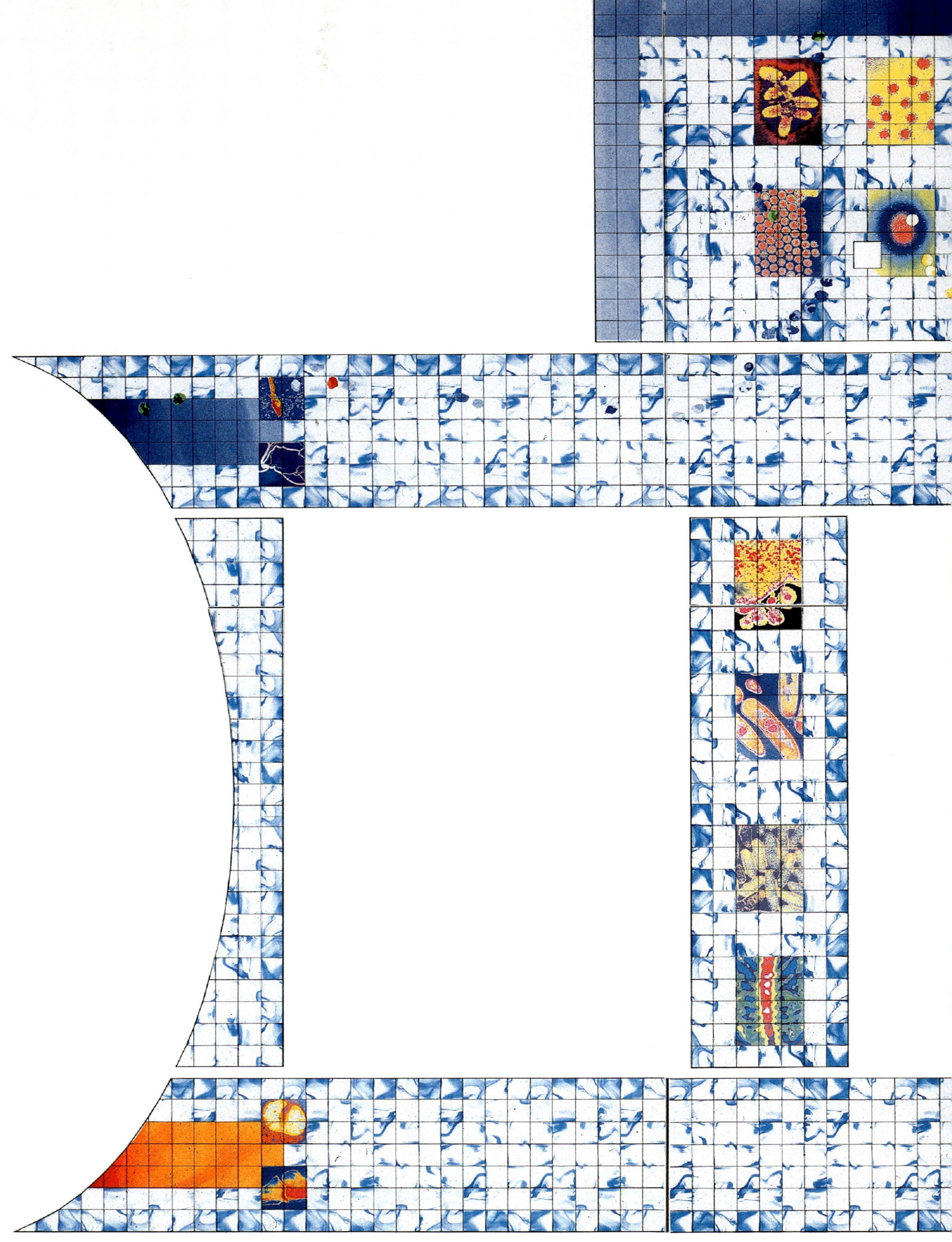

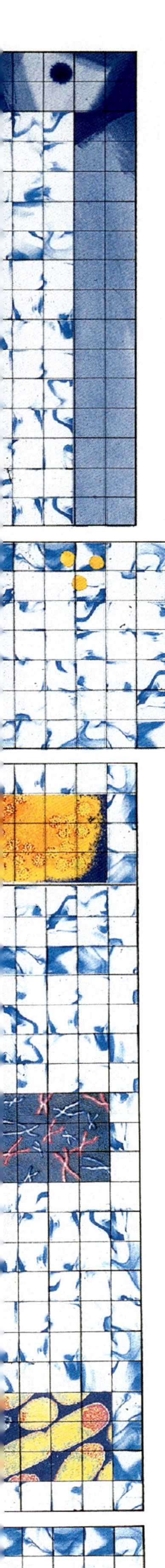

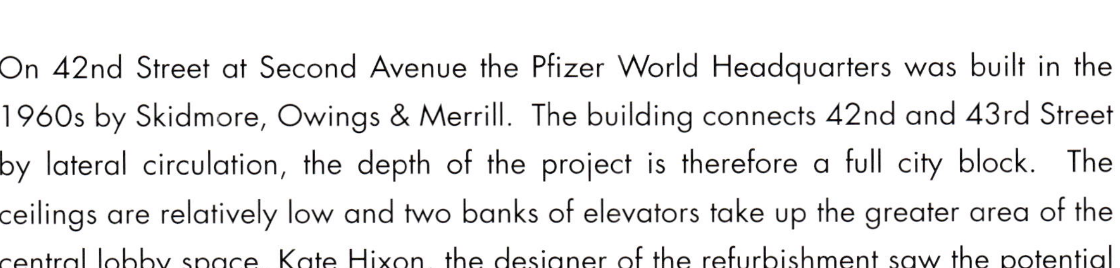

On 42nd Street at Second Avenue the Pfizer World Headquarters was built in the 1960s by Skidmore, Owings & Merrill. The building connects 42nd and 43rd Street by lateral circulation, the depth of the project is therefore a full city block. The ceilings are relatively low and two banks of elevators take up the greater area of the central lobby space. Kate Hixon, the designer of the refurbishment saw the potential in changing the sixties panel - lighted ceiling for stained glass.

My first thought was to try and visually increase the ceiling height, improving the rather pinched vertical space. I like to think that all my projects explore the specific nature of the architecture, the site and the function of the building. This means addressing problems relating to a great variety of practical and philosophical issues. Massing, layering, weight, buoyancy, light, texture, rigidity, fluidity, pedestrian and vehicular movement, climatic and seasonal change and of course function. The Pfizer Building functions as the world headquarters for a global pharmaceutical company and the imagery in the composition reflects that.

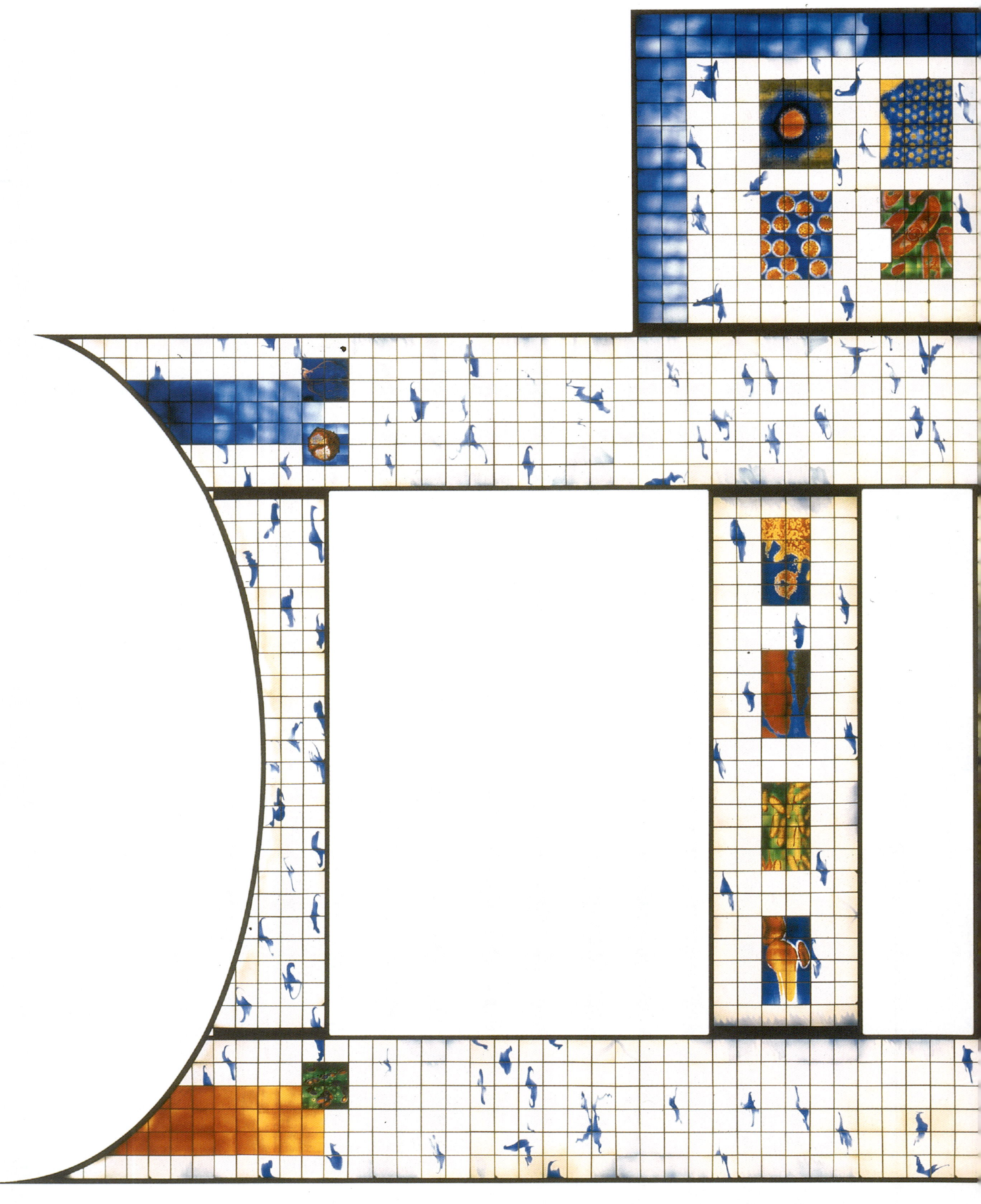

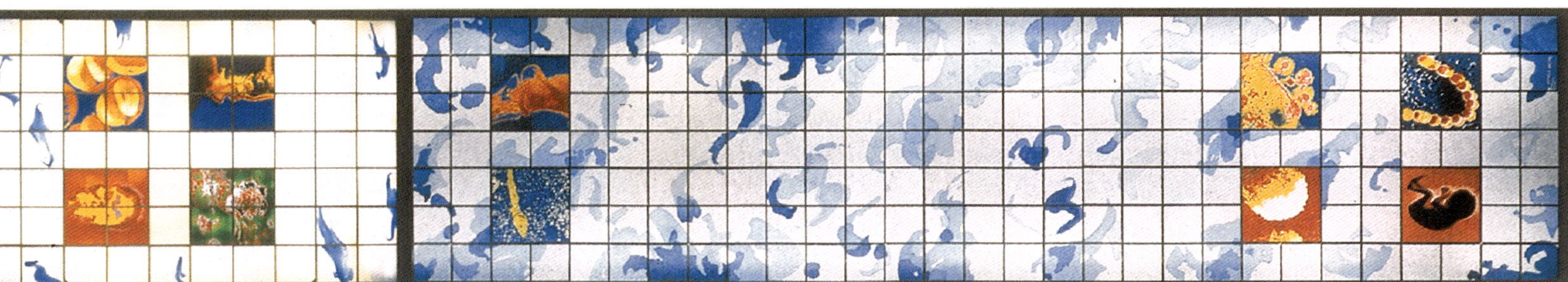

Microphotographic images of cells, bones, organs and tissues explore not only my own philosophical inquiry to try and understand something of our human condition but also an expression of the "genius loci" of this building.

The "amorphic" forms that constitute the active blue areas within the opal white field are my first attempt at creating such forms out of shapes born during the molten stage of glass production.

Moving into mosaic for the North corridor ceiling was a decision informed by subjective desire as much as objective need. The change of medium at this point creates a physical and emotional shift analogous to the architectural change occasioned as we move from the spacious central lobby into the confined corridor.

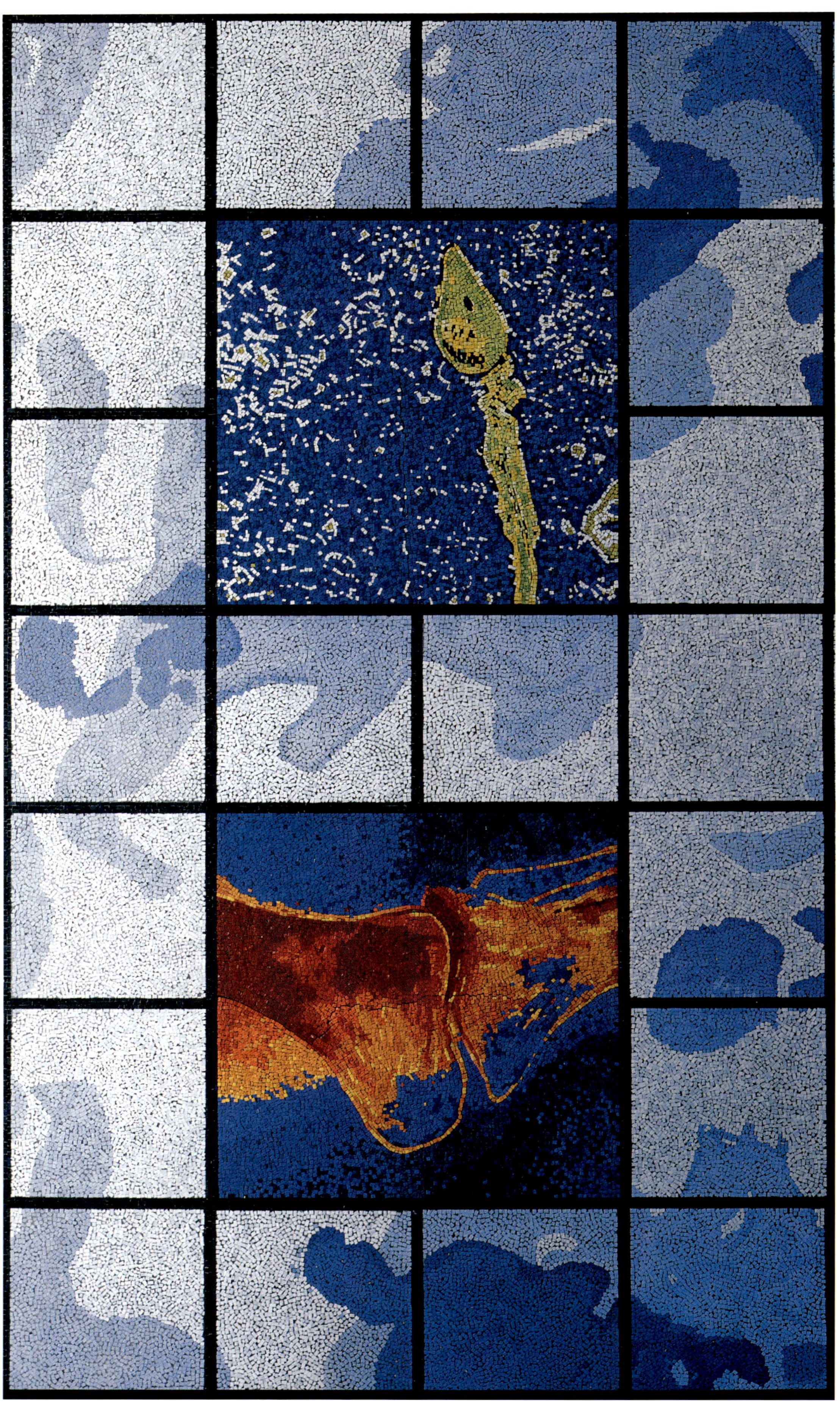

Ceiling mosaic showing sperm and X-ray: rheumatoid arthritis of knee

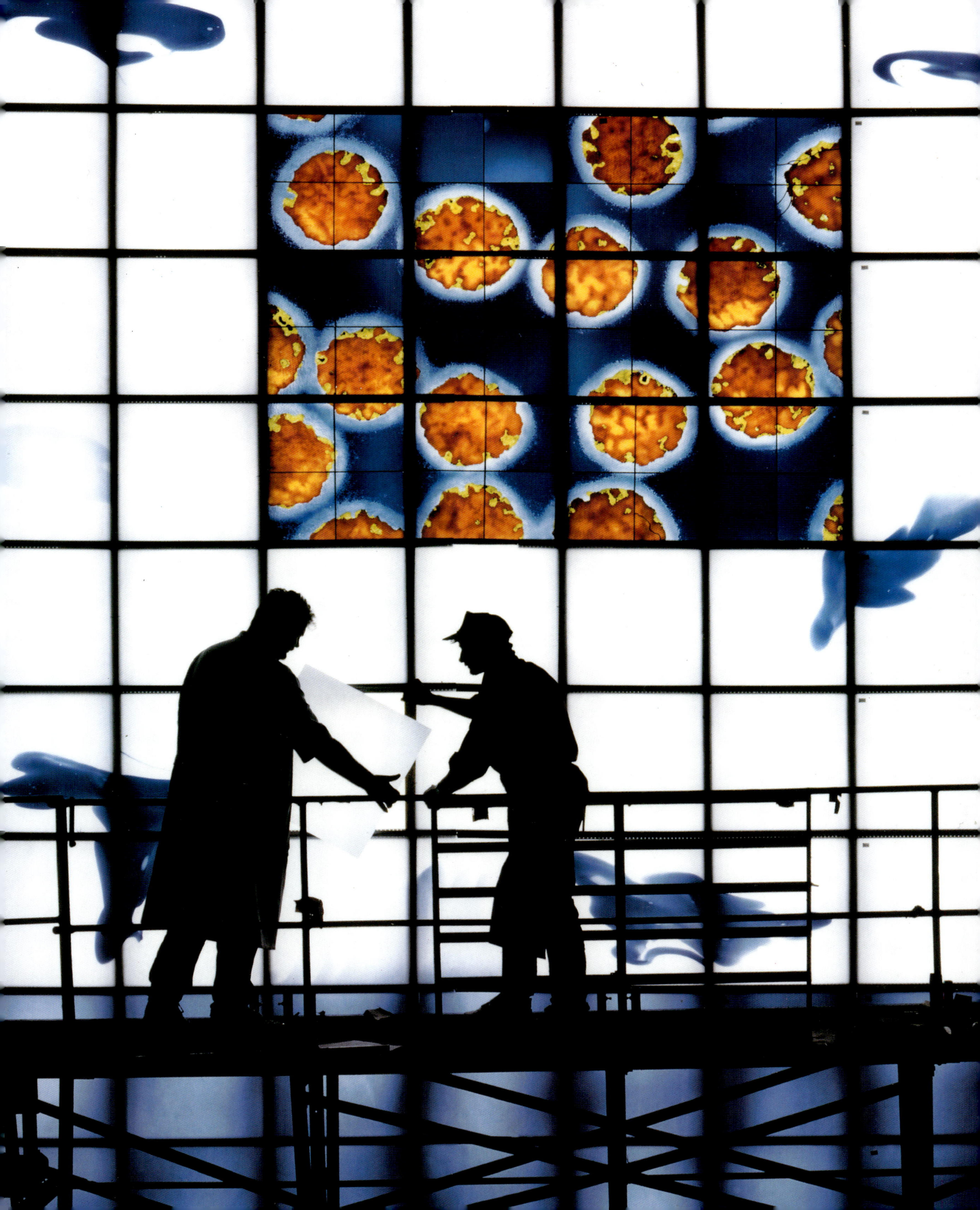

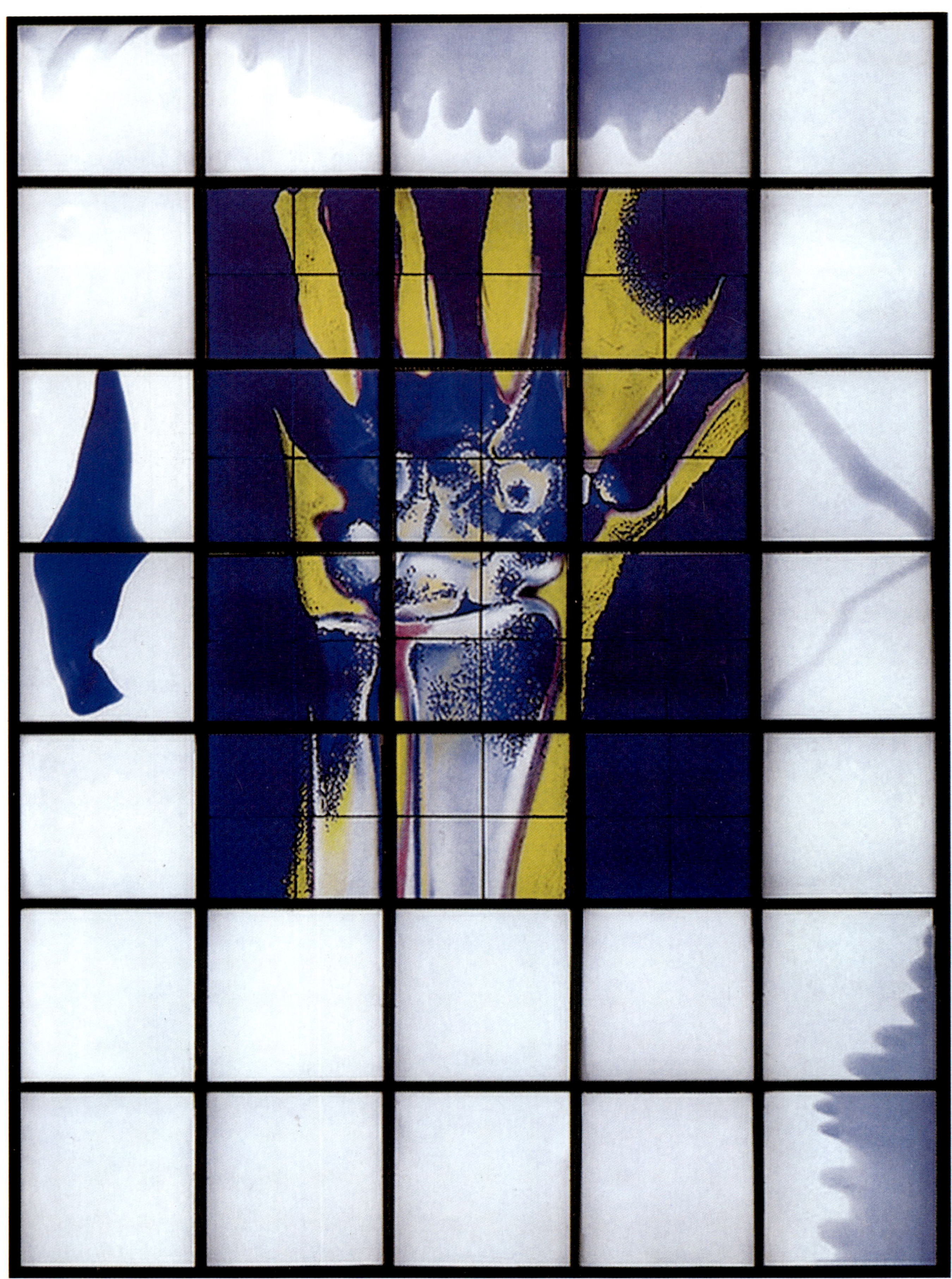

Ceiling stained glass showing X-ray: normal wrist

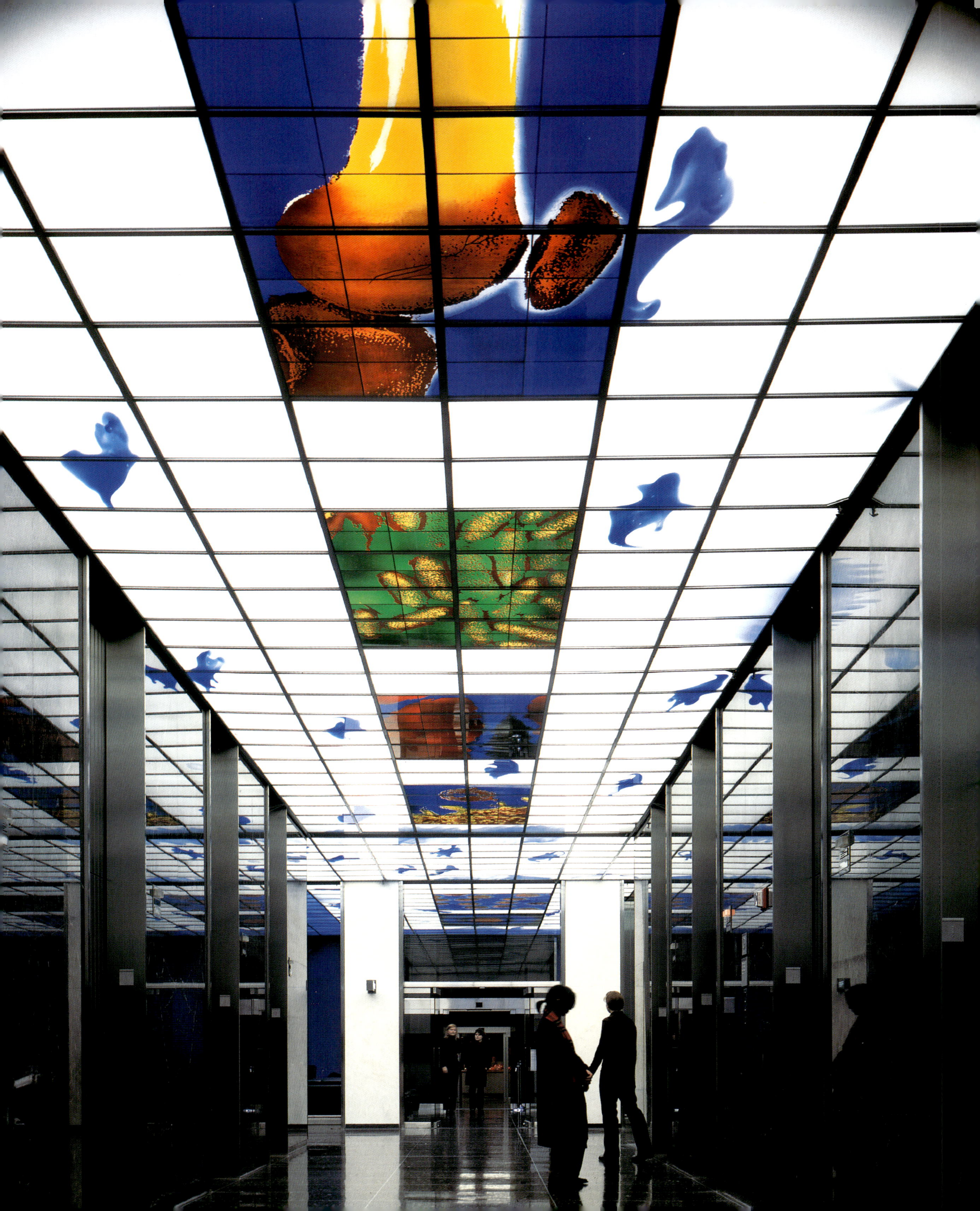

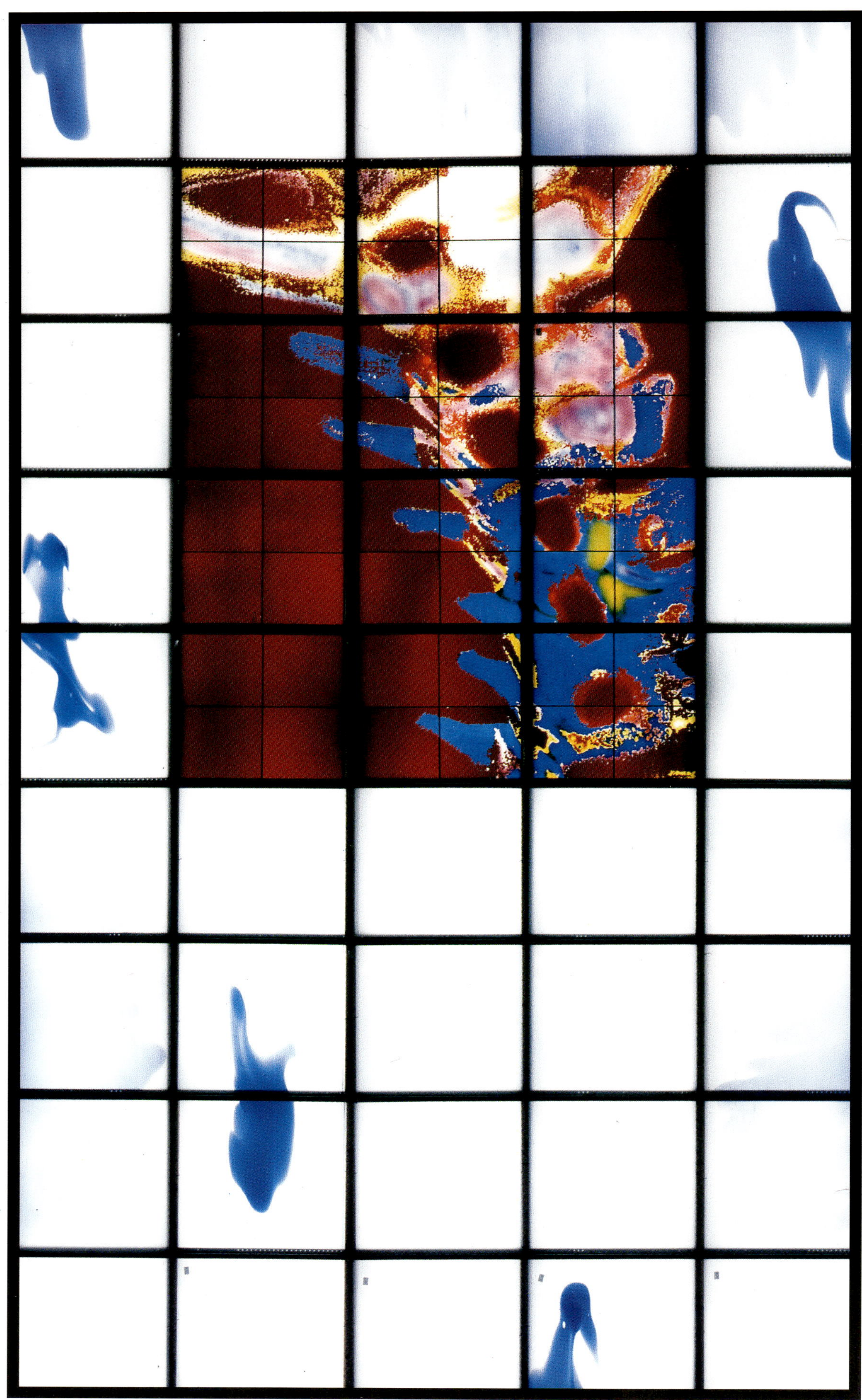

Ceiling stained glass showing X-ray: cervical vertebrae

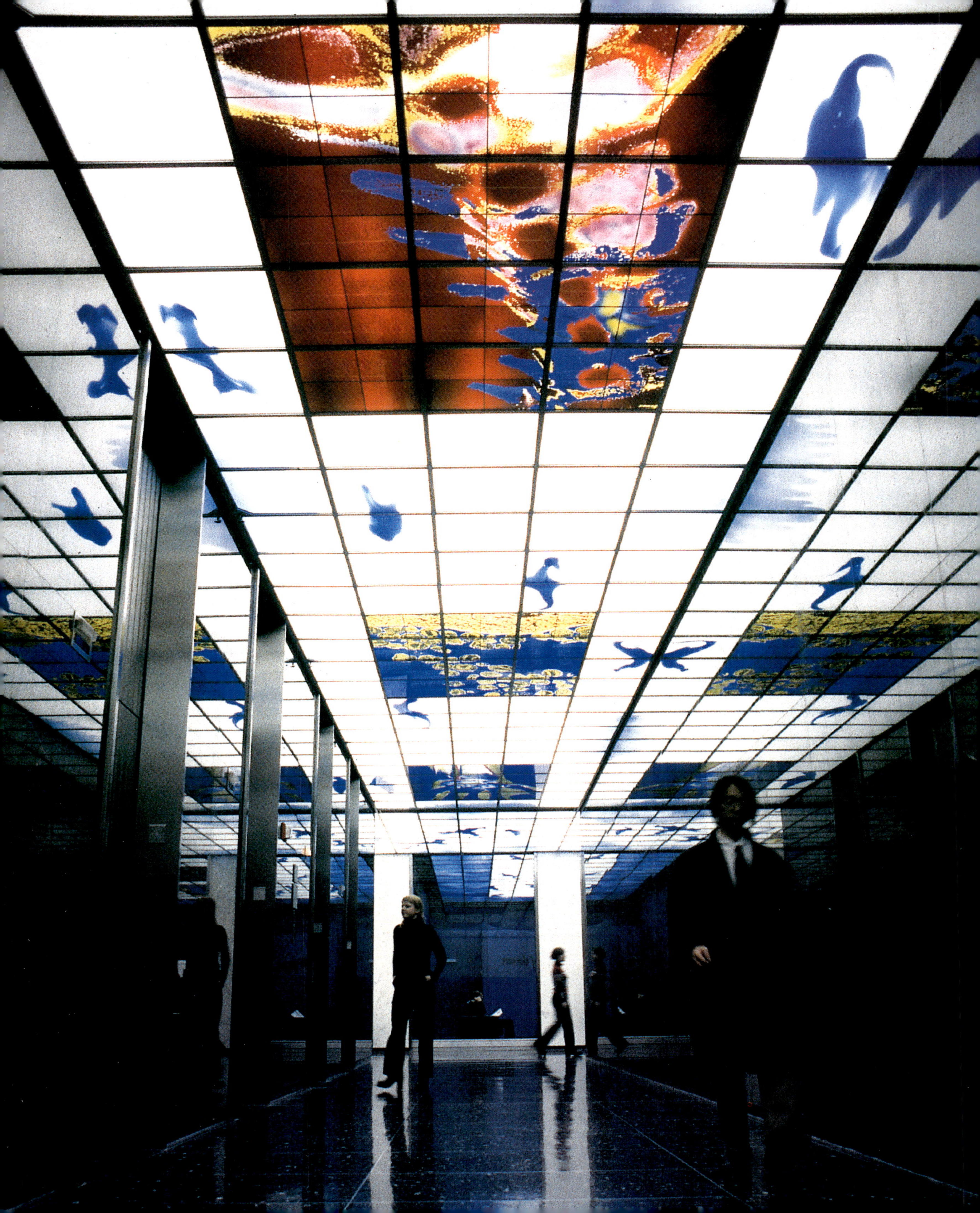

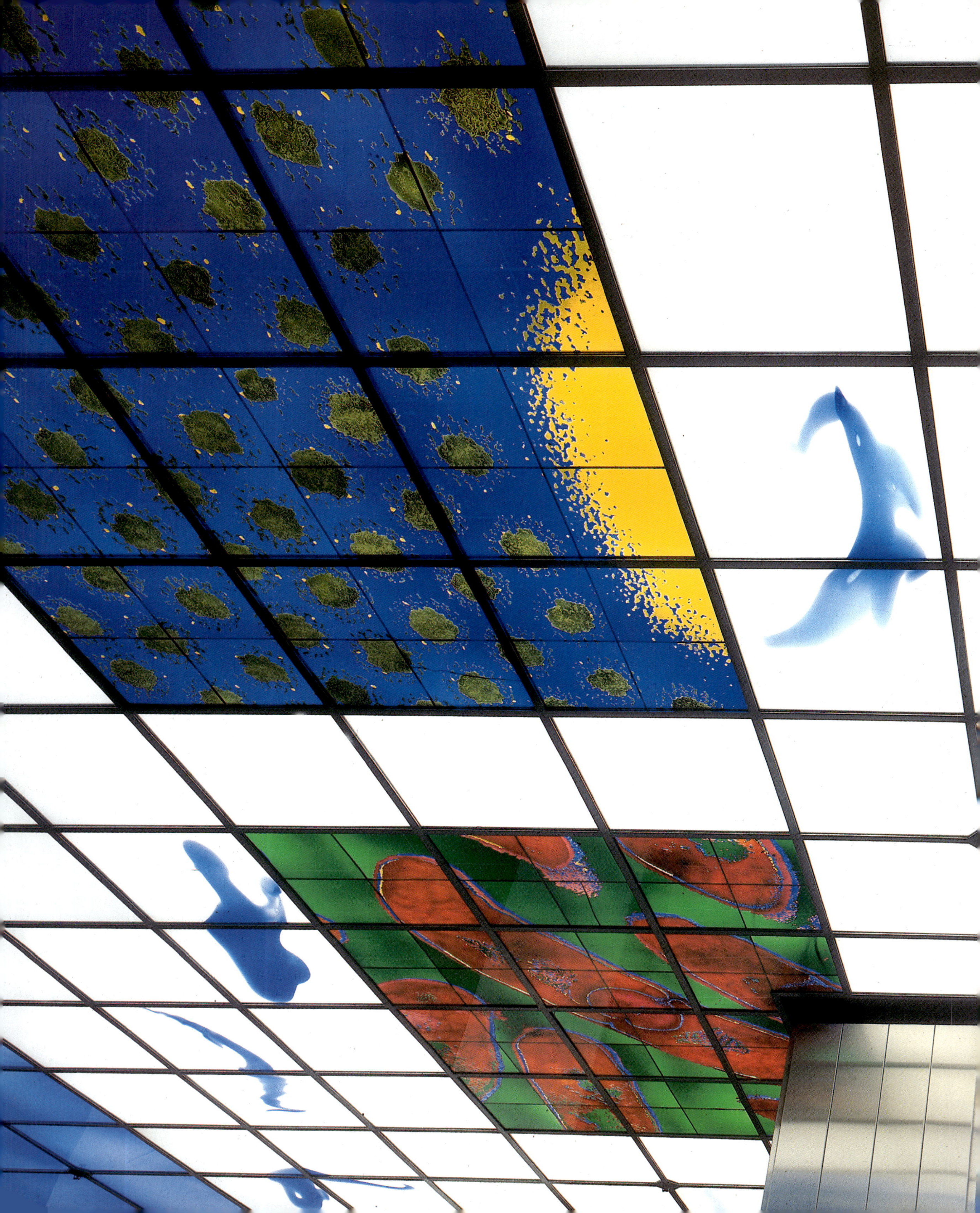

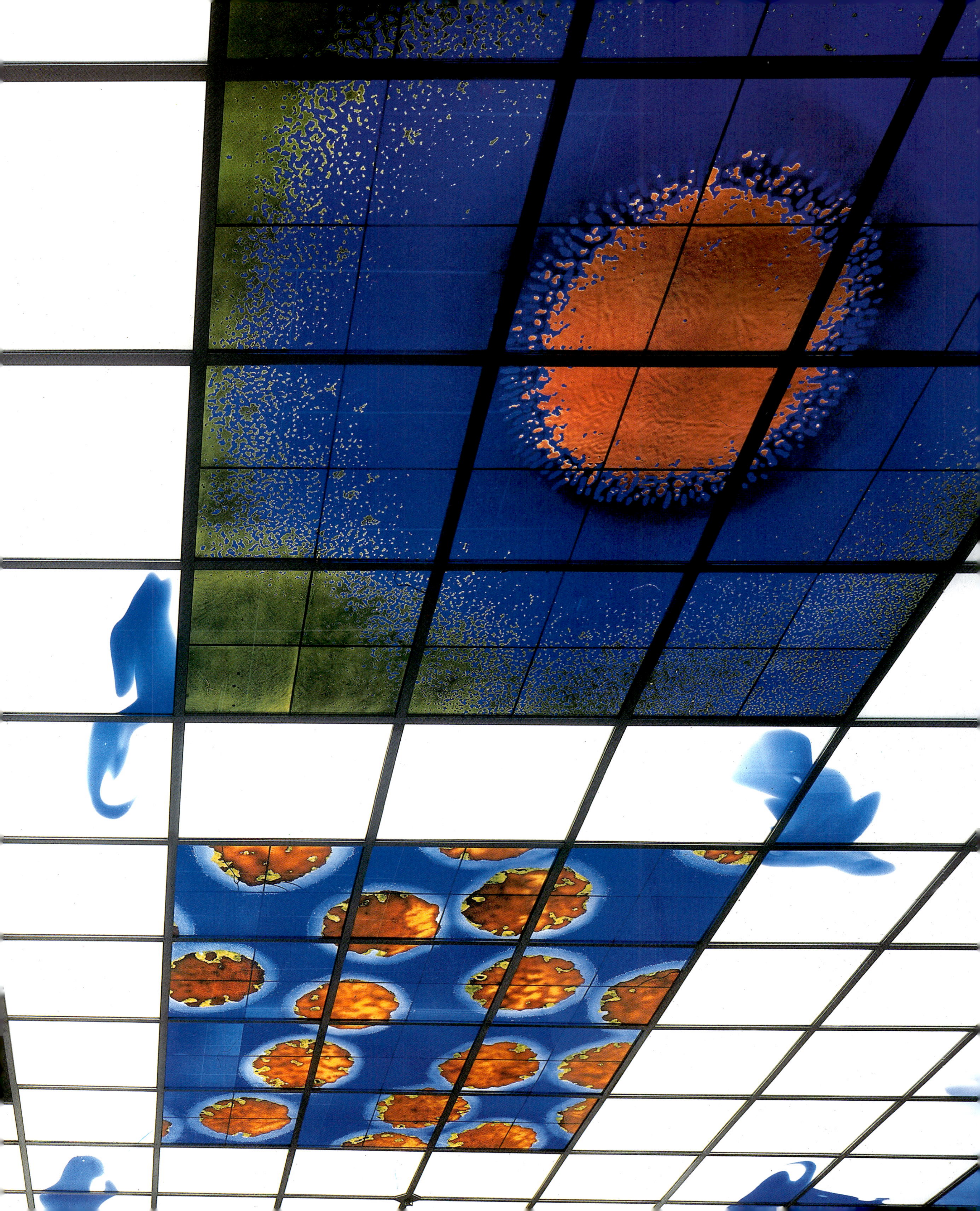

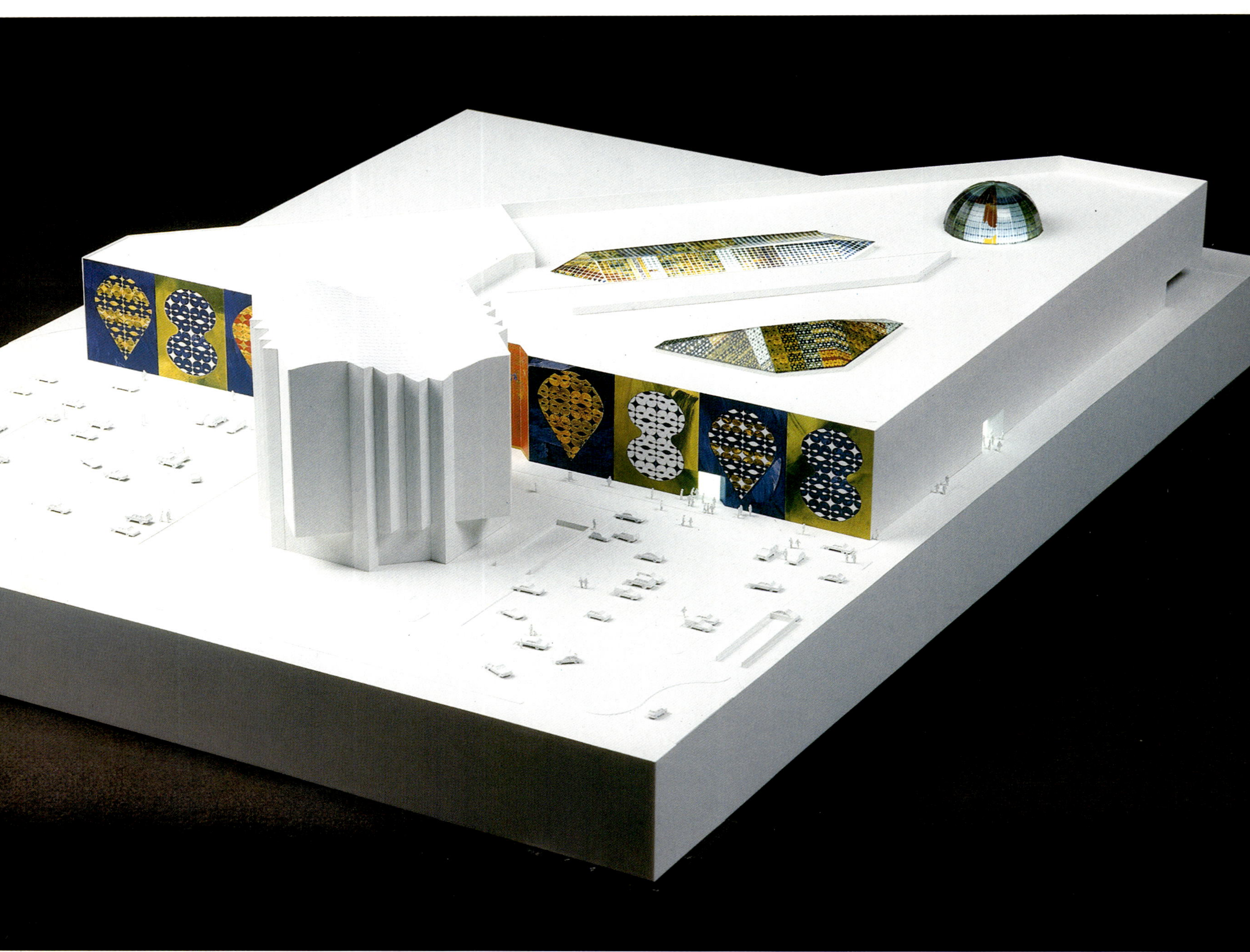

Architect: Julio Neves, São Paulo, Brazil

Proposals for stained glass and mosaic
21,700 sq ft (glass)
33,800 sq ft (mosaic)

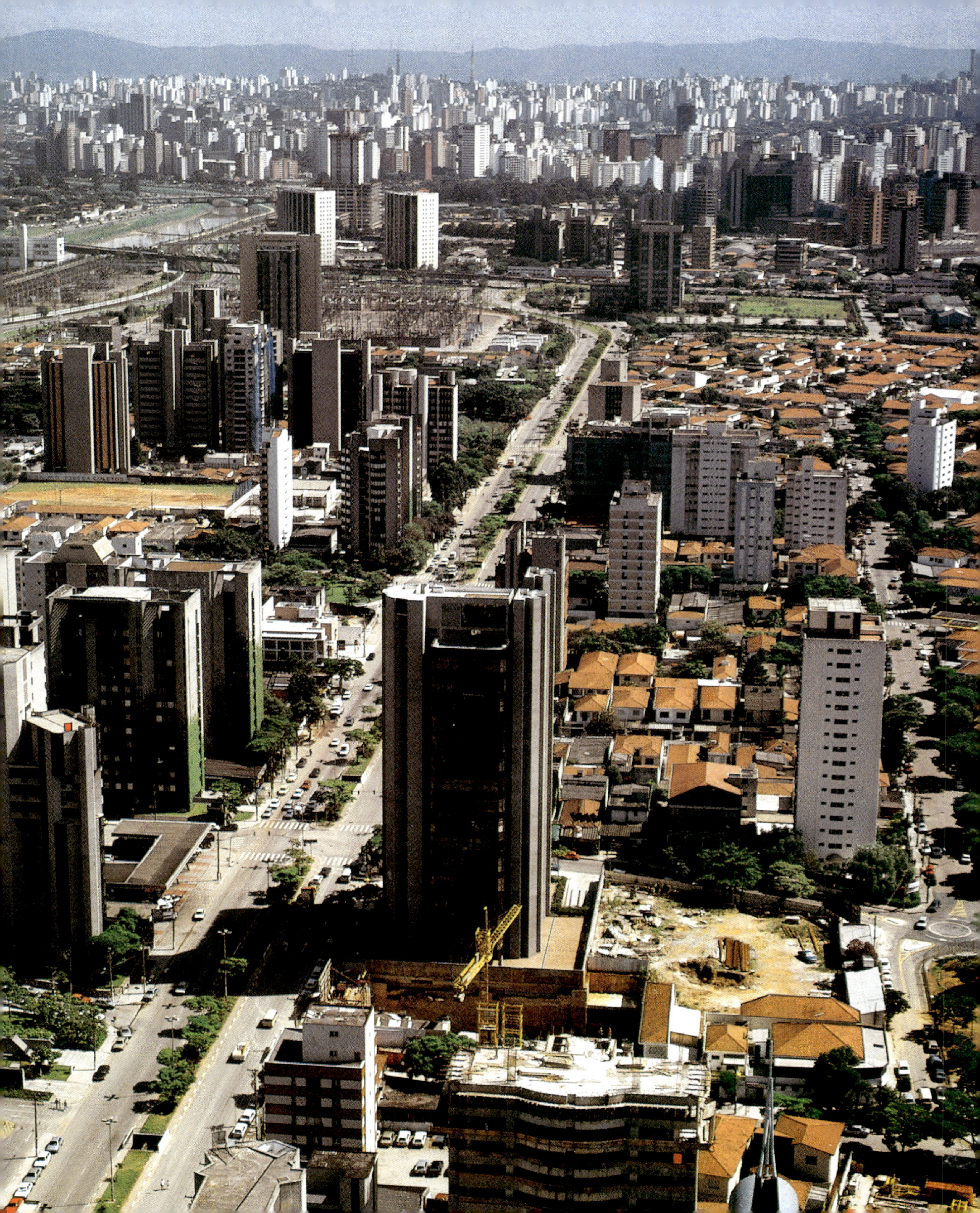

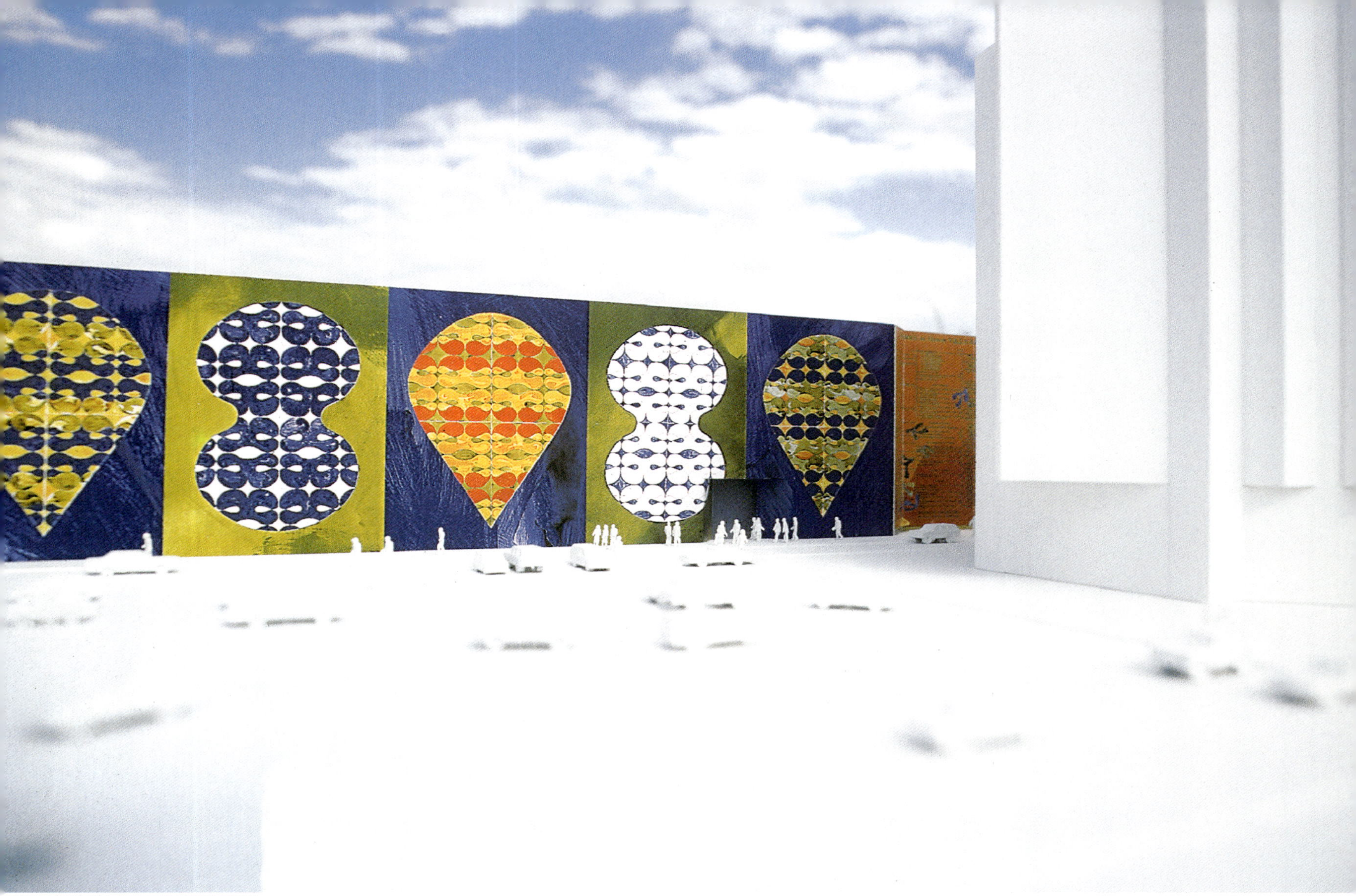

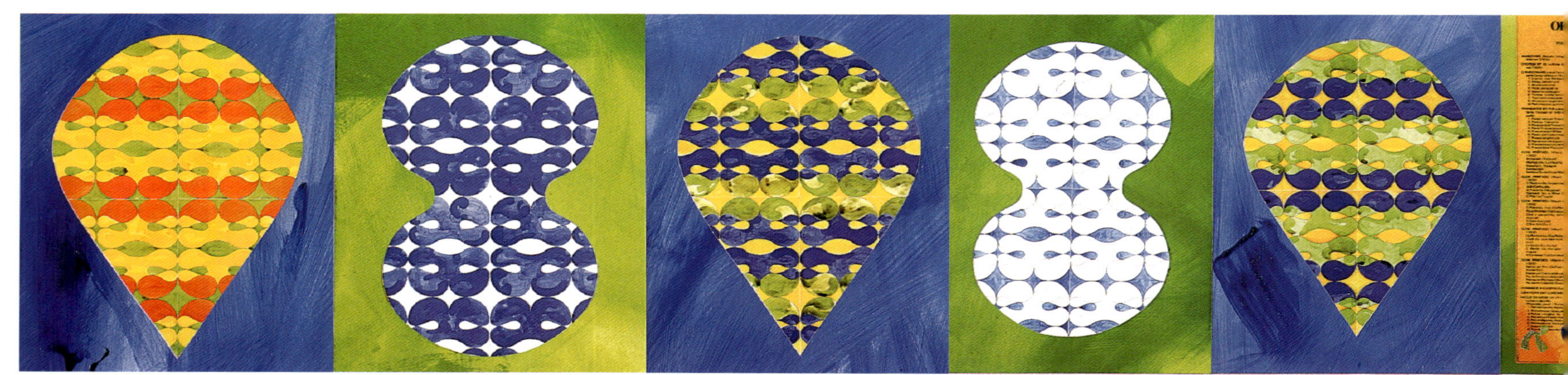

Model

Design

The intensity of downtown São Paulo is difficult to describe to those who don't know it. Somewhere between Charles Dickens' *Hard Times* and Ridley Scotts' *Bladerunner*, the frenzied complexity of this ultimate urban experience needs to be both acknowledged and contrasted. This is just the beginning of that task. I feel it may open some interesting doors.

The musician, Hector Villa Lobos, combined folk tradition with avant-garde composition. This new center in São Paulo, located by the university, is named after him. The gigantic external mosaic and the skylights are all an attempt to bring something of contemporary and historical São Paulo into a transparent fusion of color. Using ciphers particular to Villa Lobos, the plectrum and guitar, I've made here a first attempt at creating a canopy of flickering translucent interconnected shapes that replicate the impact of a net of foliage suspended above a forest.

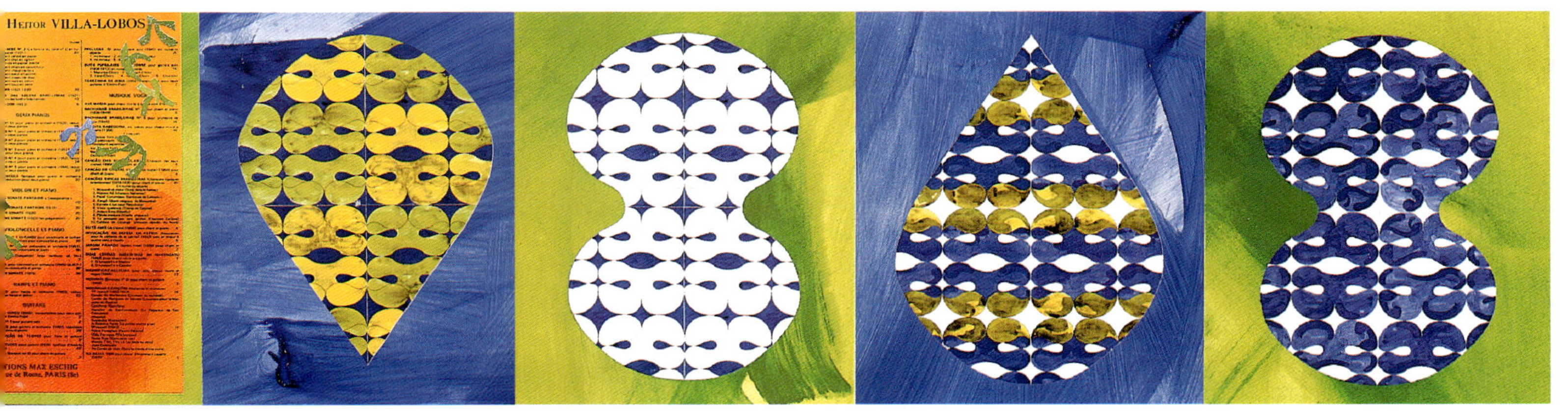

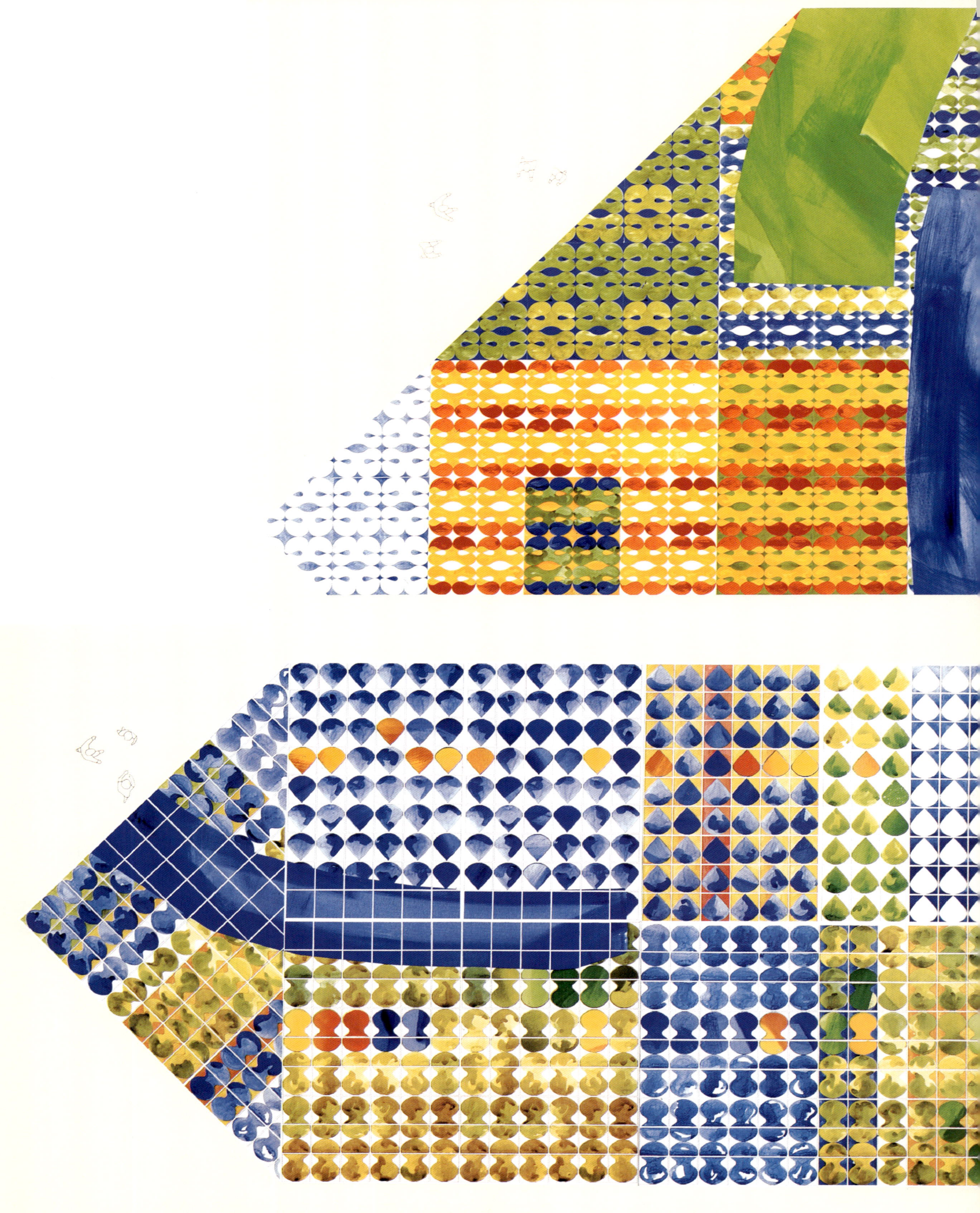

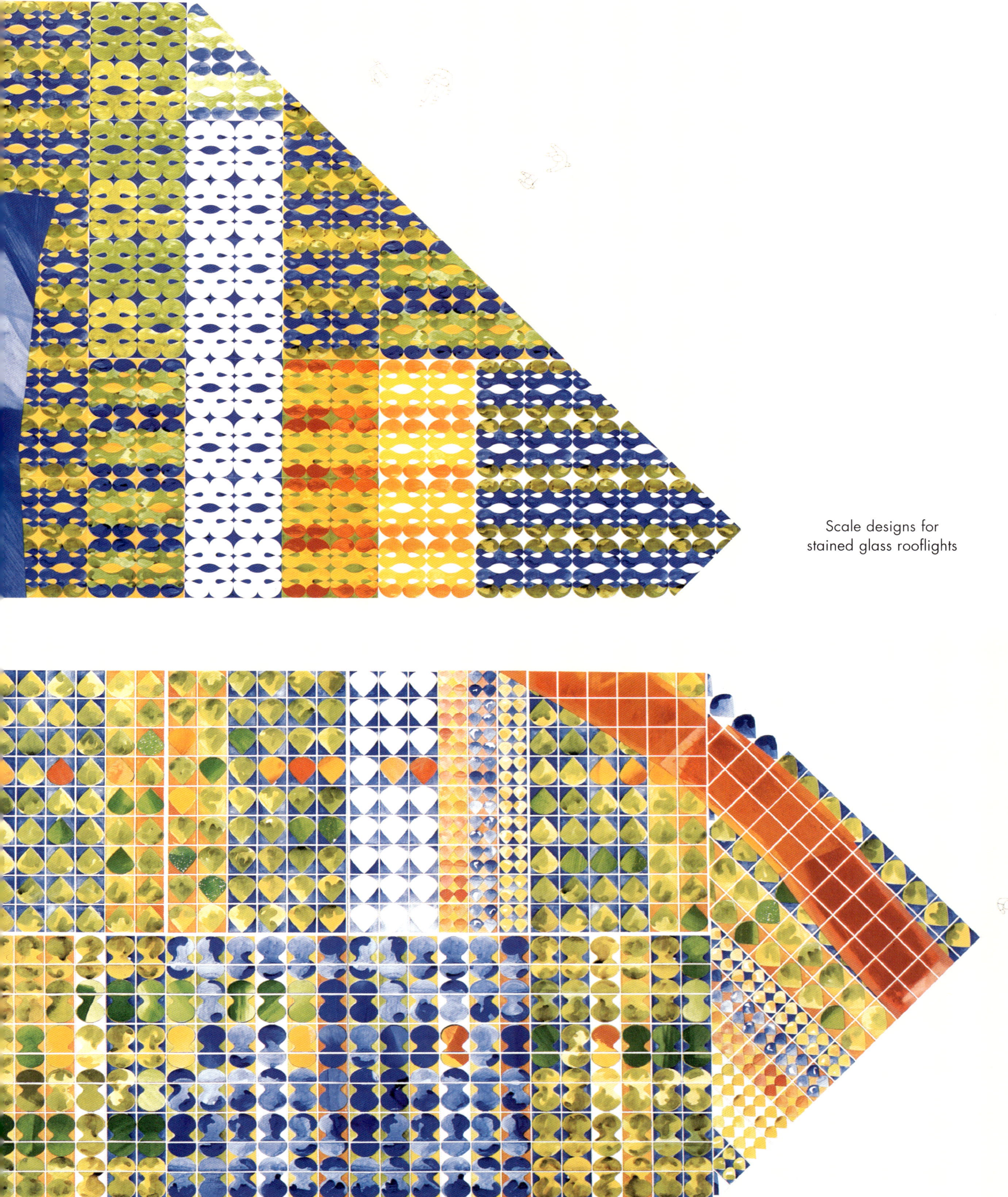

Scale designs for
stained glass rooflights

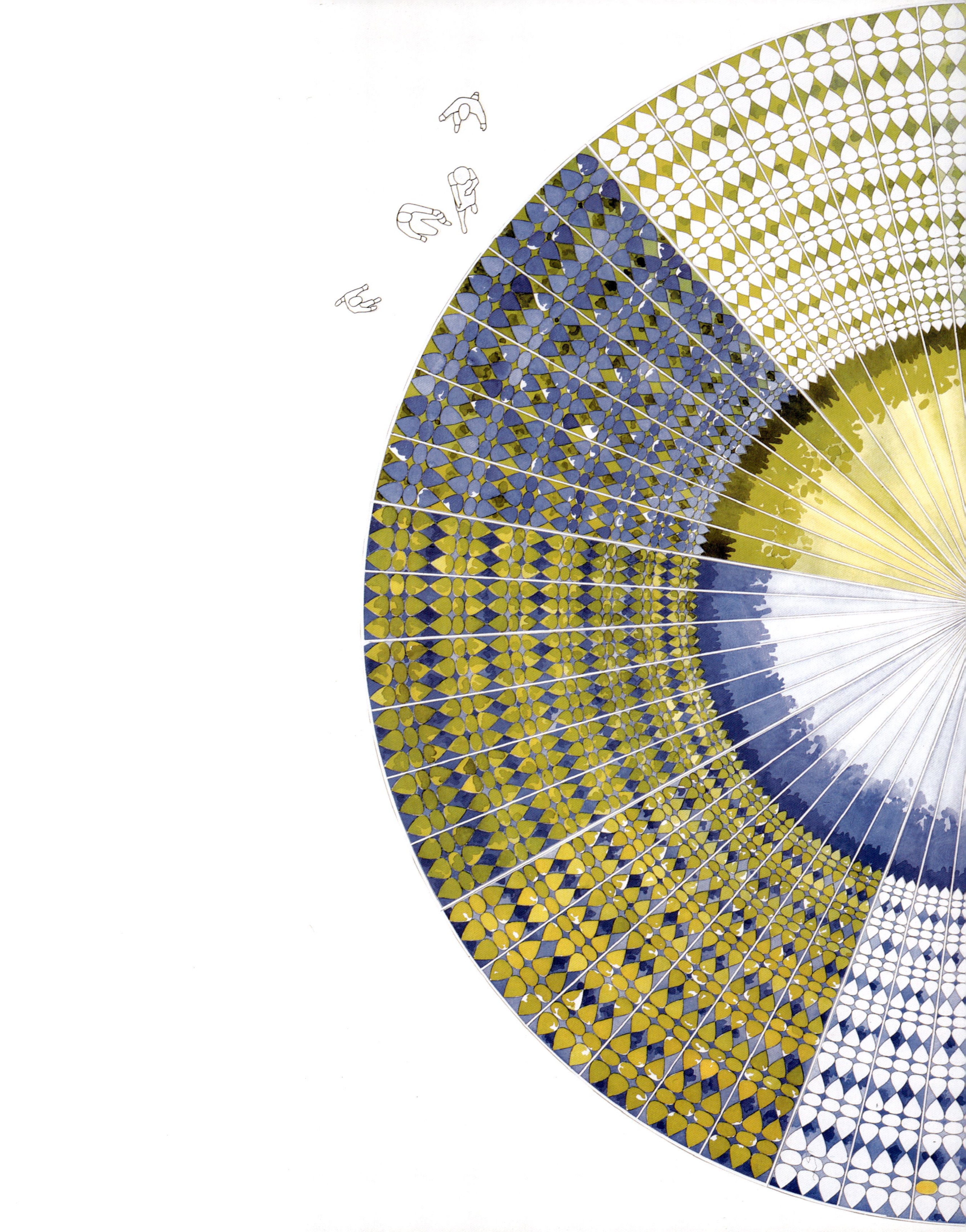

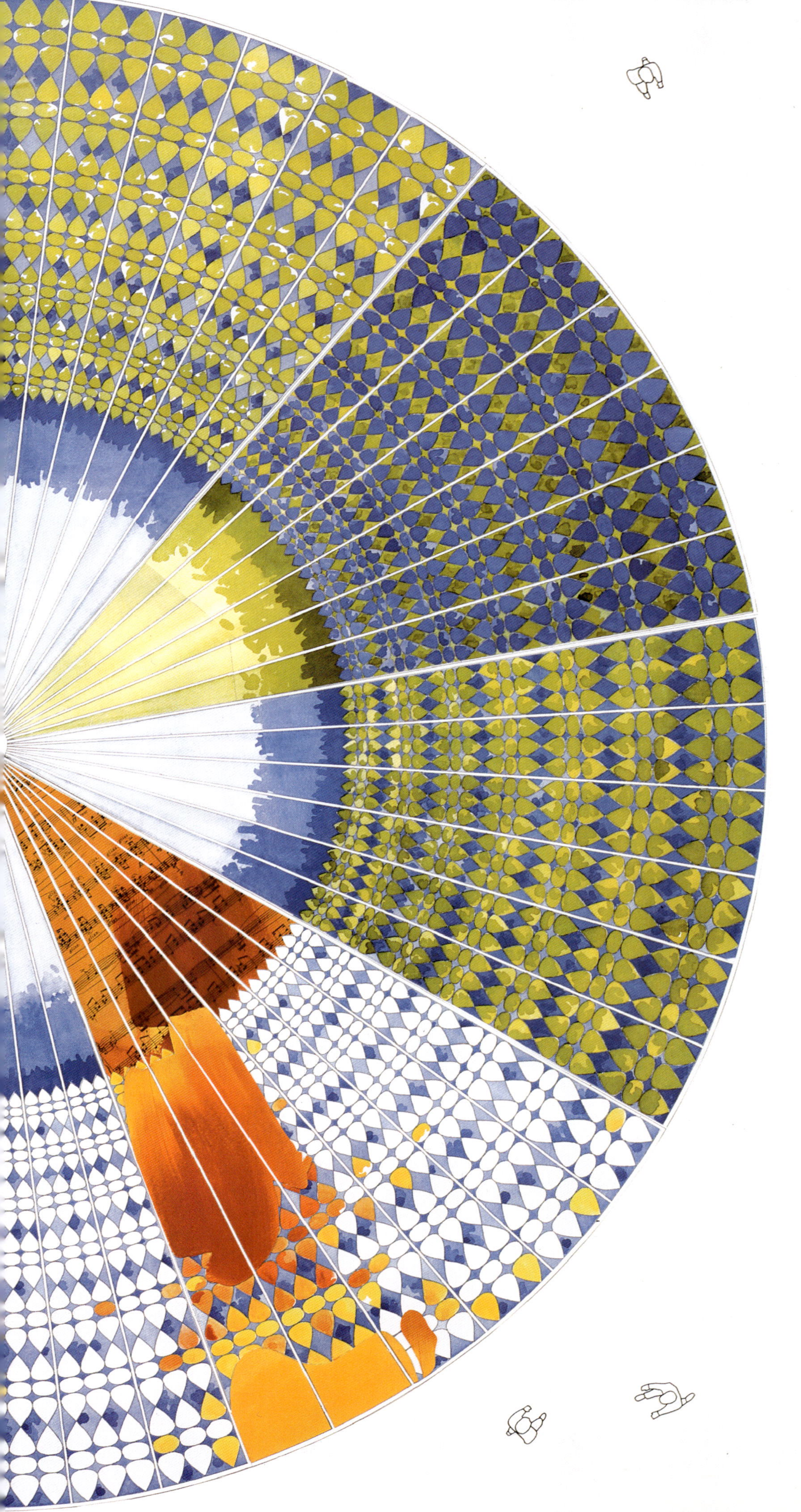

Scale design
for stained glass dome

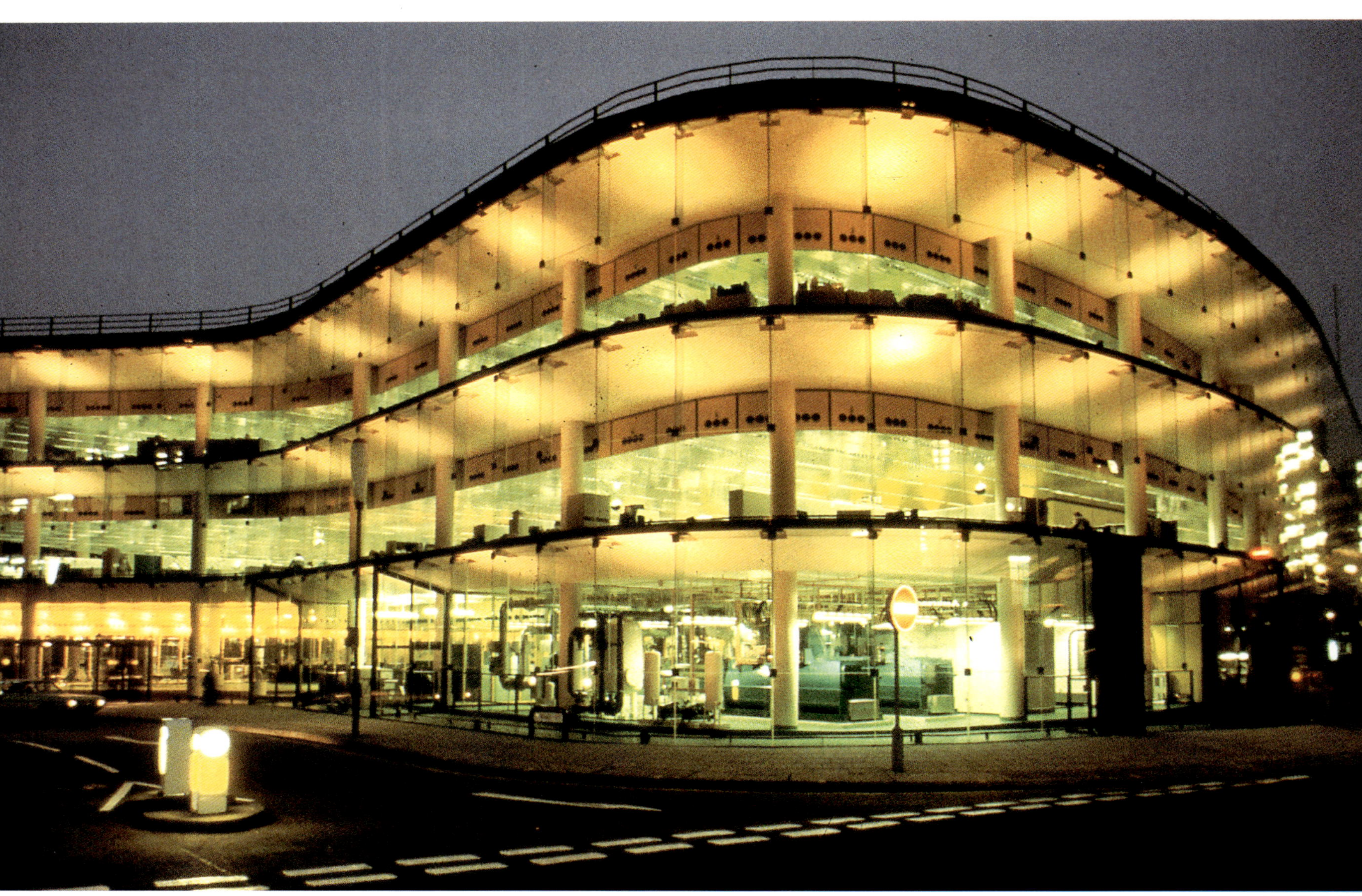

Architects: Sir Norman Foster & Partners

Cut pile tapestry
6 ft 6 in x 19 ft 8 in

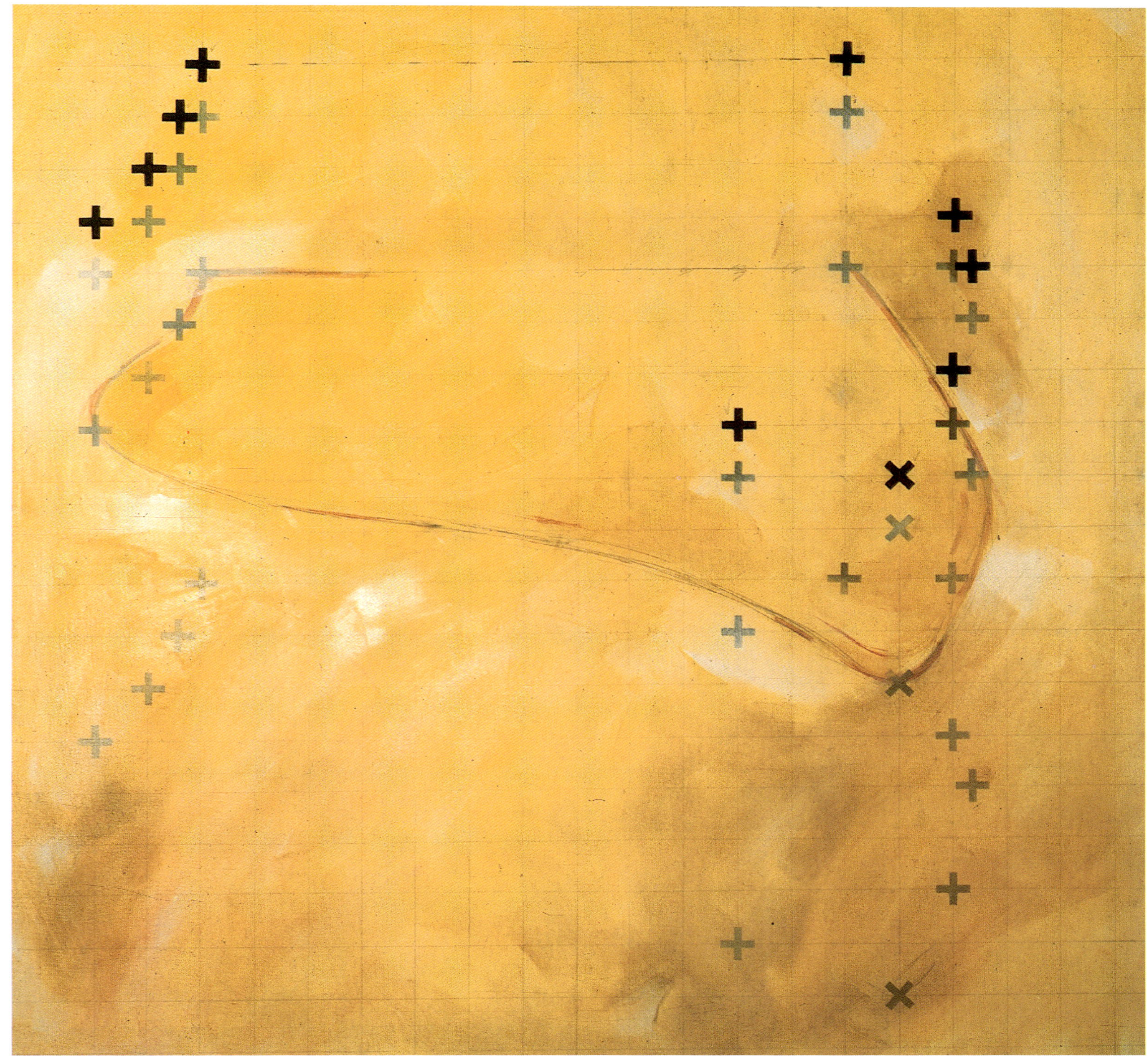

Site Plan, Acrylic on canvas 60in x 60in, 1978, Sheffield City Art Gallery

Sir Norman Foster's magnificent Willis Faber Building in Ipswich, built 1973–74, is recognized as an architectural landmark and a major contribution to contemporary debate on modern design in the urban landscape. The tapestry, sited at the head of the large entrance vestibule, is a recent addition to the interior and is a testament to the continuing involvement I have with this site and one of my greatest friends.

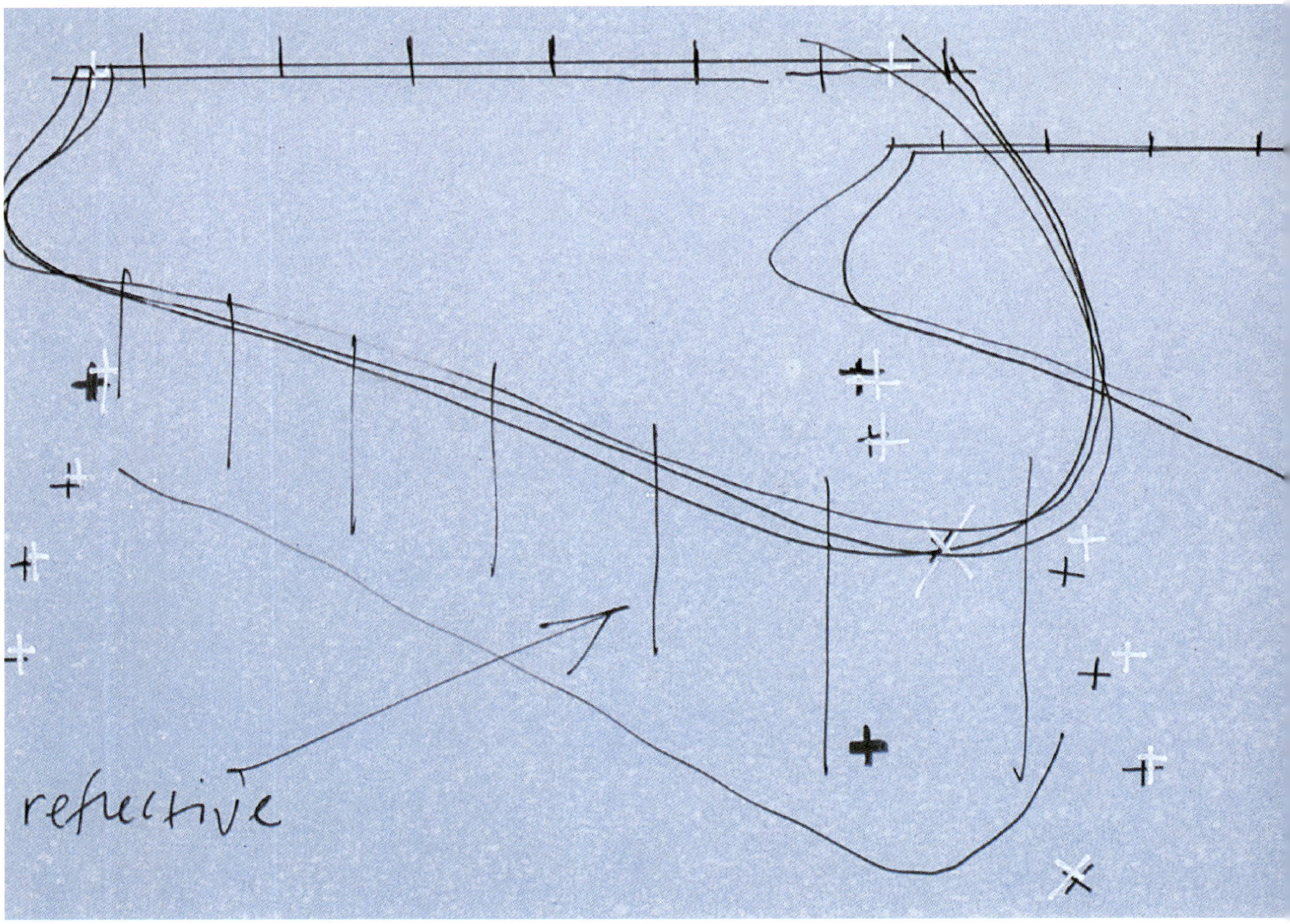

reflective

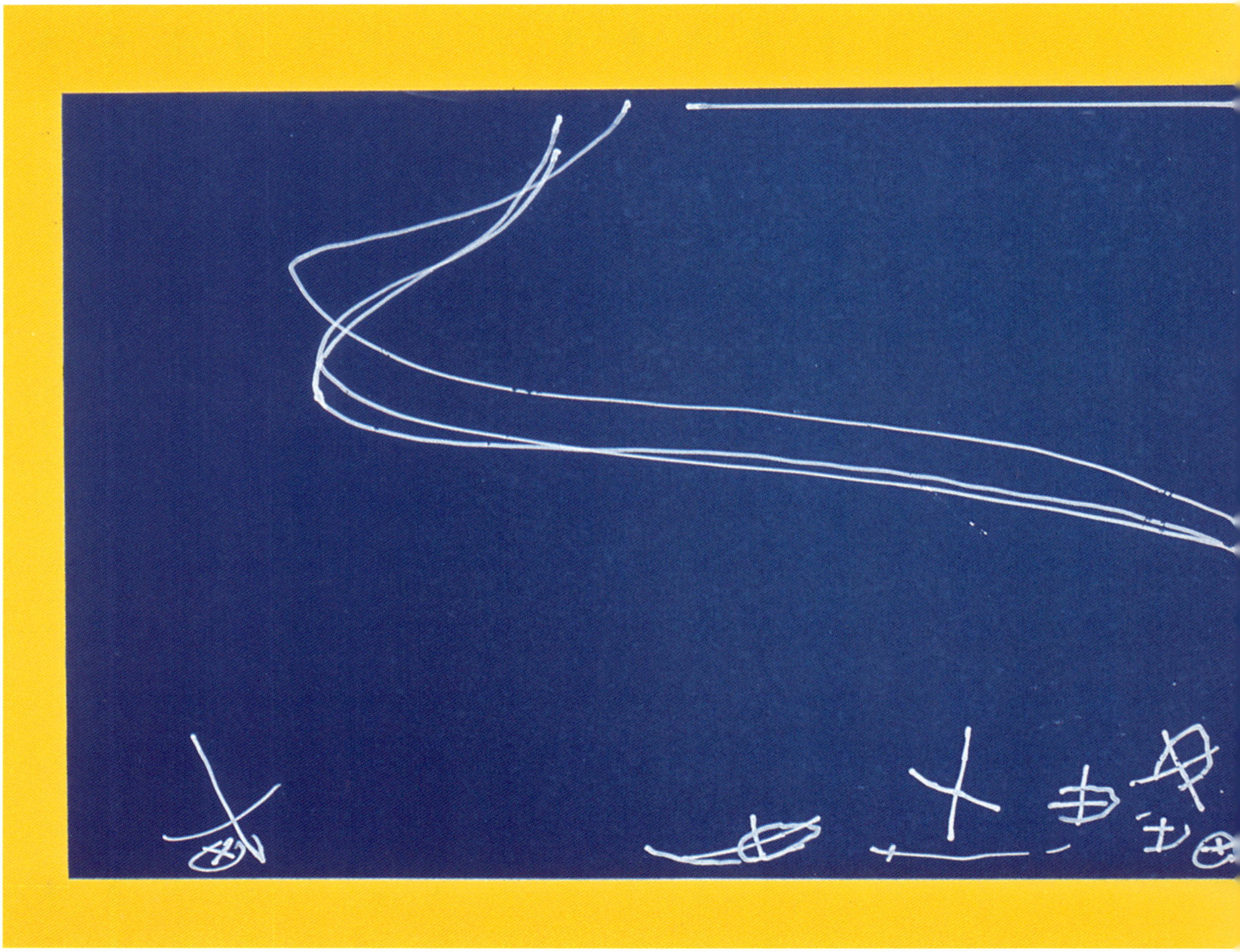

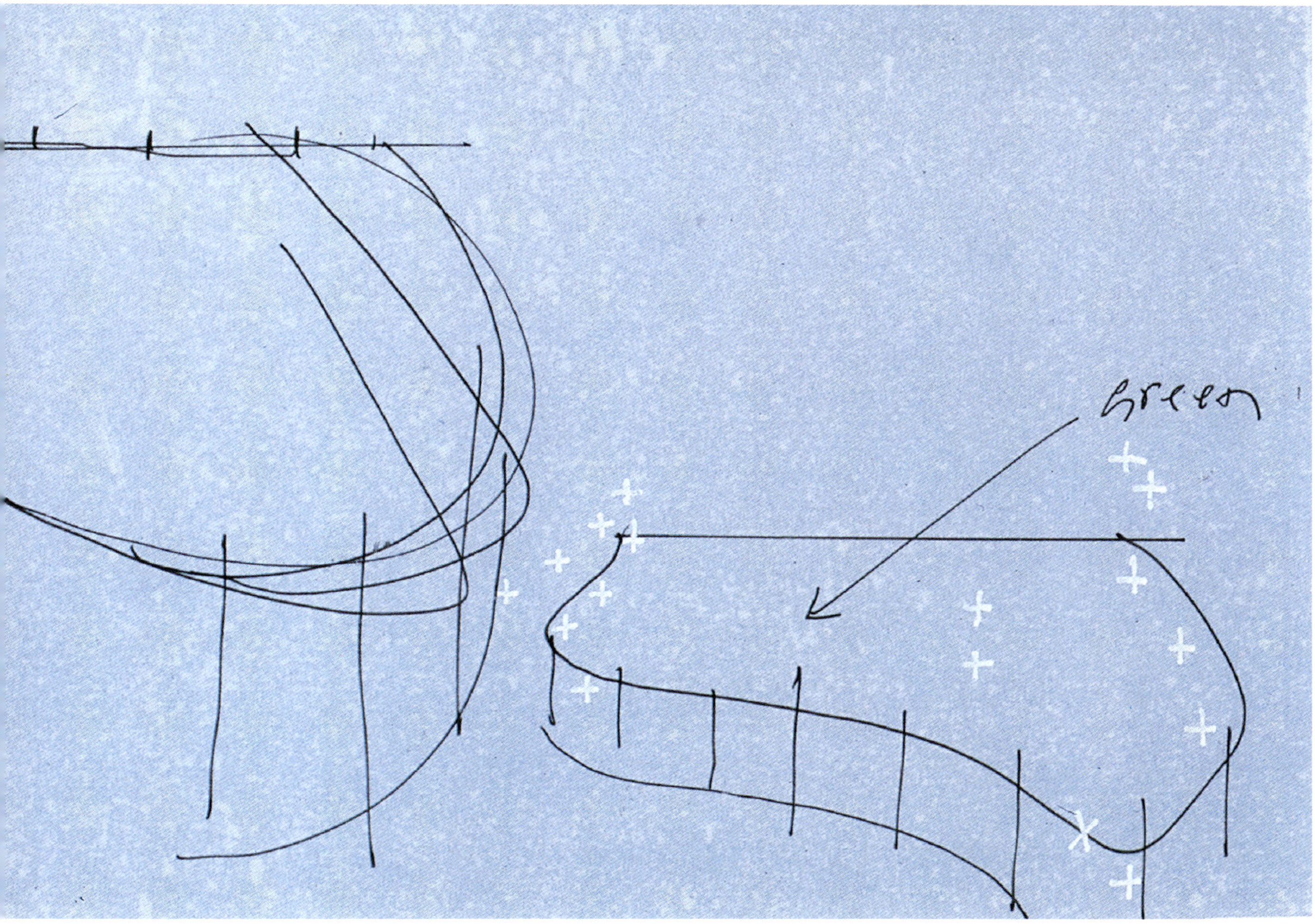

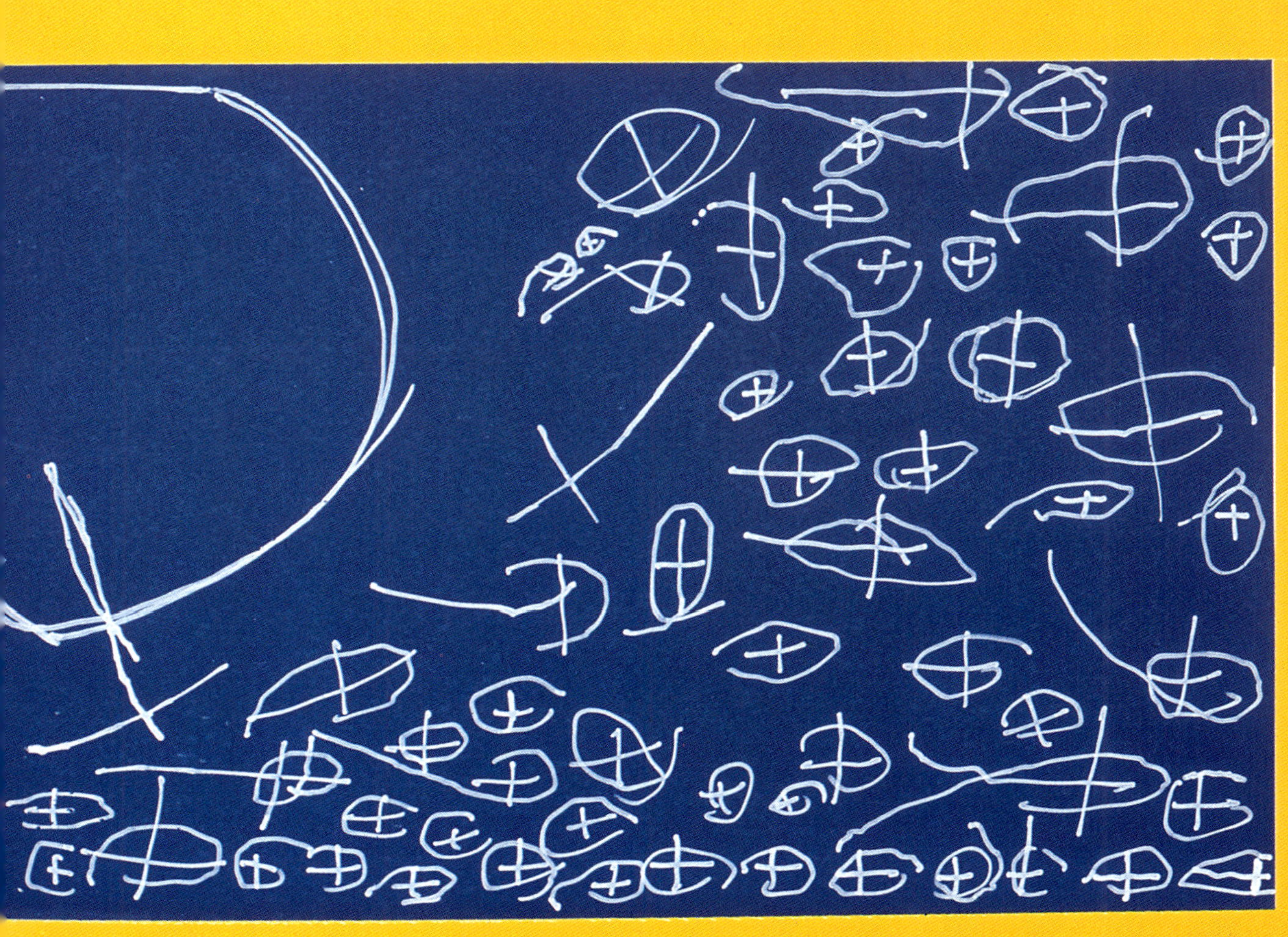

Pages from sketchbook

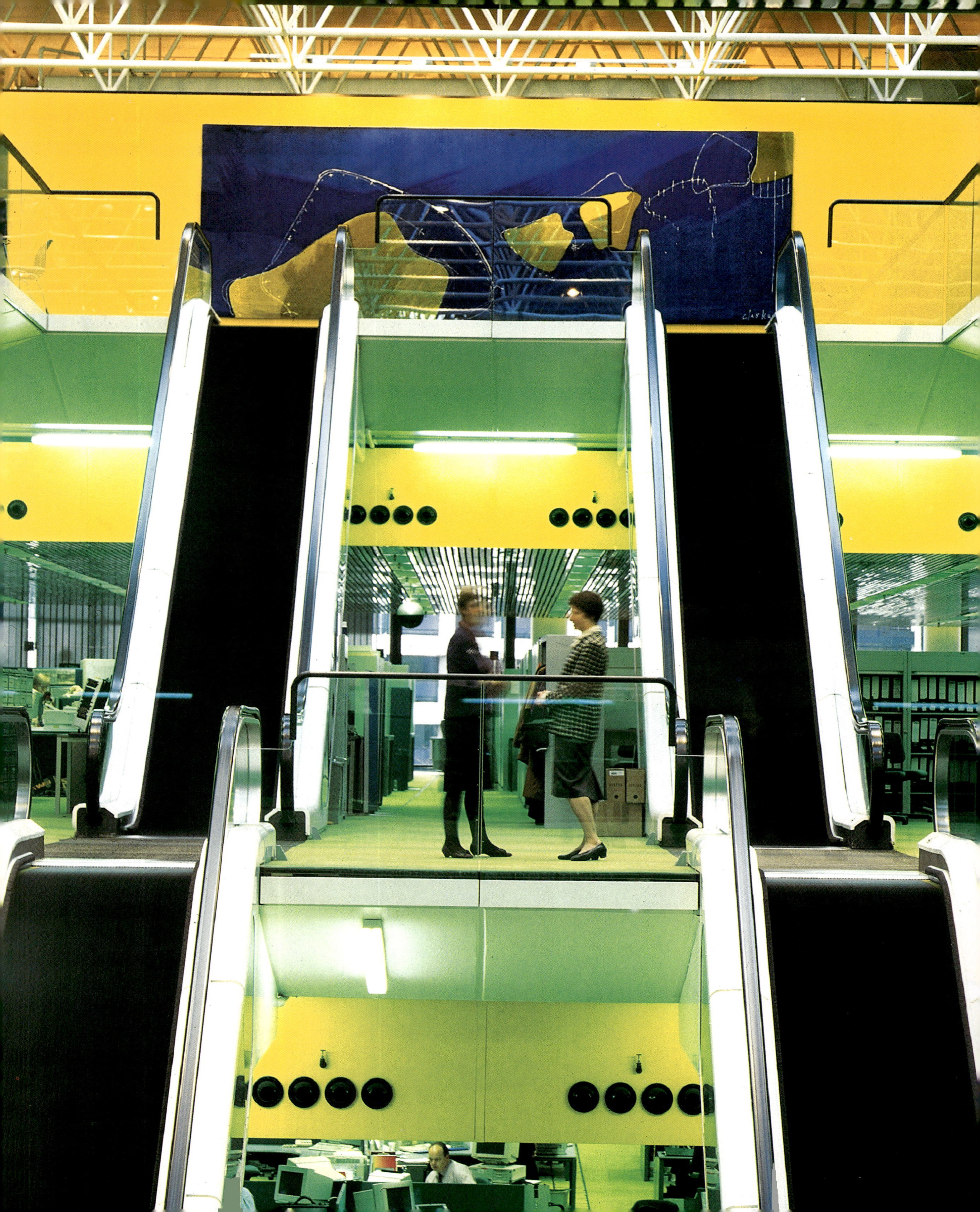

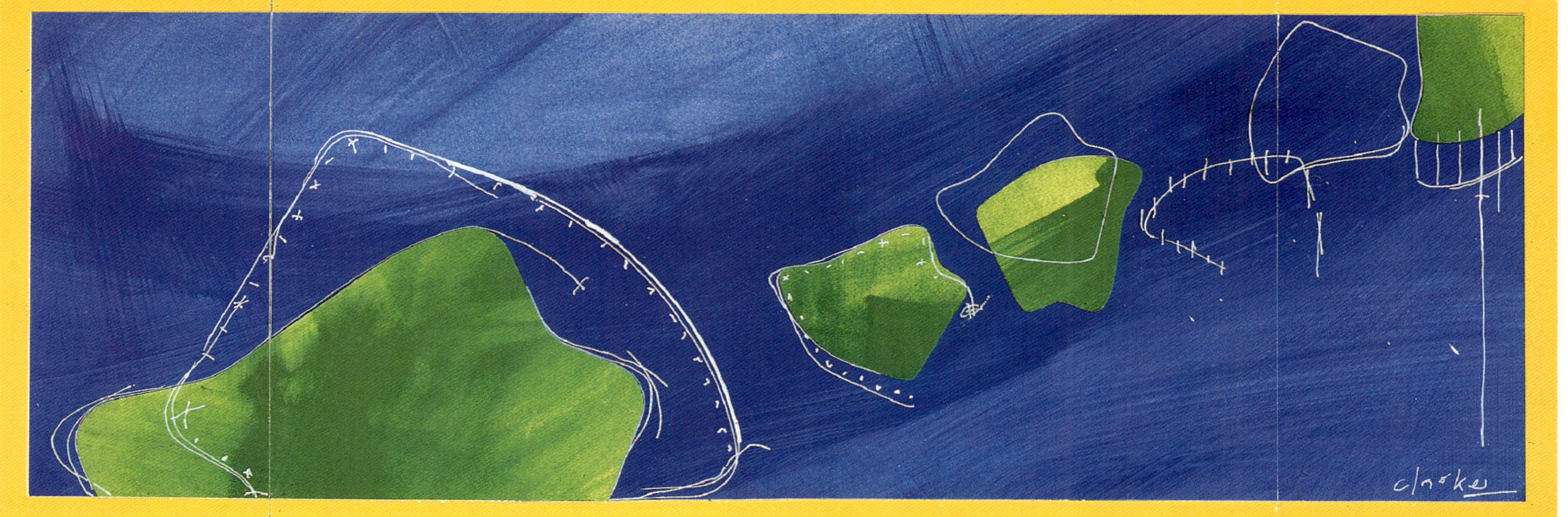

Design: Site Plan II 1997

Willis Faber is one of my favorite buildings in the world. In the late 70s I based a painting upon it and have visited it countless times over twenty years. Being asked to make a tapestry for this central circulation space was like being invited home. I see this as a small victory in my work.

'Site Plan II' tapestry installed at head of entrance vestibule (below and left)

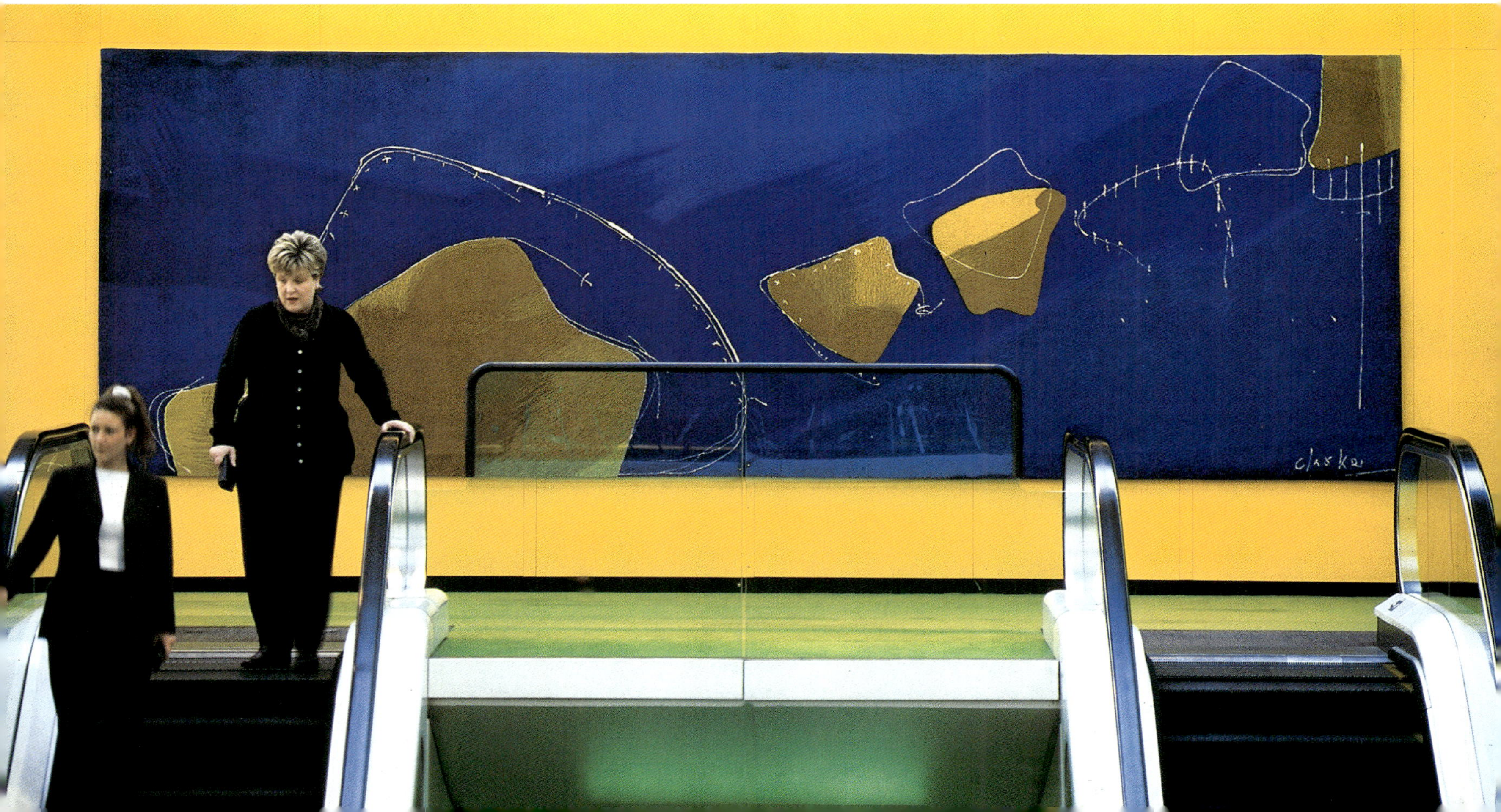

CHICAGO SINAI SYNAGOGUE
CHICAGO, ILLINOIS, USA   1997

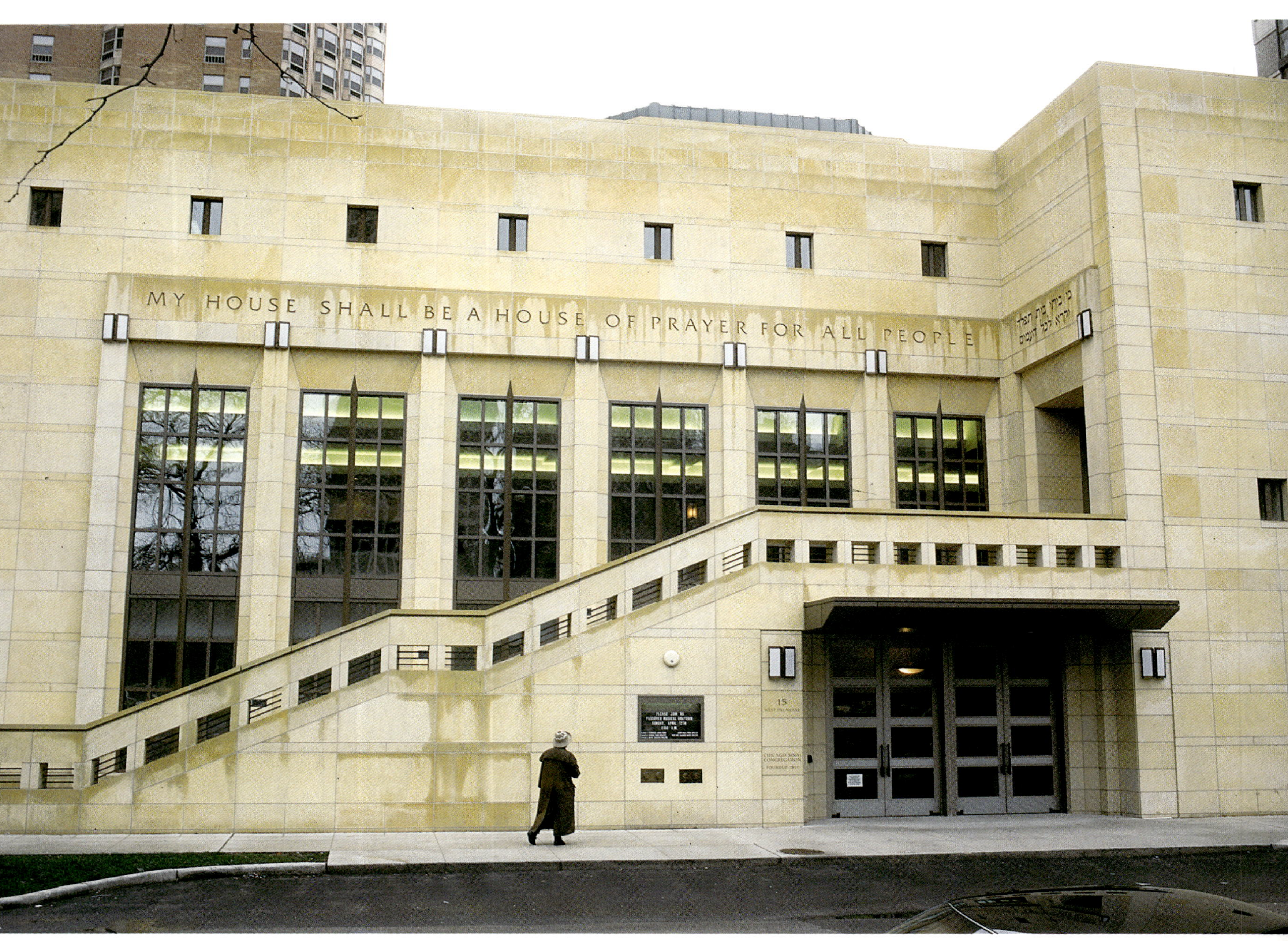

Architect: Dirk Lohan Associates

Stained glass window
140 sq ft

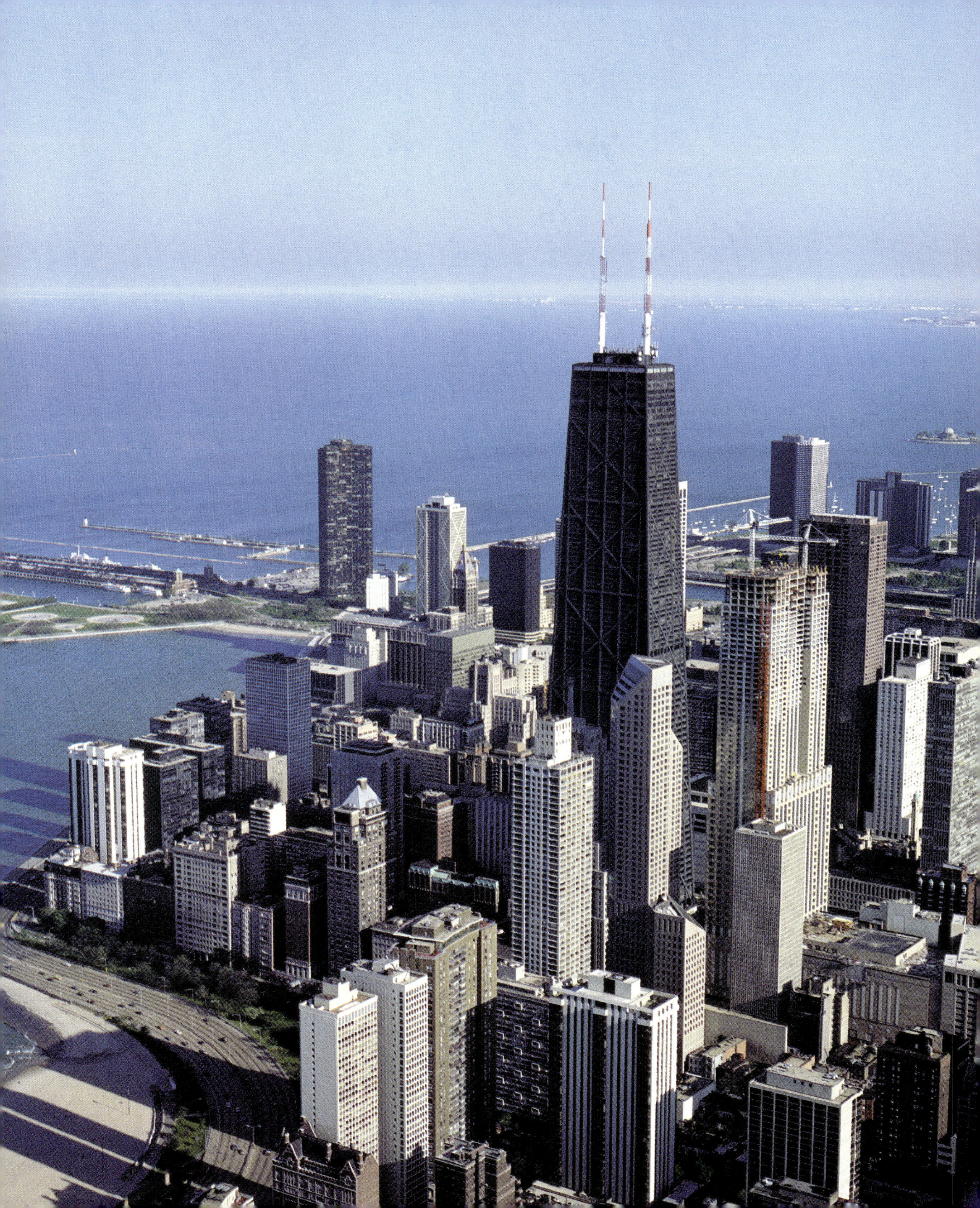

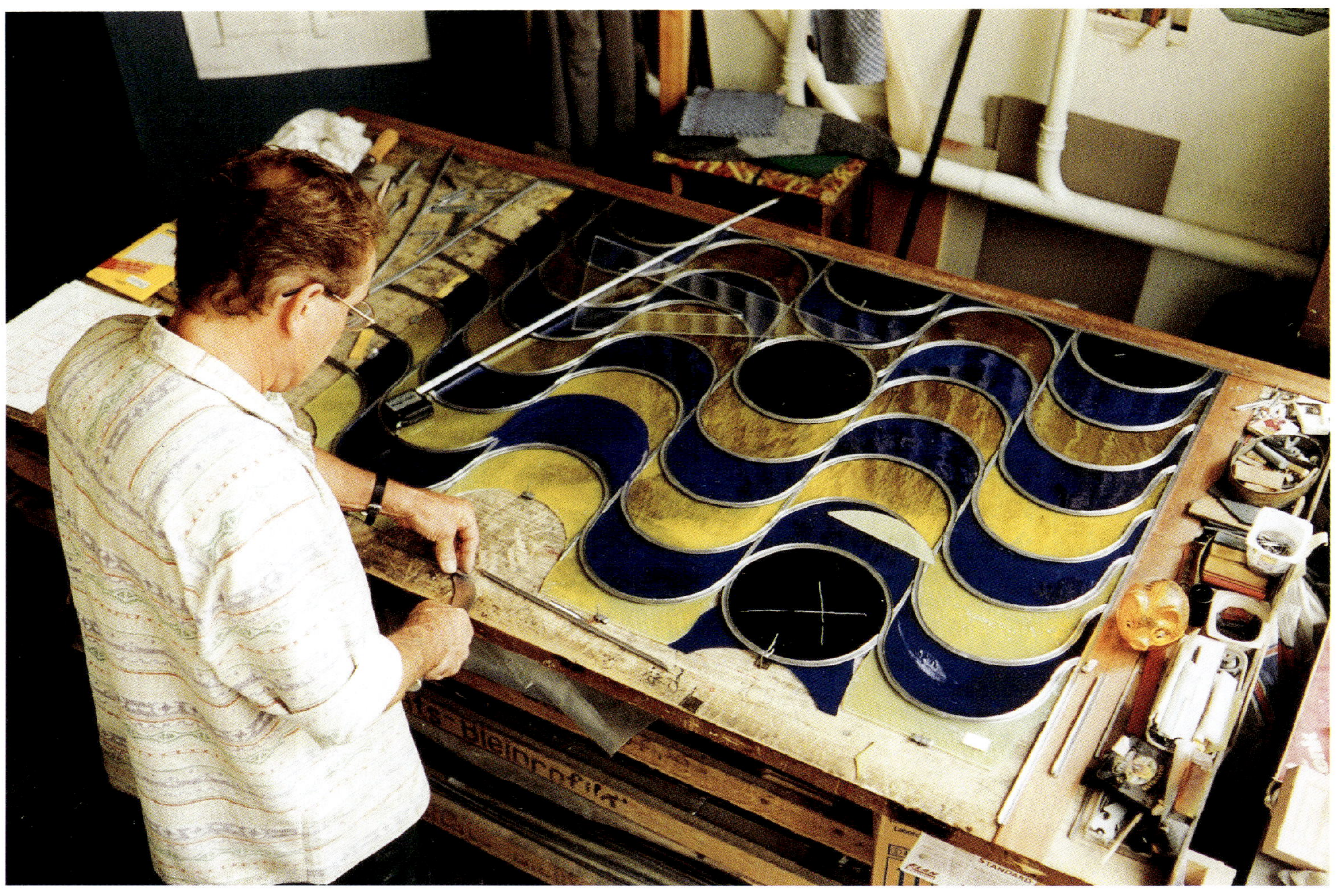

Chicago is extraordinary. I find it as architecturally compelling as Venice. This synagogue is the fourth I've worked in and my first in the U.S. It was important to create a focal point of concentration that at the same time did not distract from the building's primary function. The color and forms had to obscure the prosaic mundanities of the car-lot behind and at the same time obscure the internal activities of the building from outside view. I see this work as a kind of huge "Kabinettscheibe" or jewel fixed into the architectural setting of Dirk Lohan's building's. Refracting and transmitting liquid color into the cylindrical form of the building...

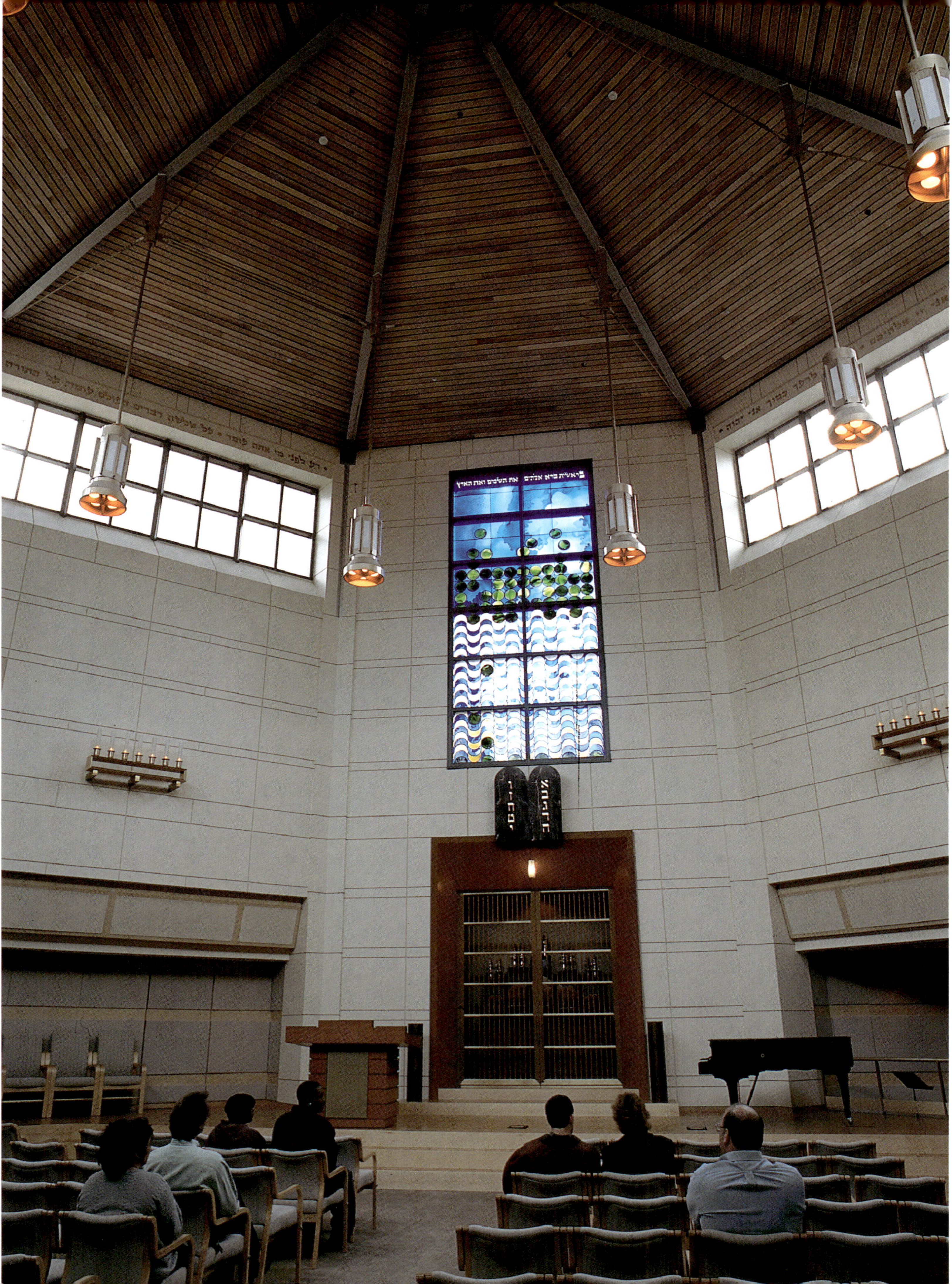

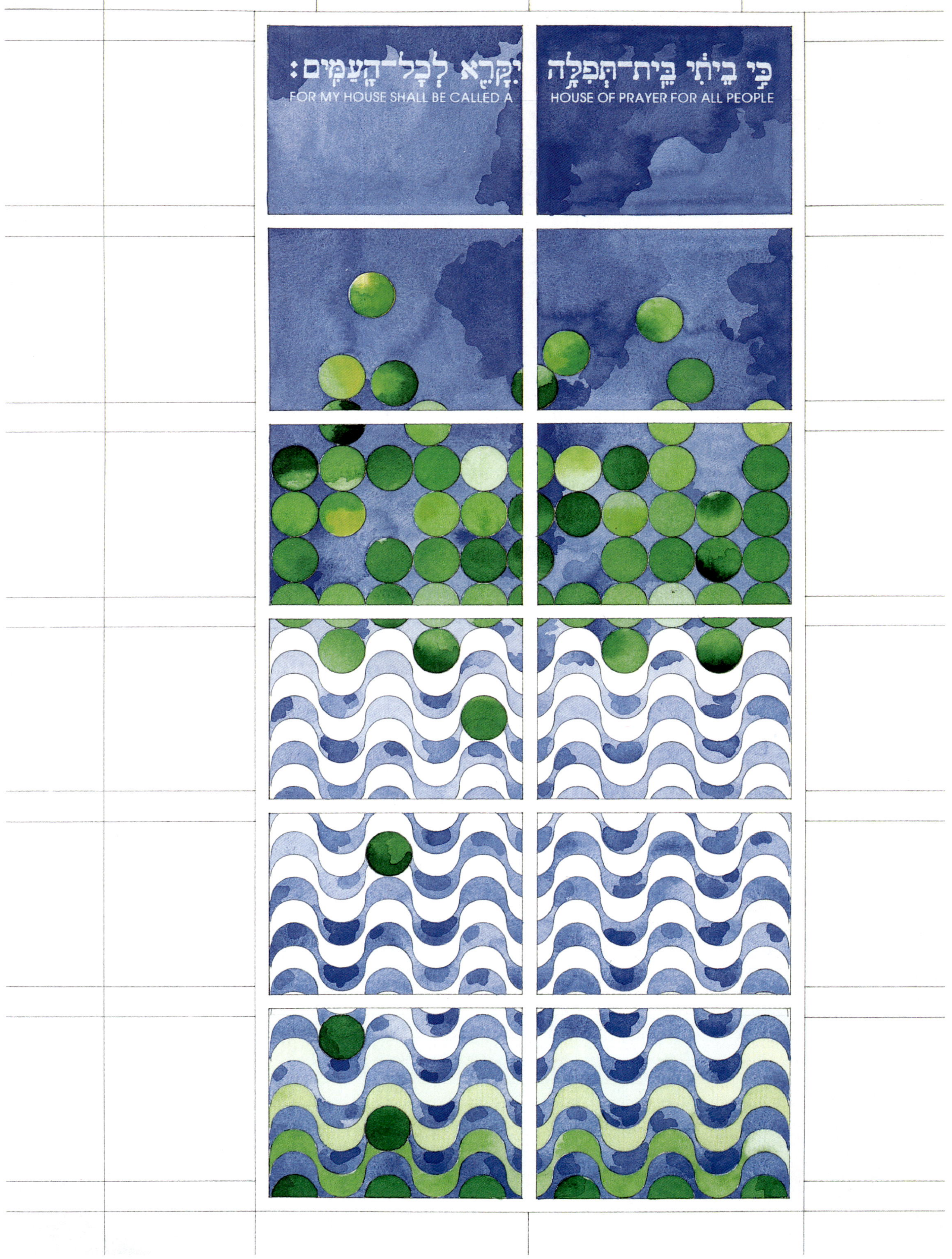

Watercolor design (above)
Completed window installed (opposite)

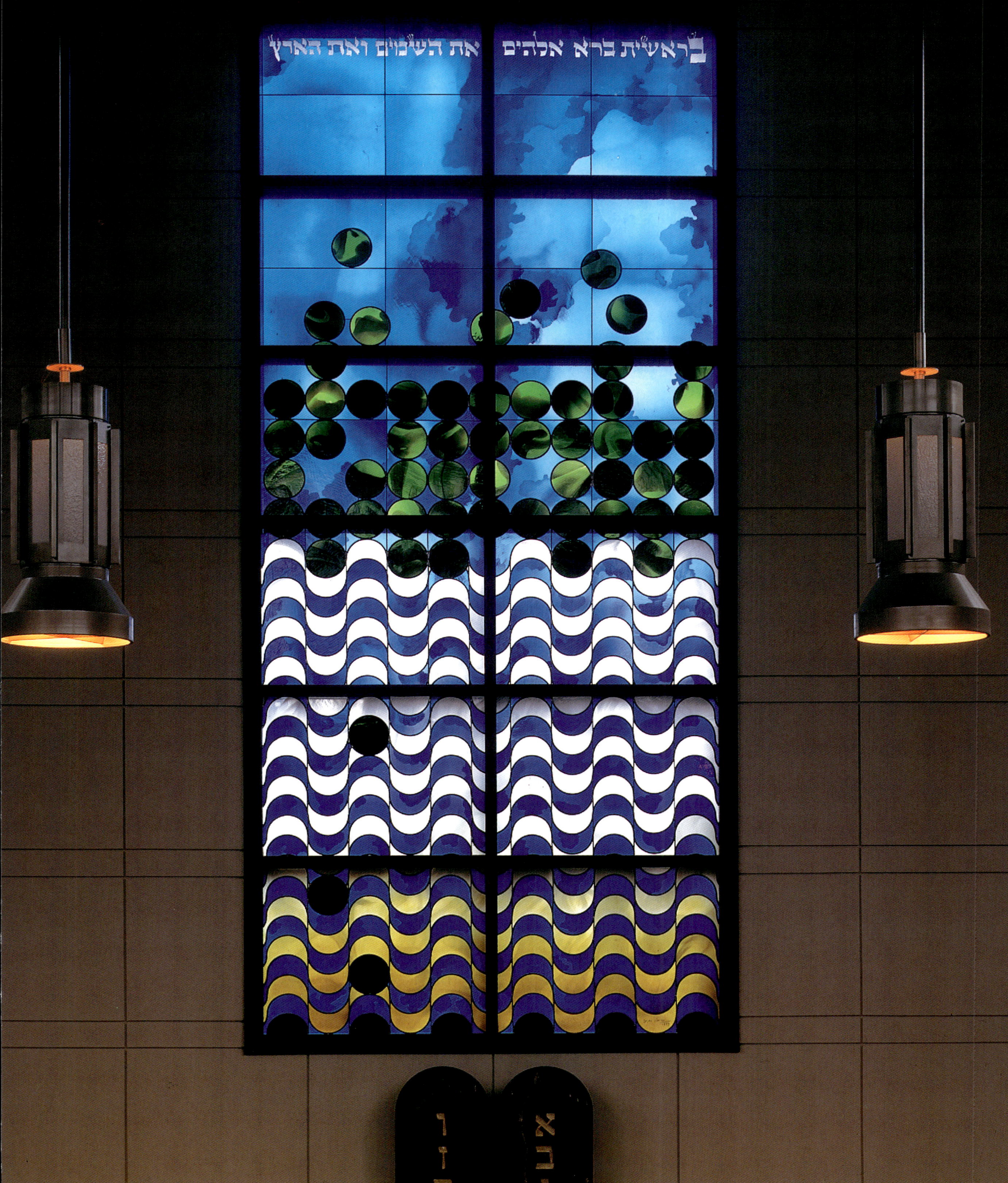

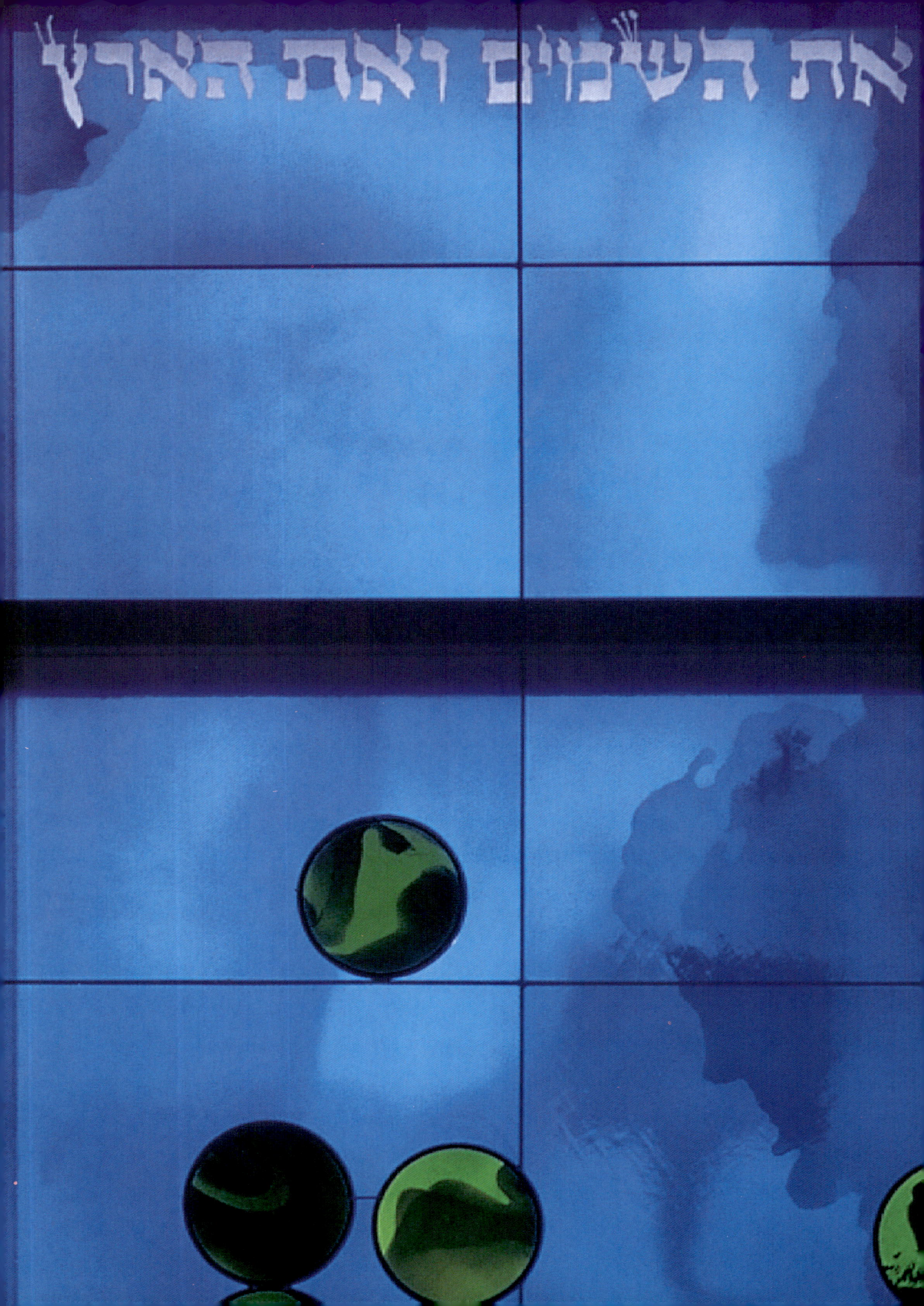

את השמים ואת הארץ

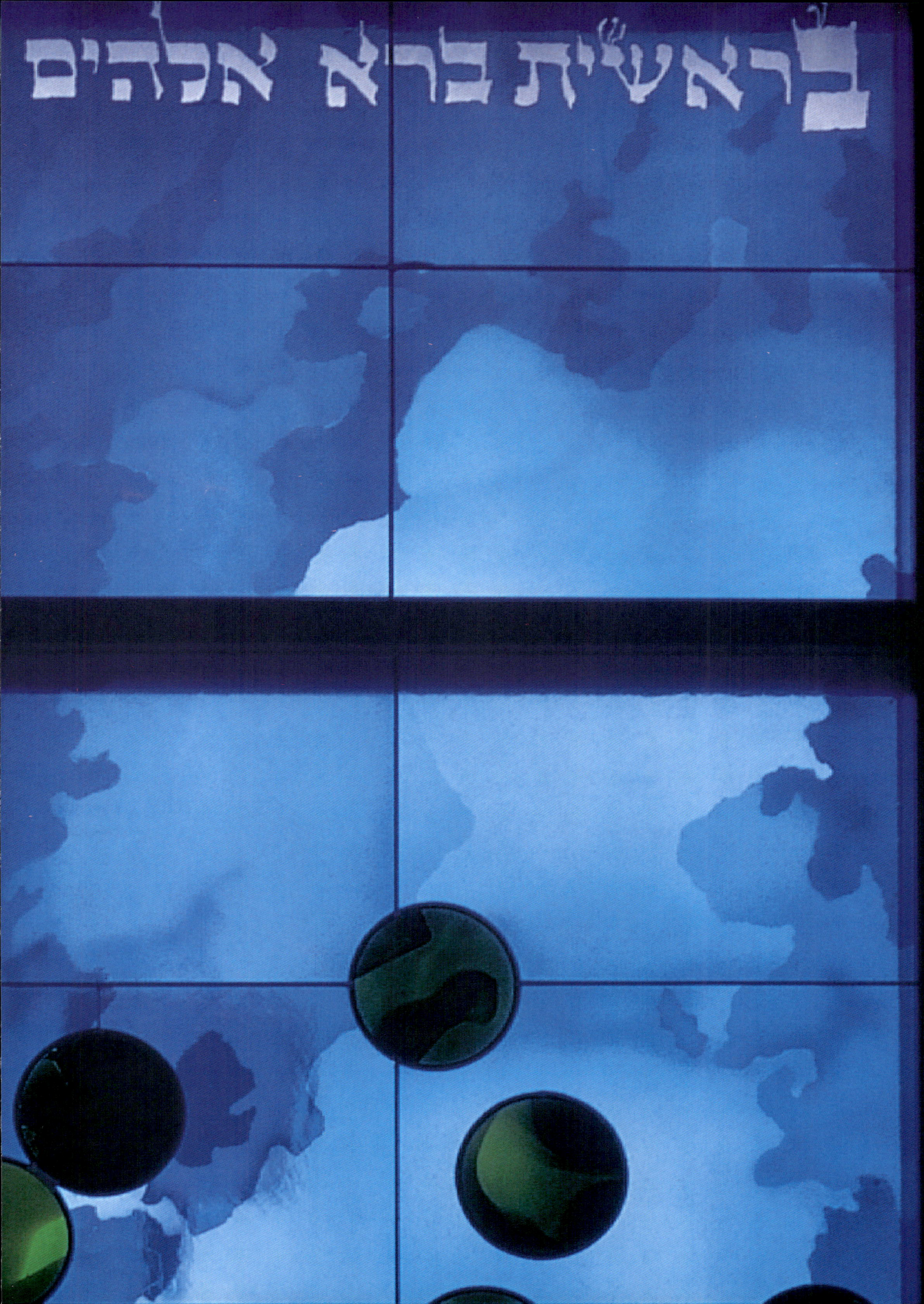

בְּרֵאשִׁית בָּרָא אֱלֹהִים

SWISS BANK CORPORATION
STAMFORD, CONNECTICUT, USA 1996 - 1998

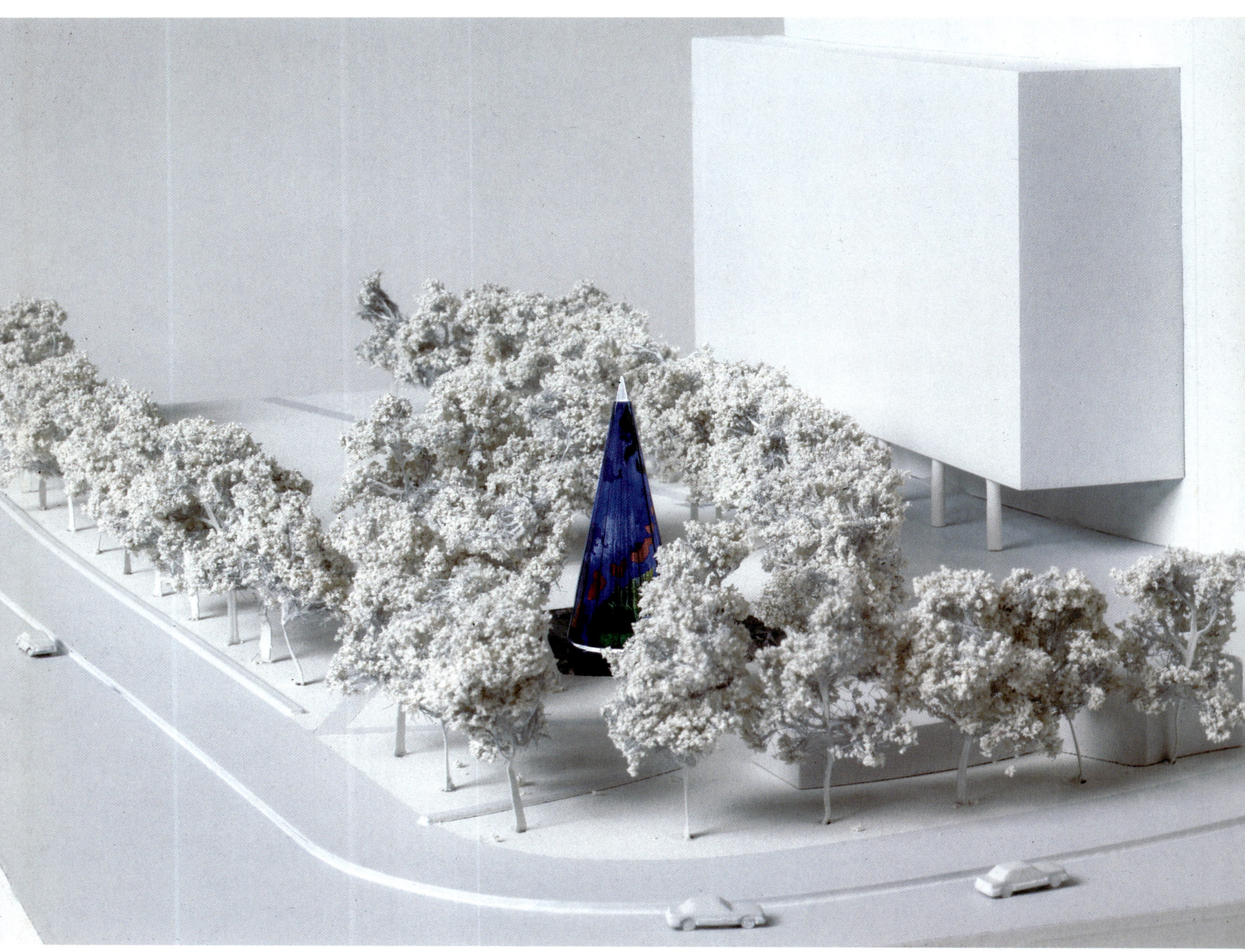

Site model 1996

Engineers: Dewhurst Macfarlane & Partners

This project is currently under construction and will be completed by fall 1998
Stained glass cone
861 sq ft (glass artwork)

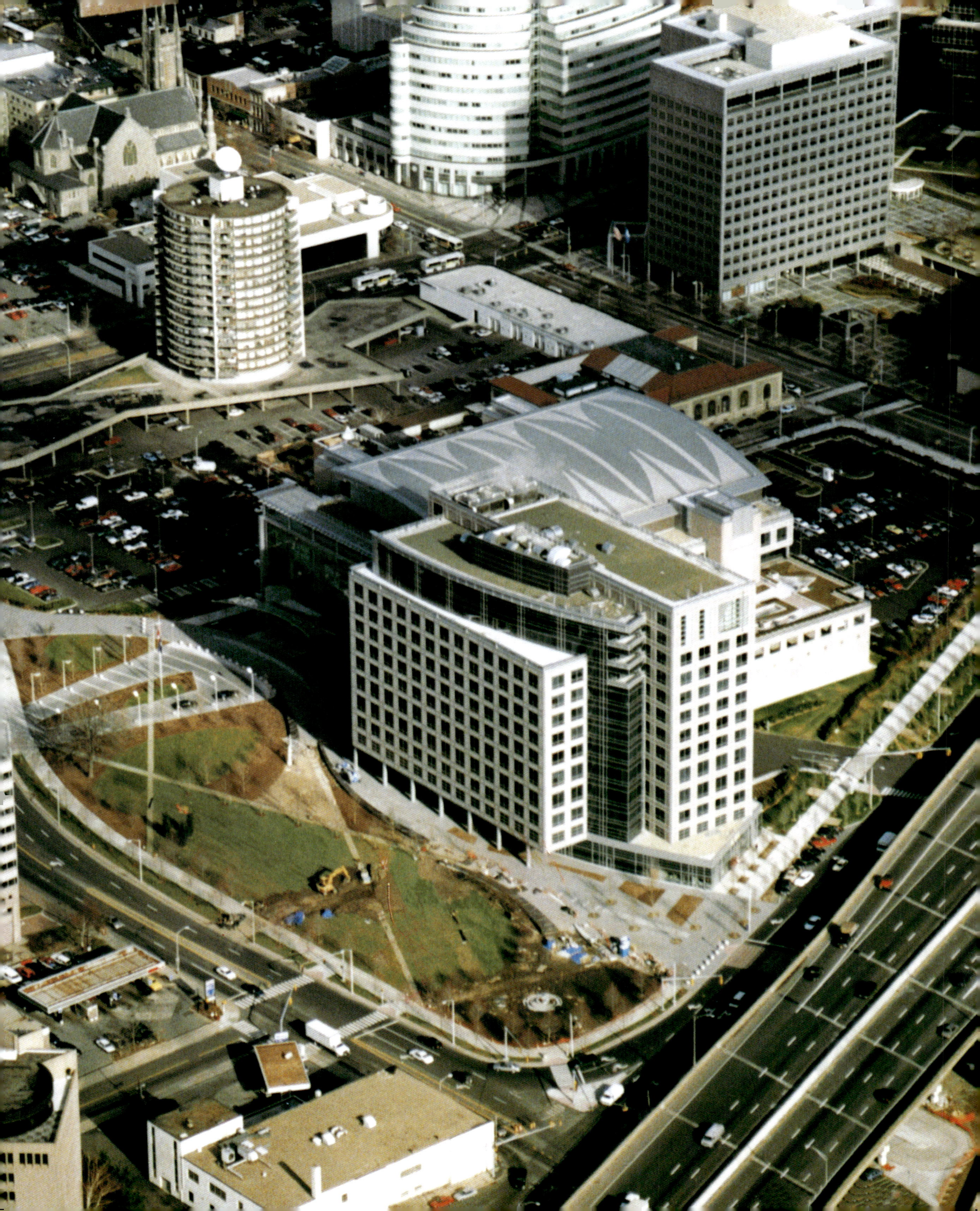

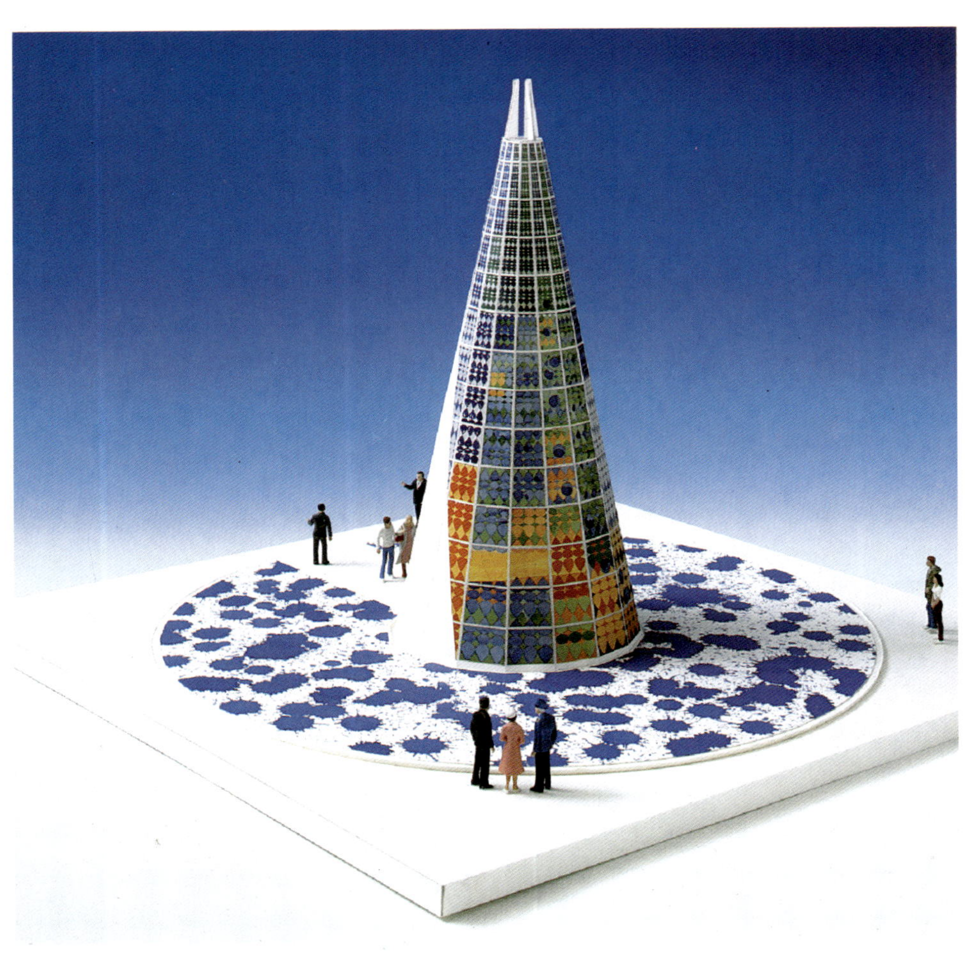

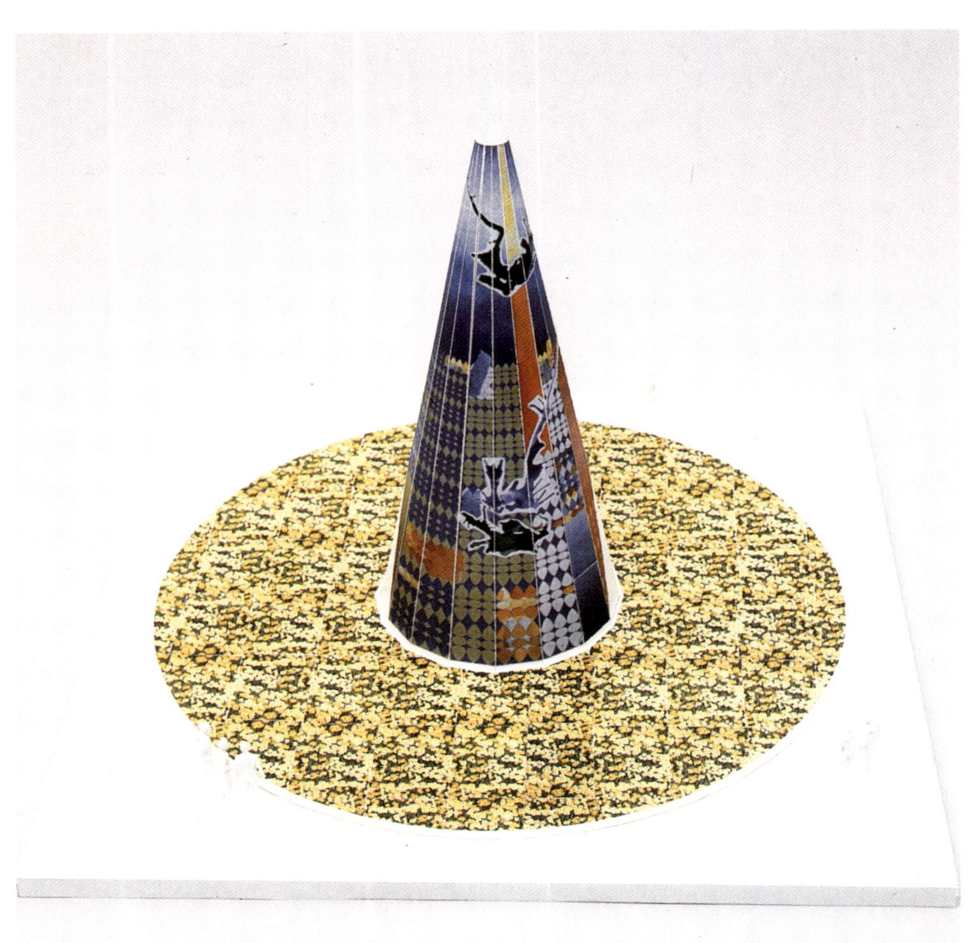

Working models (above)
First preliminary study (right)

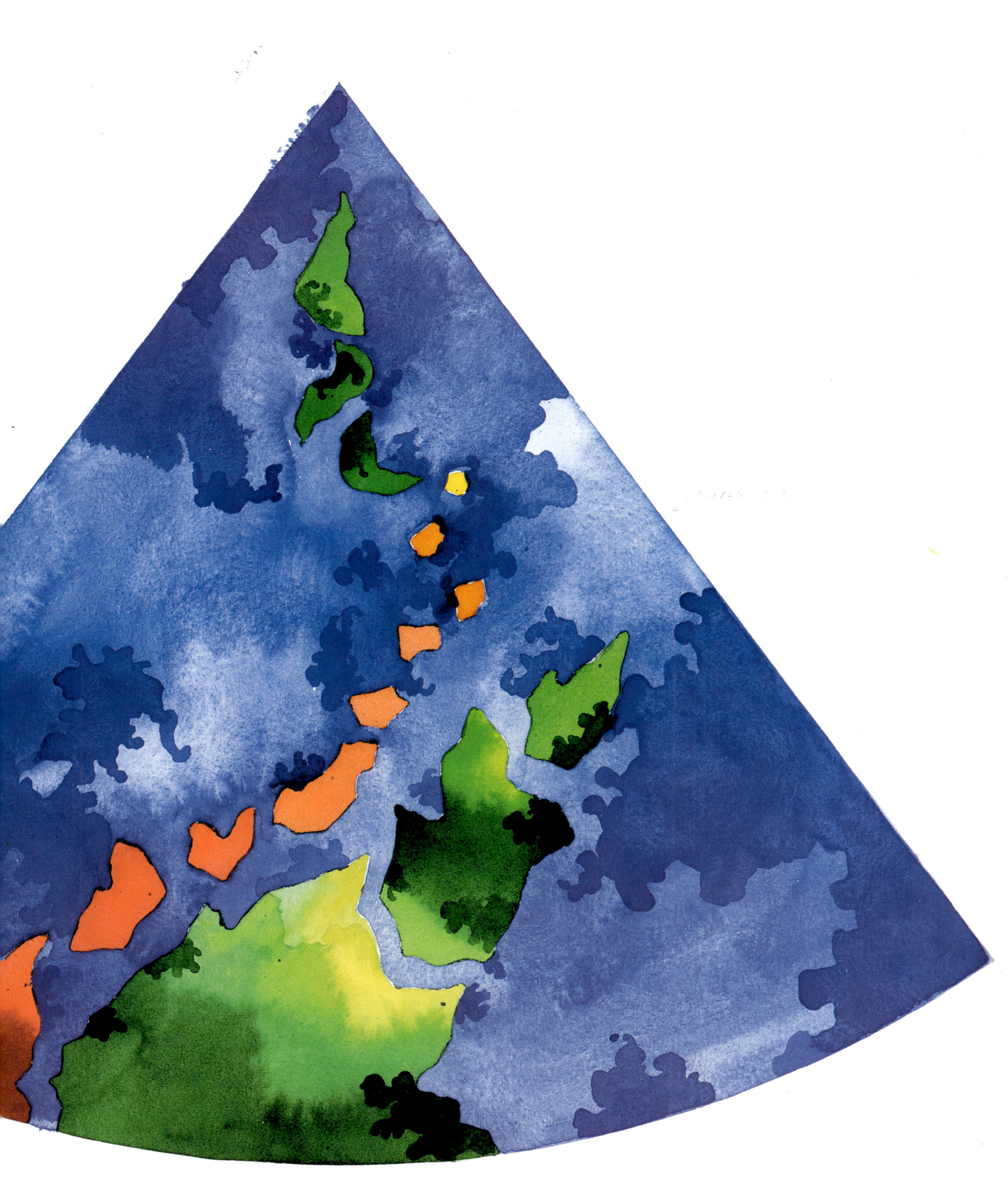

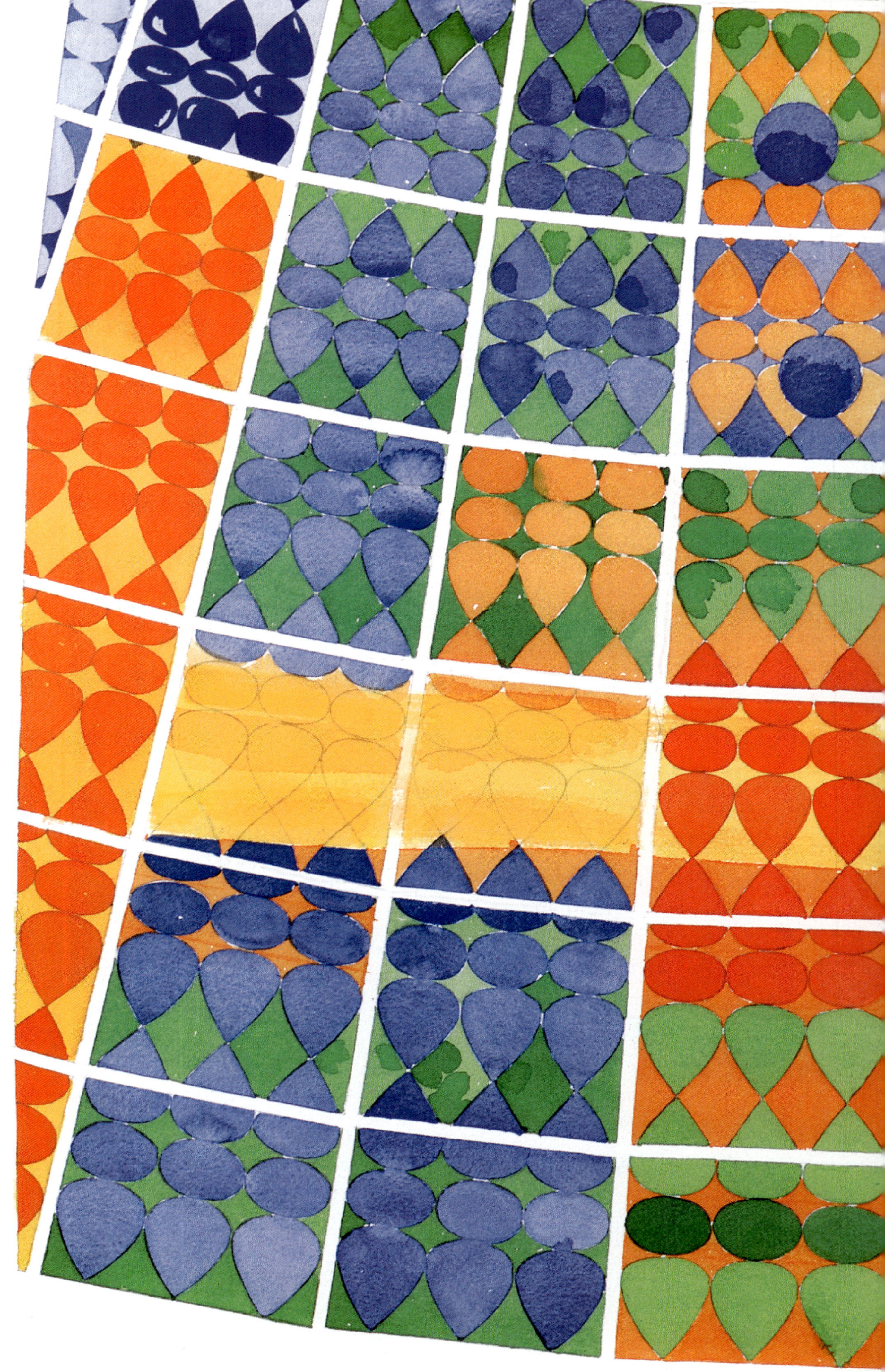

Detail of final
watercolour schematic
design

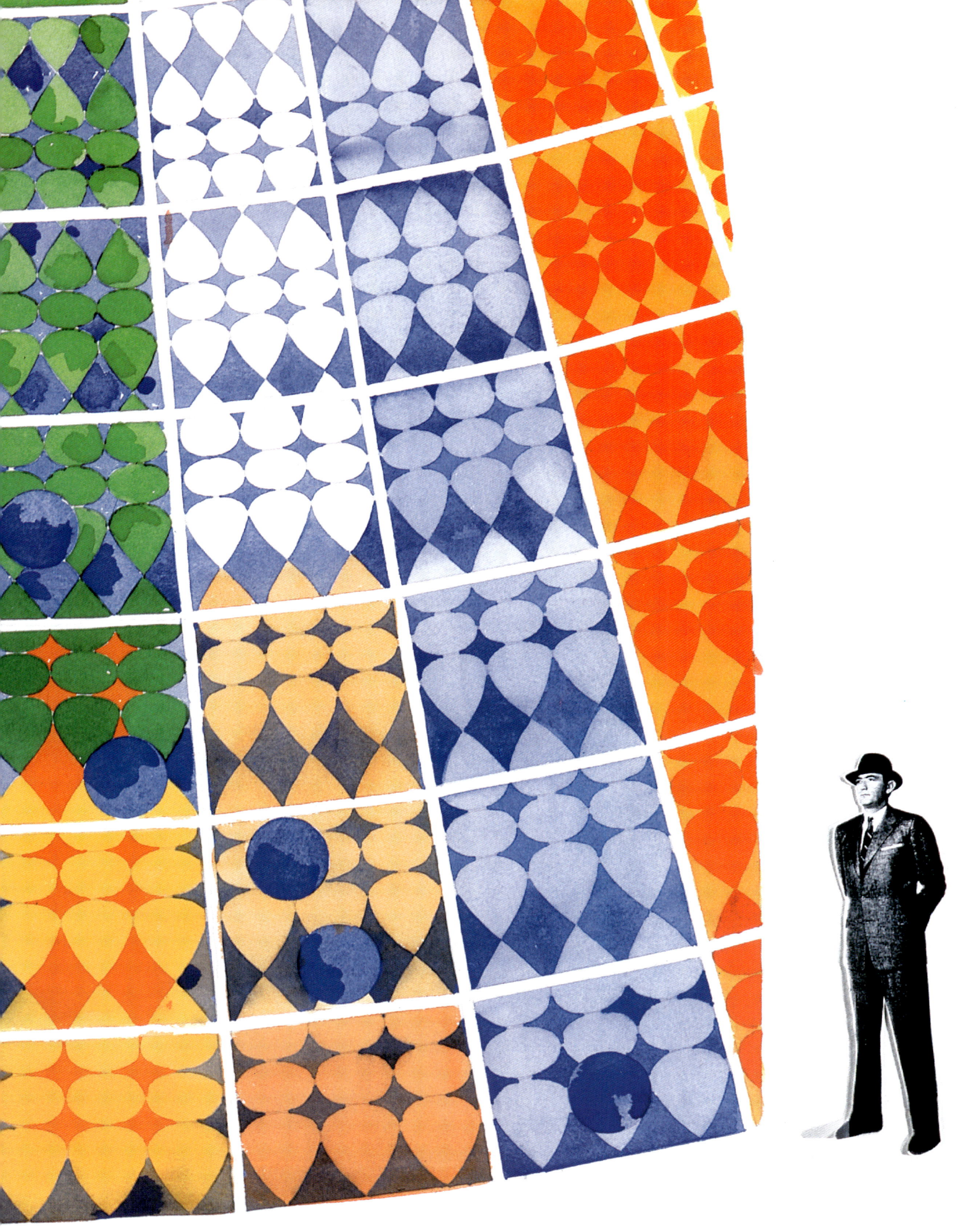

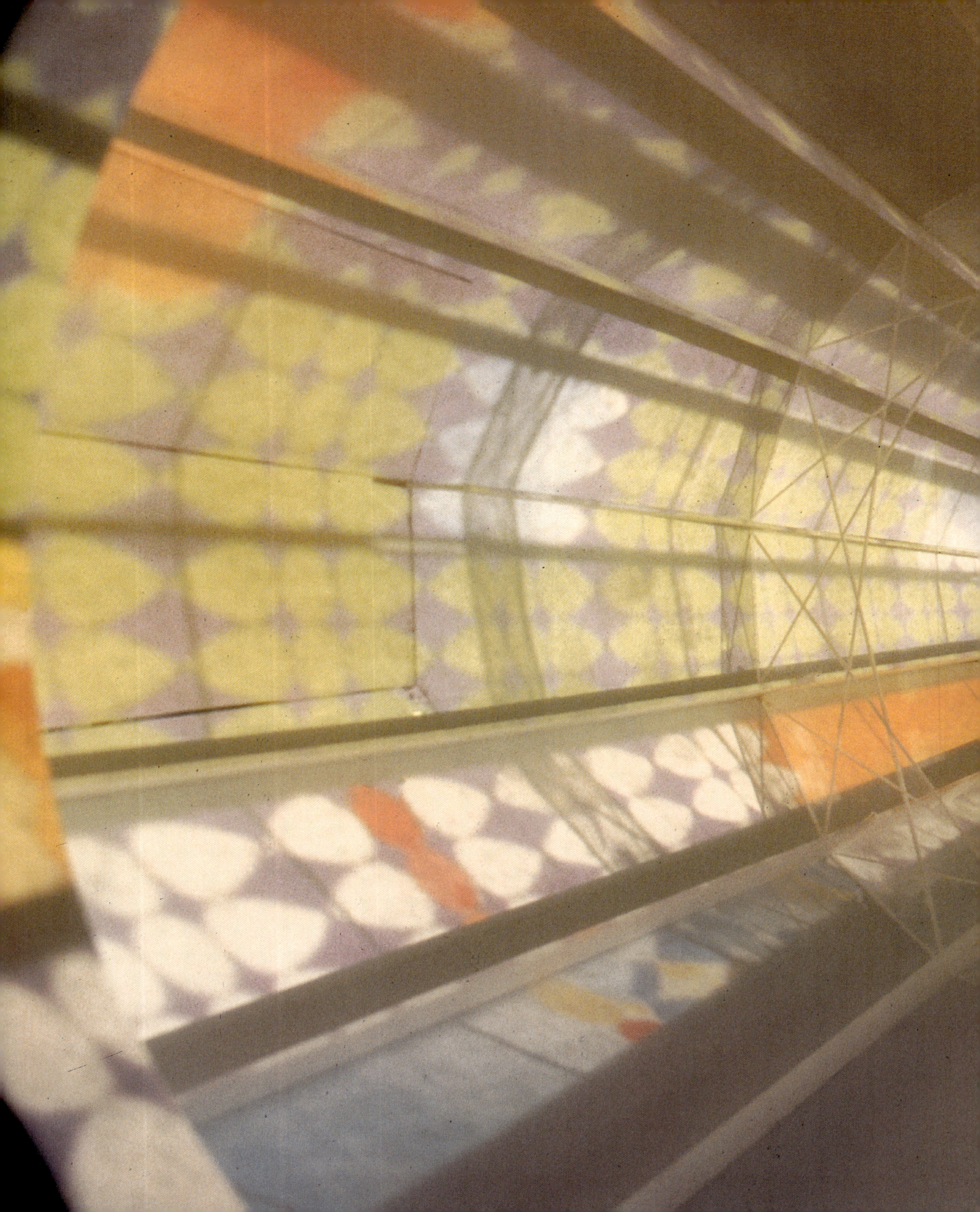

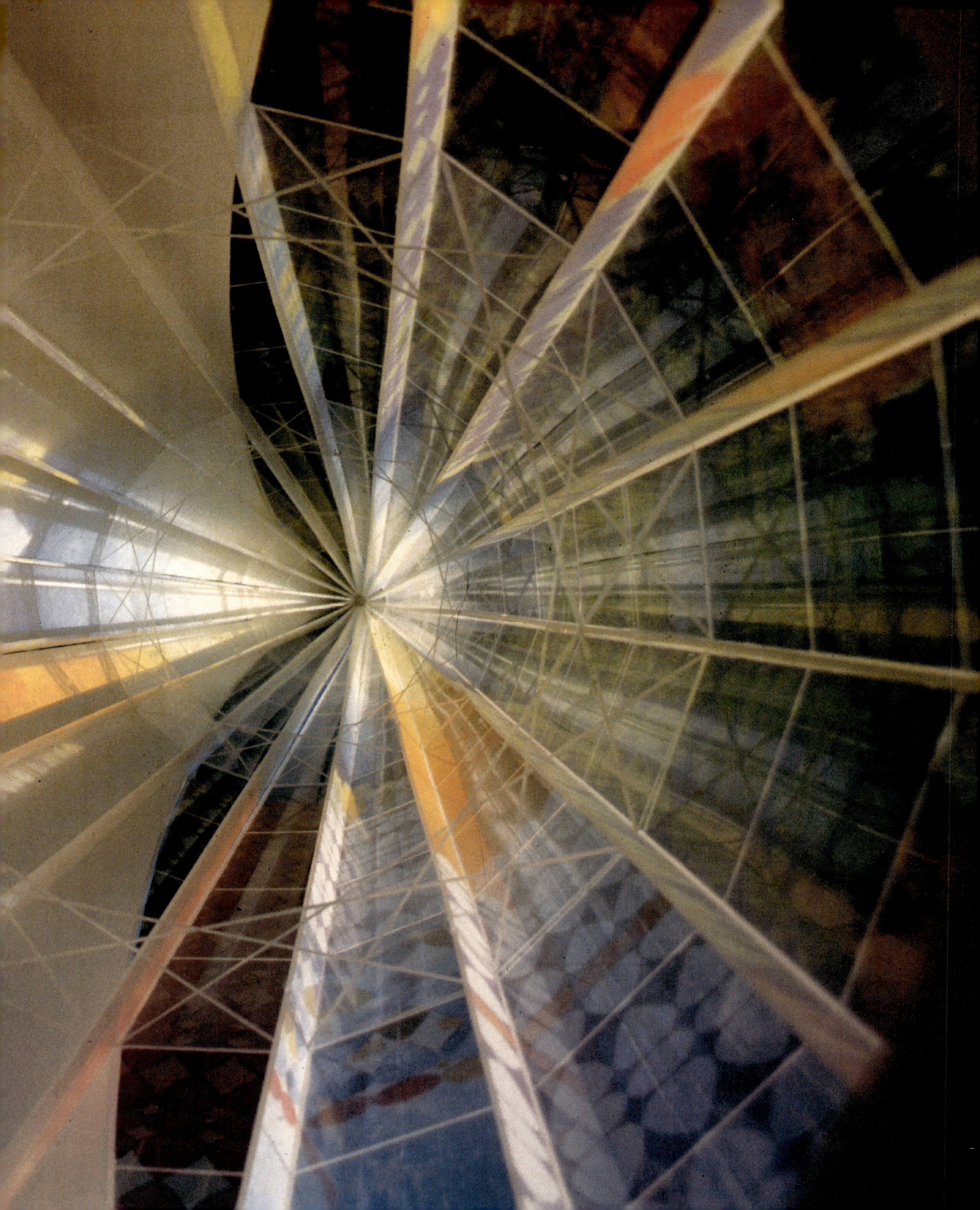

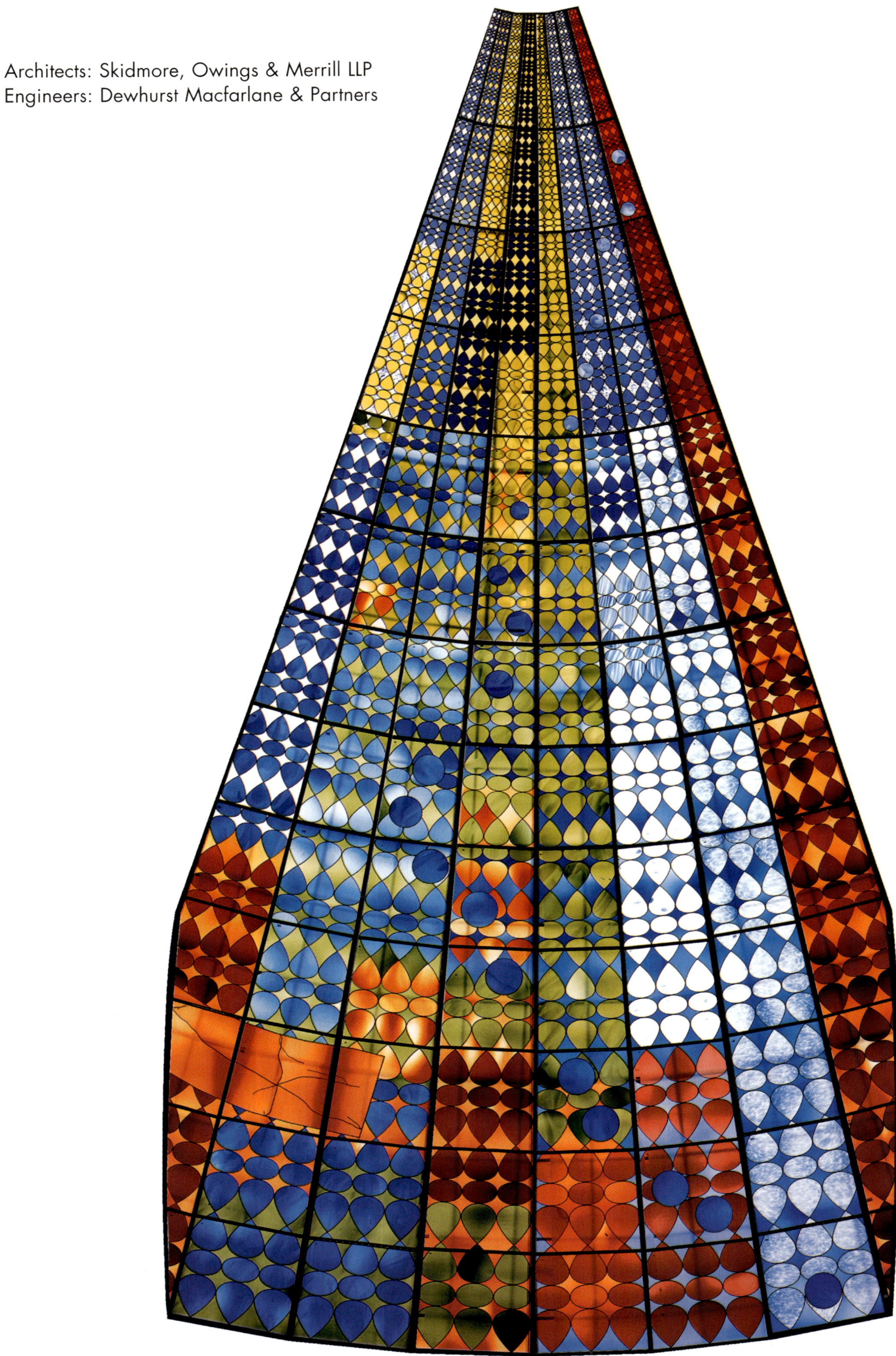

Composite of actual stained glass

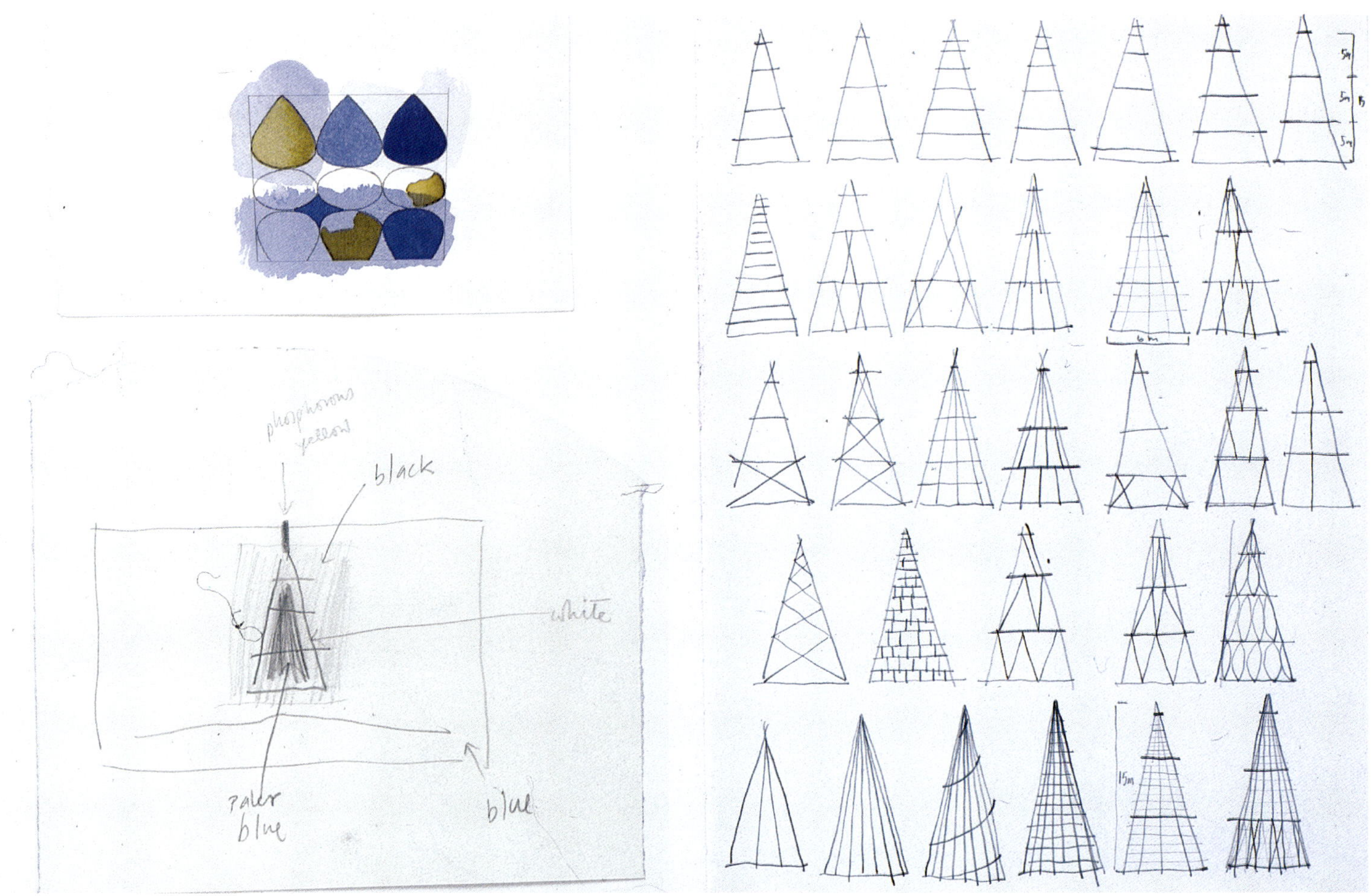

Pages from sketchbook

Most artists who work in two dimensions feel the regular desire to explore a third. In the early hours of the morning a couple of winters ago (in Chalet Gin Gin in Gstaad) I crudely carved a small cone from cheddar cheese. That early half-idea has today grown into a radical structure almost entirely formed from glass. The cone which stands 14 metres high and has a footprint diameter of 6 metres will be located in front of the new American Swiss Bank Headquarters Building in Stamford, Connecticut (architects: Skidmore, Owings & Merrill LLP). It will be visible to the countless commuters who daily thunder along Interstate 95, and to the railroad users who are disgorged by Amtrak into the center of town. Open to the public and staff of the Swiss Bank, it is one of my first real 3D pieces in stained glass. A solid "baffle" or sail forms part of the glass structure and it is onto this that pools of transmitted color will fall during direct sunlight. This same baffle will act as a reflector screen by night when powerful internal illumination will render the cone as arresting by night from outside as it will be by day from within. Steel tension cables and ring beams at various intervals are the only non-glass structural elements in this work. An 18 metre circle of scented flowers surrounds the base and a skybeam searchlight will radiate from the center of the stone base up through the open apex 1 mile into the sky.

I like to think people will spend time alone in the cone when they need that kind of emotional uplift.

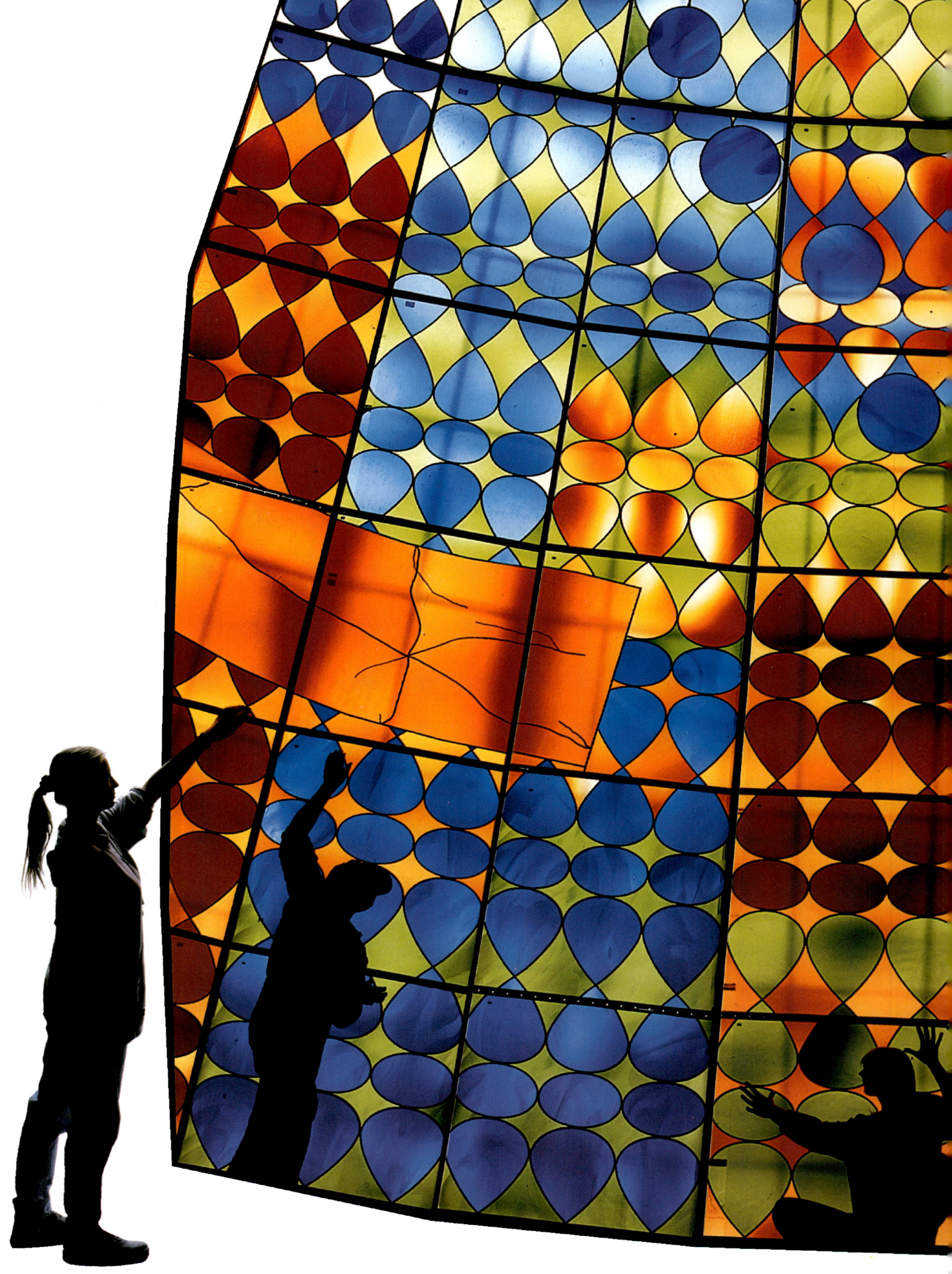

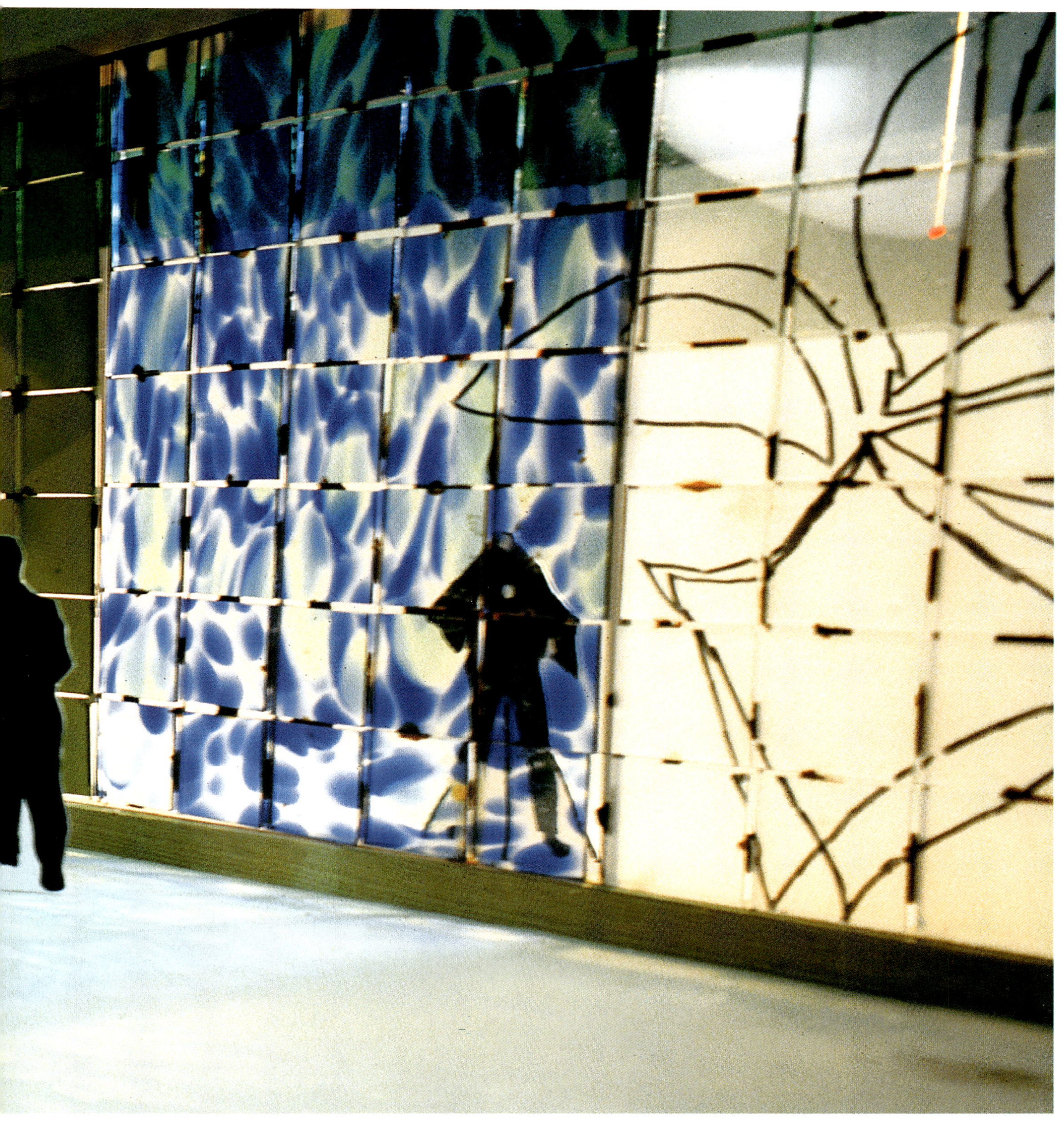

Scale model of installation using actual materials

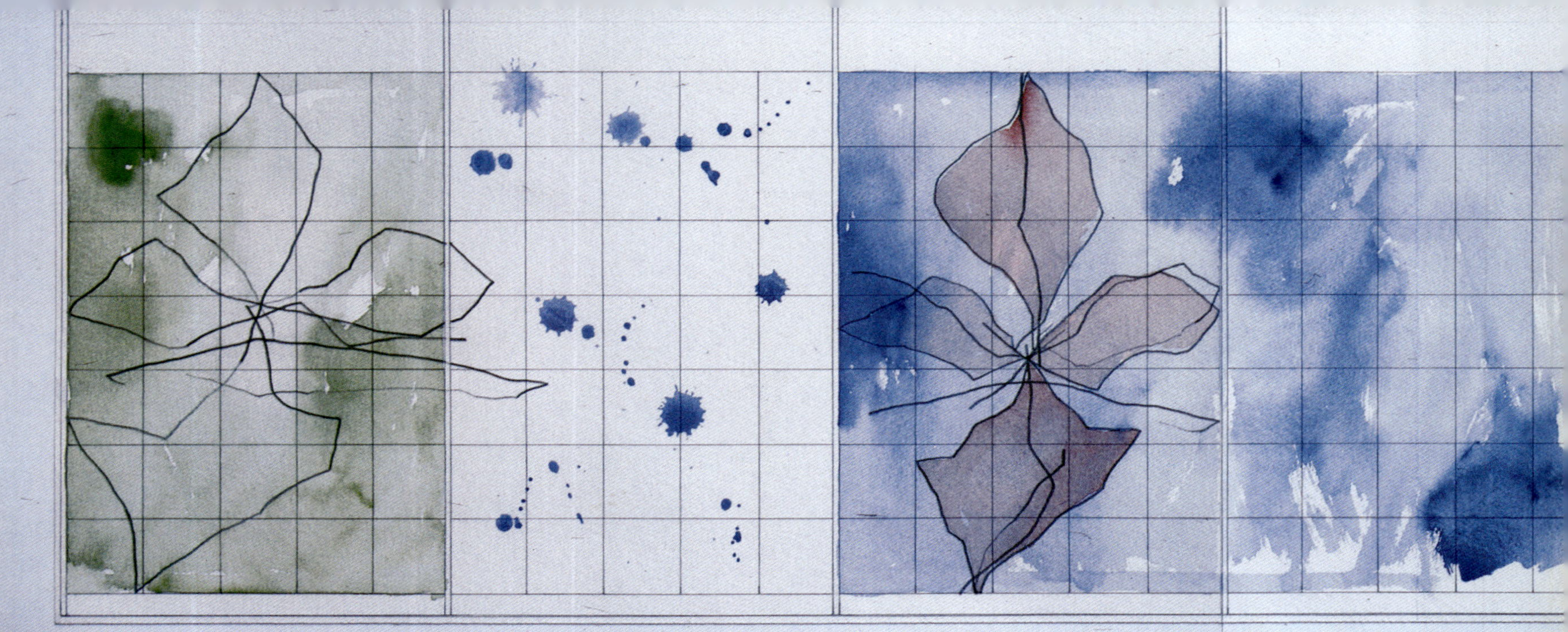

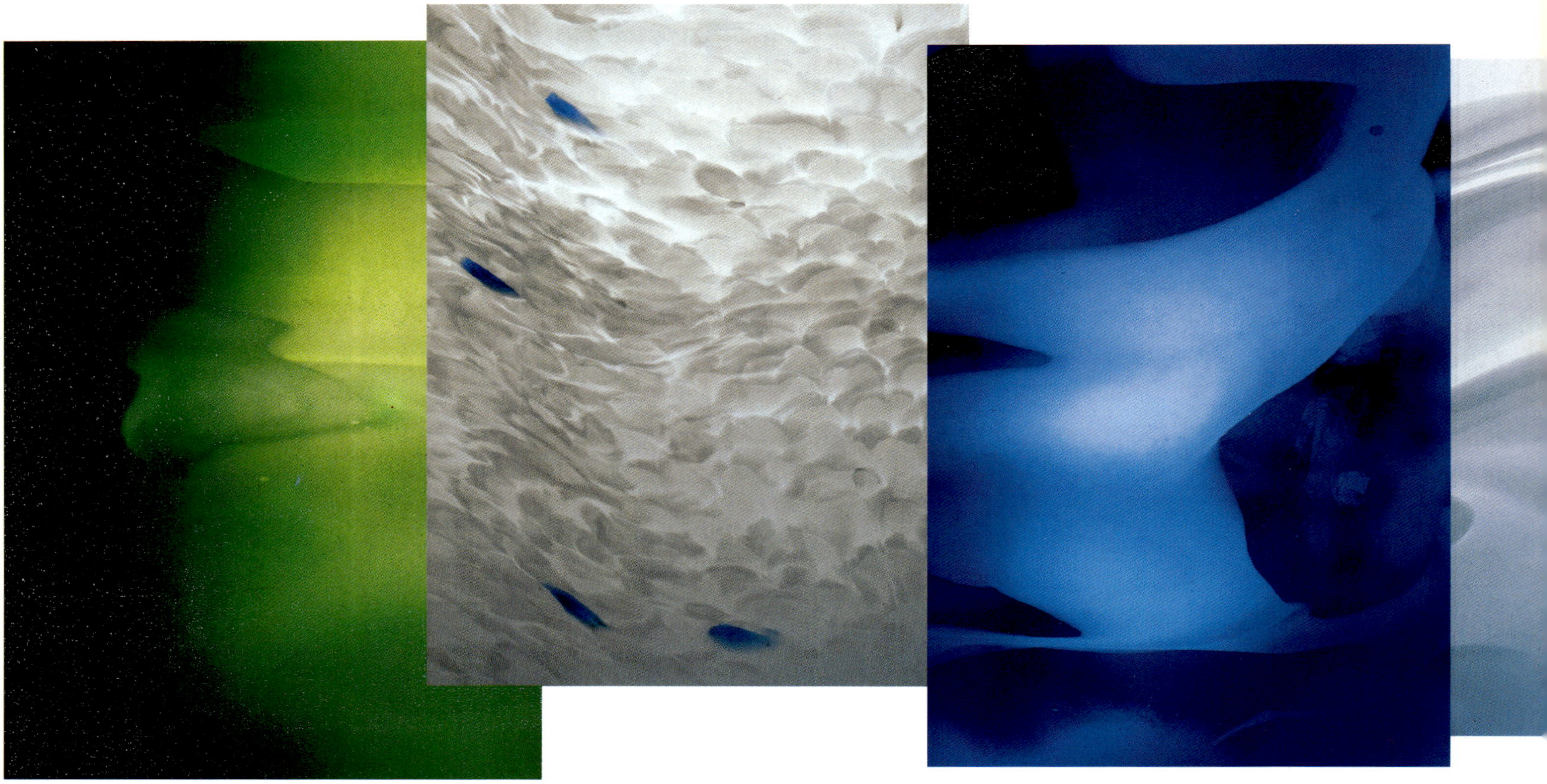

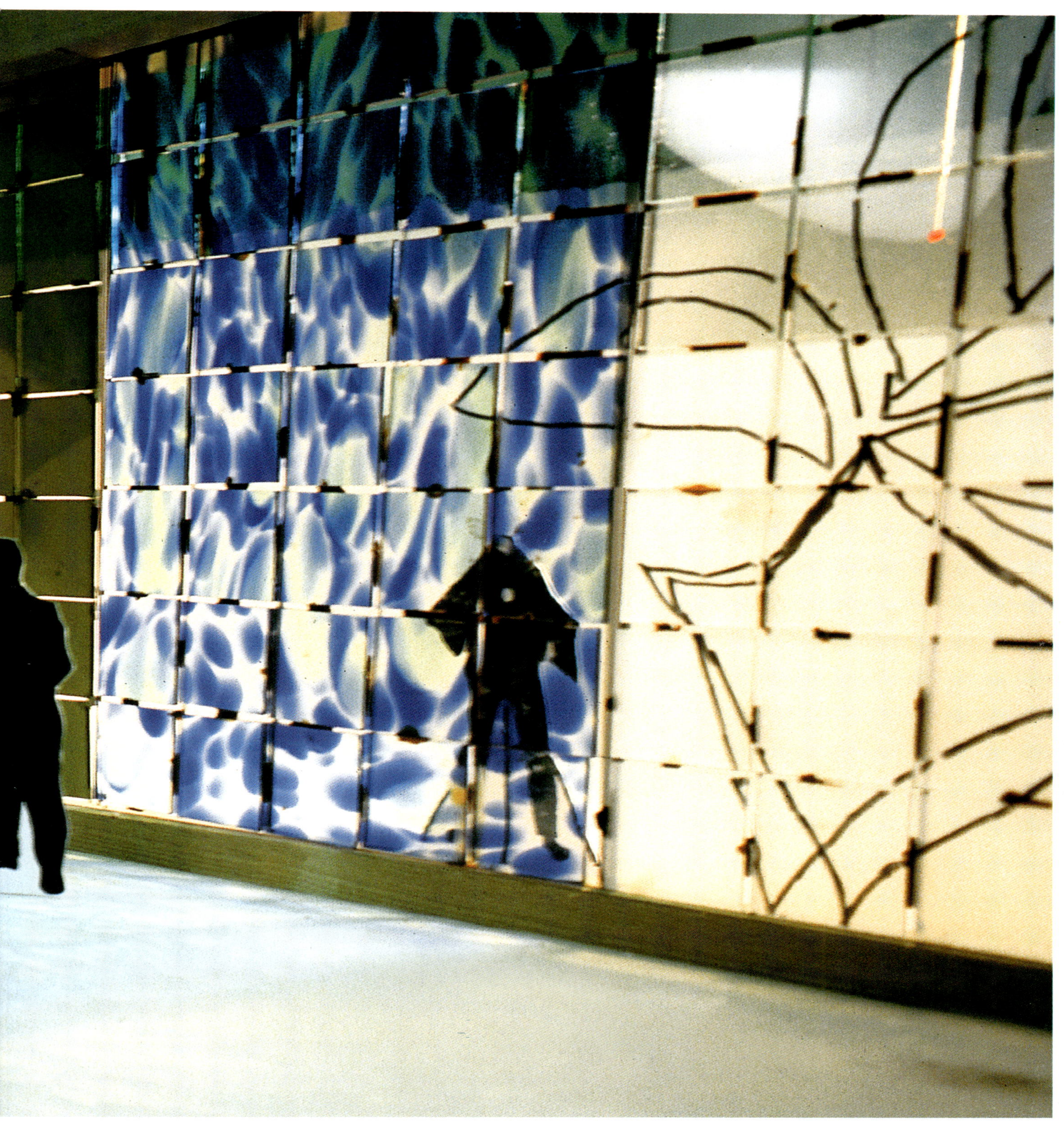

Scale model of installation using actual materials

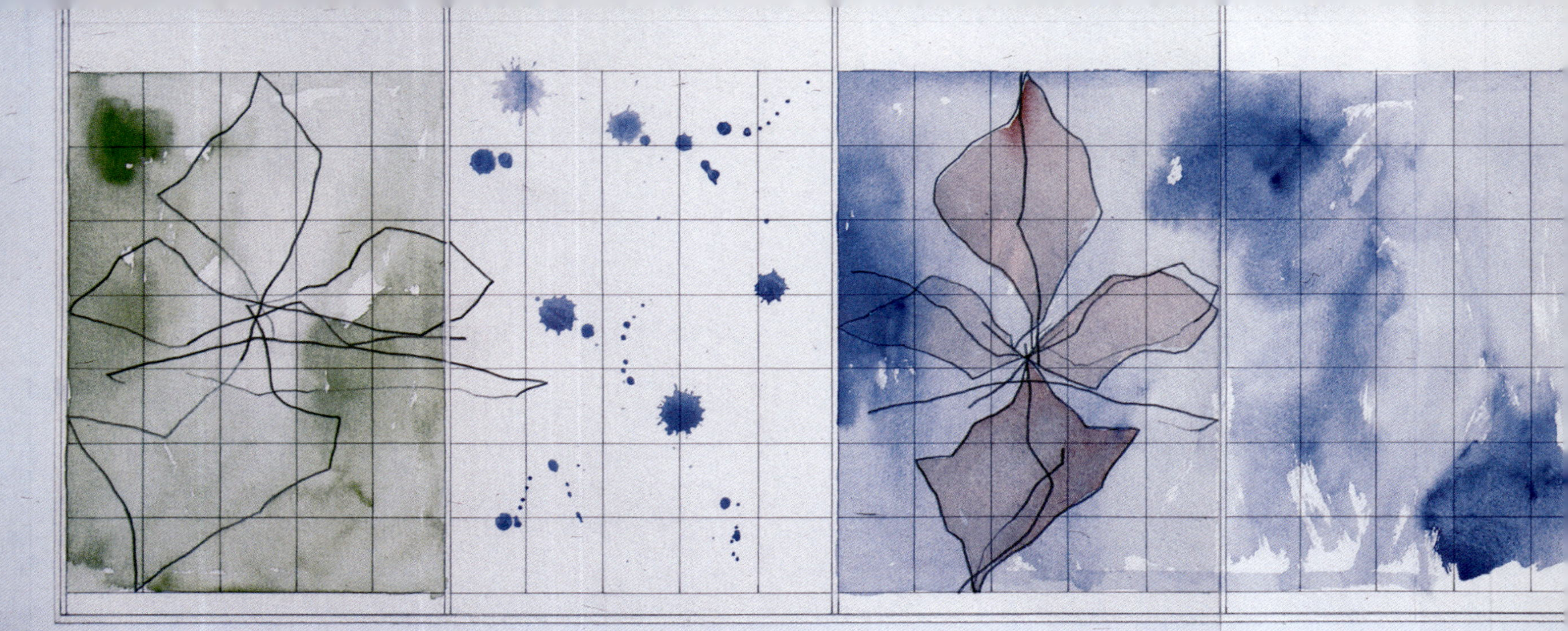

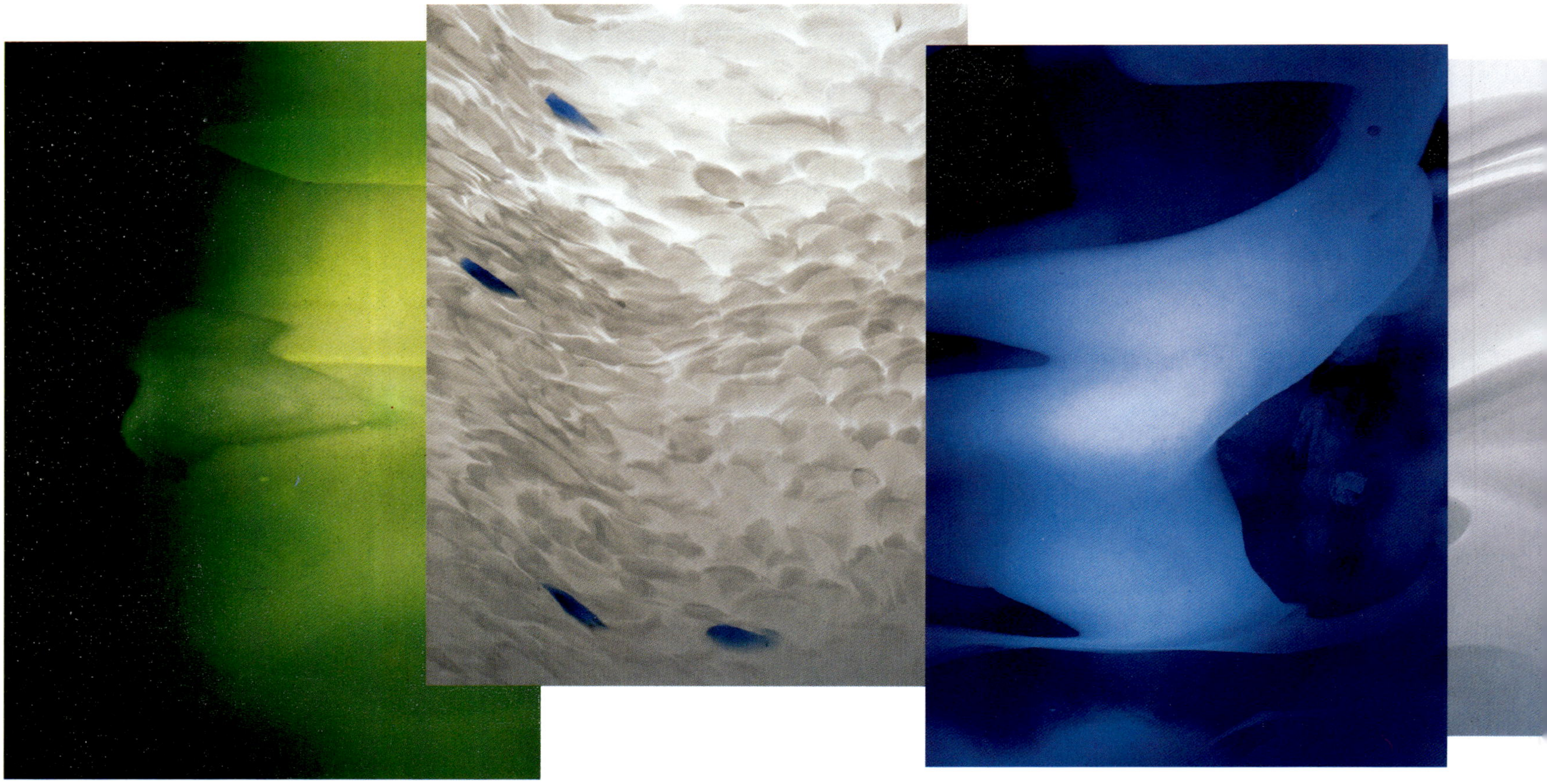

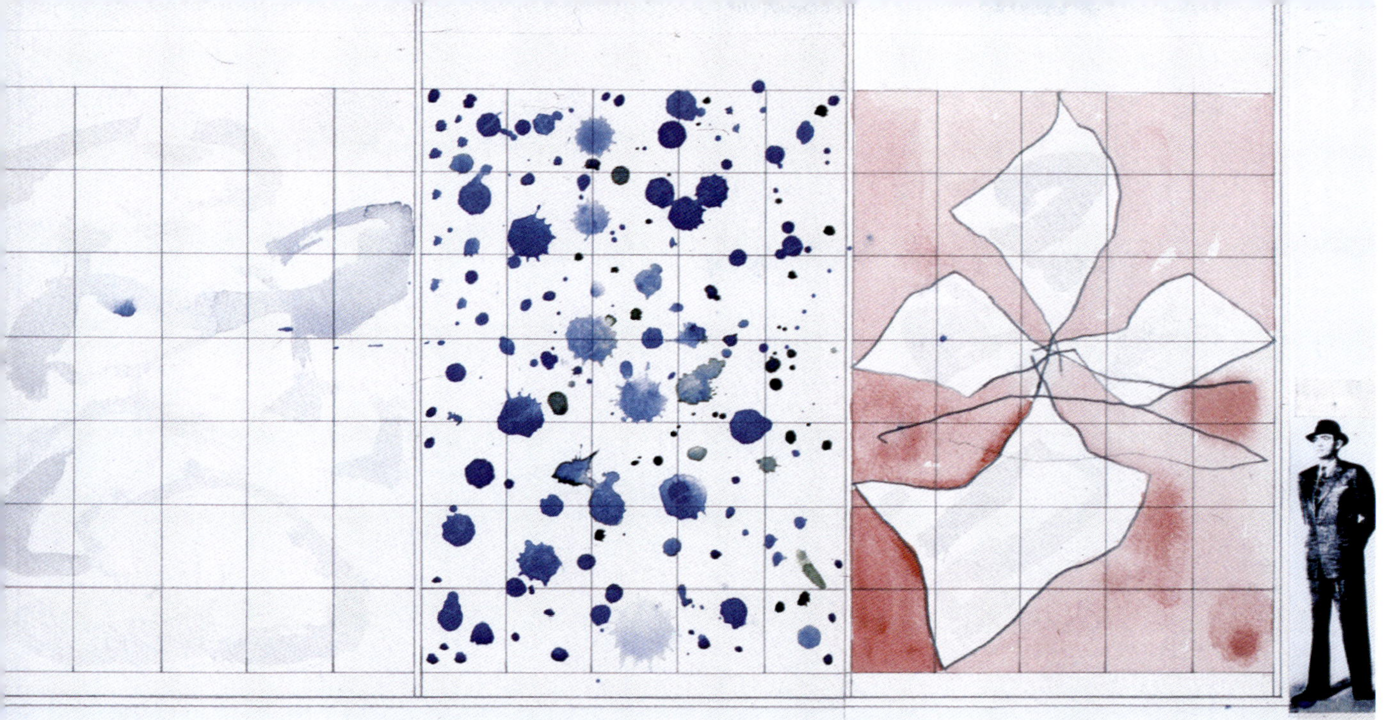

Scale design

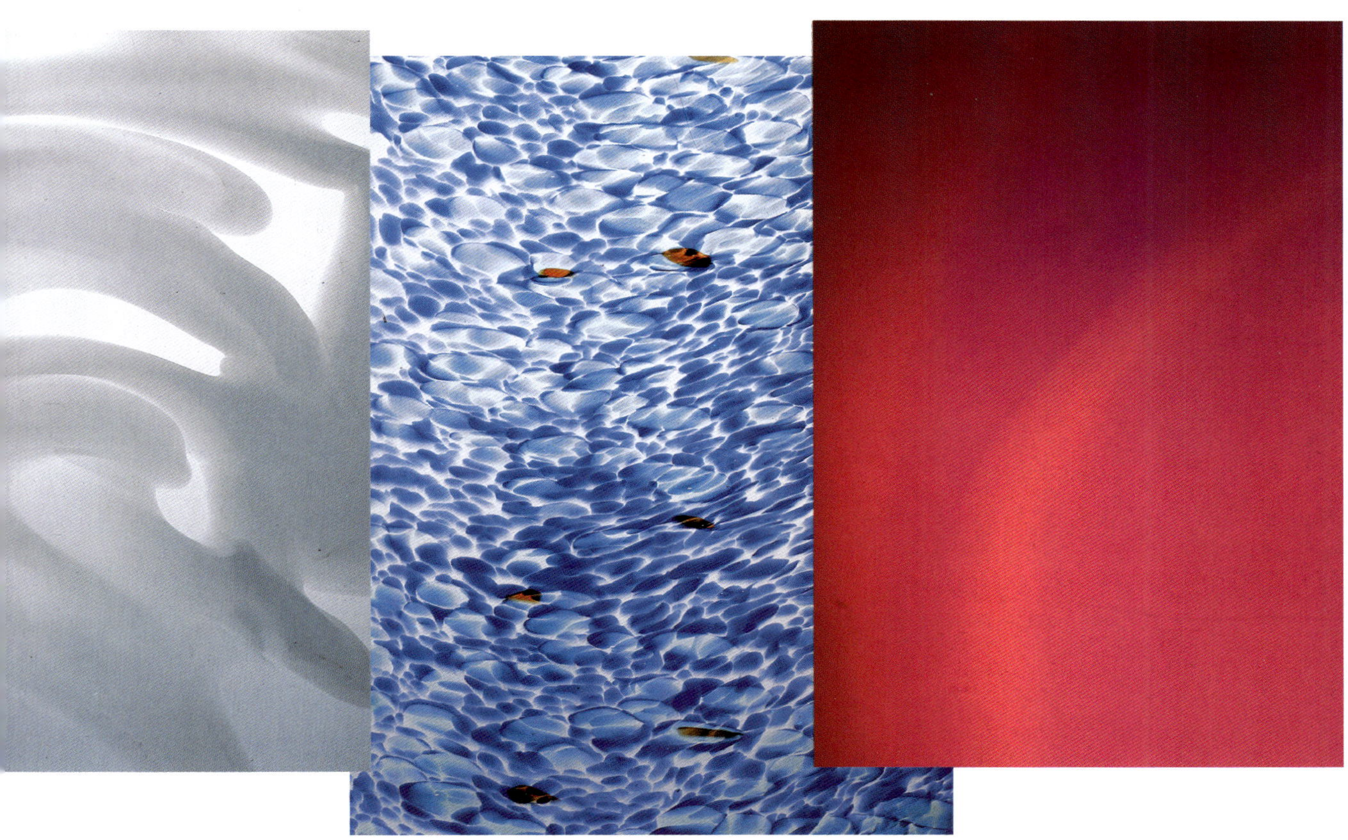

Glass samples corresponding left-to-right with the above design

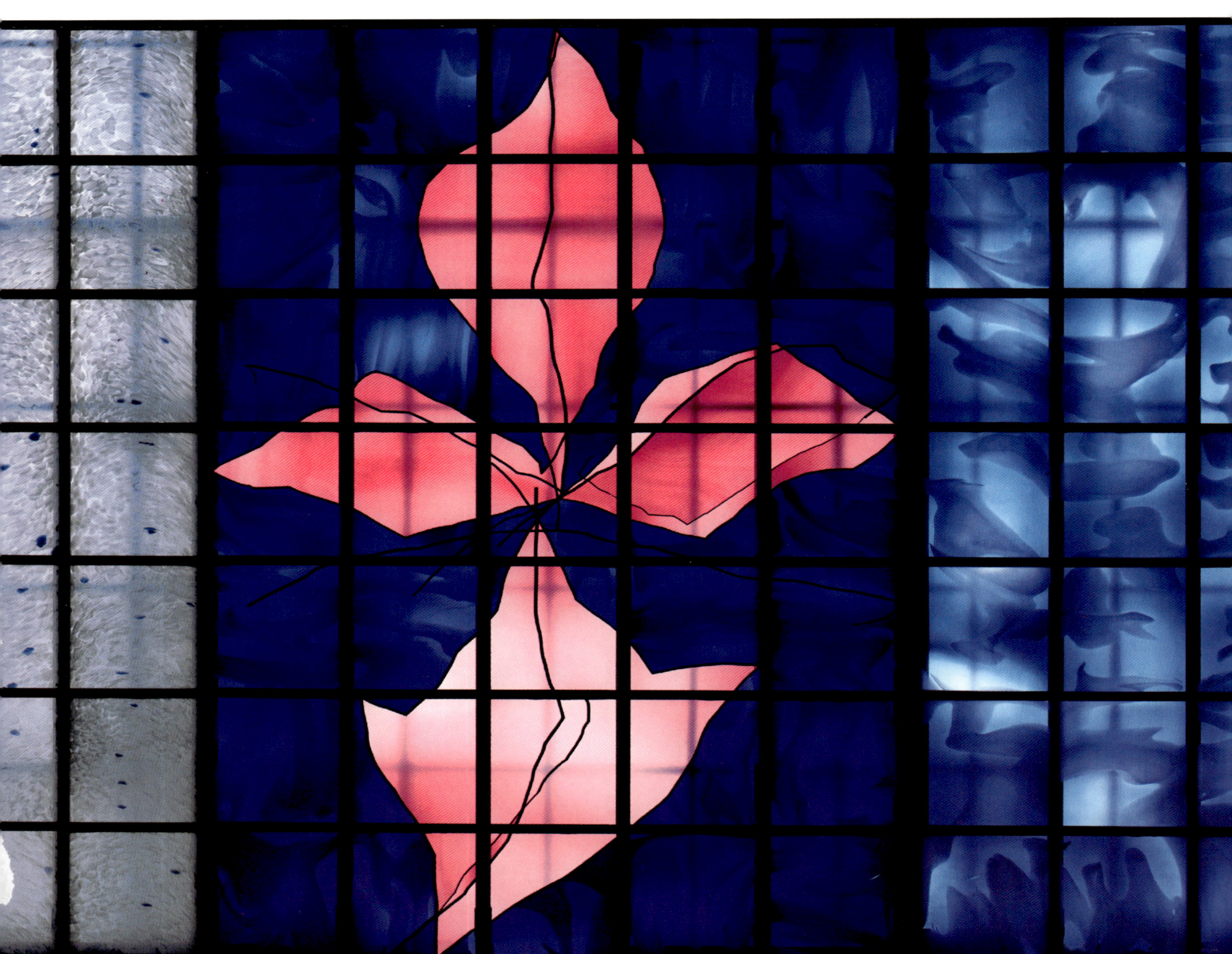

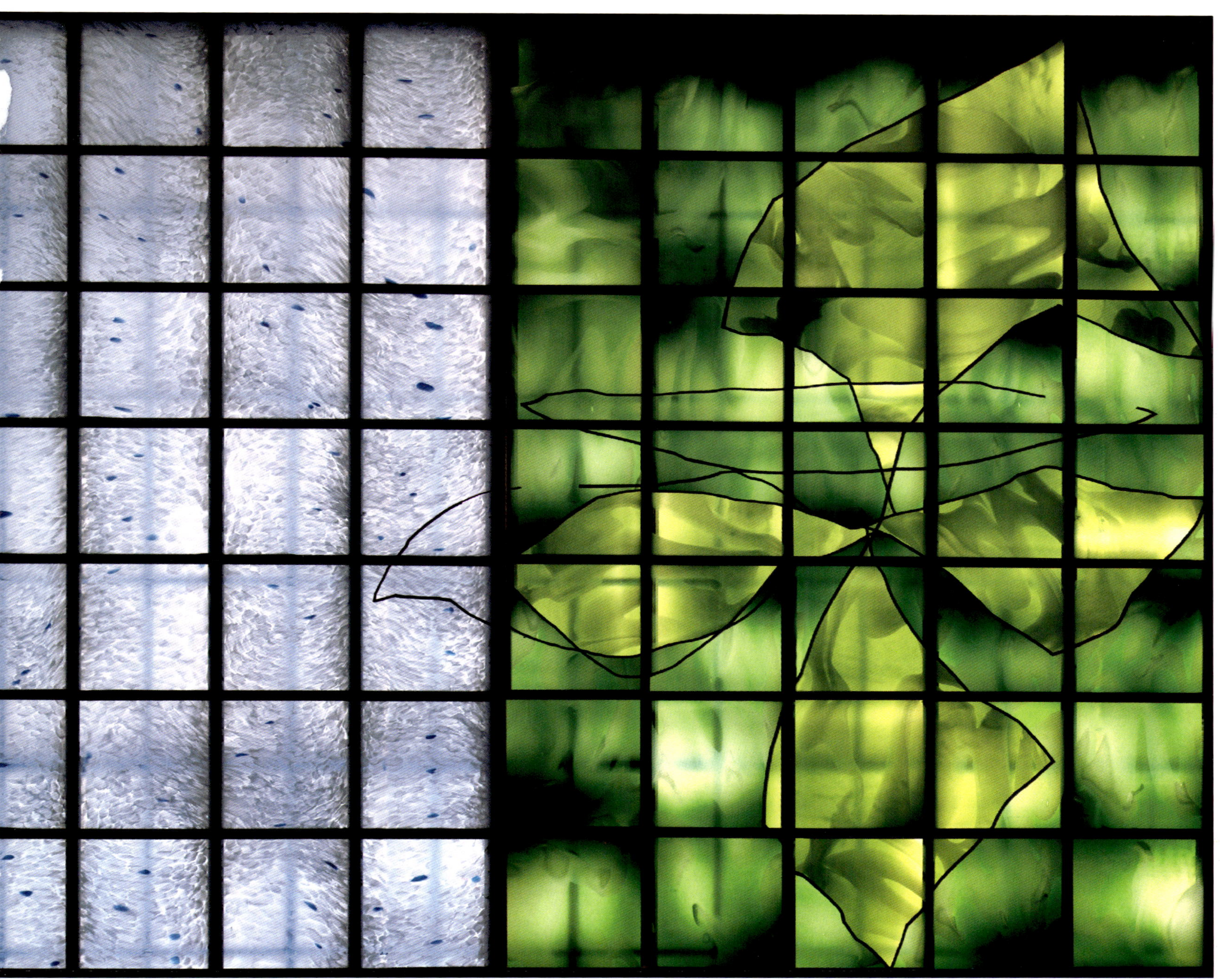

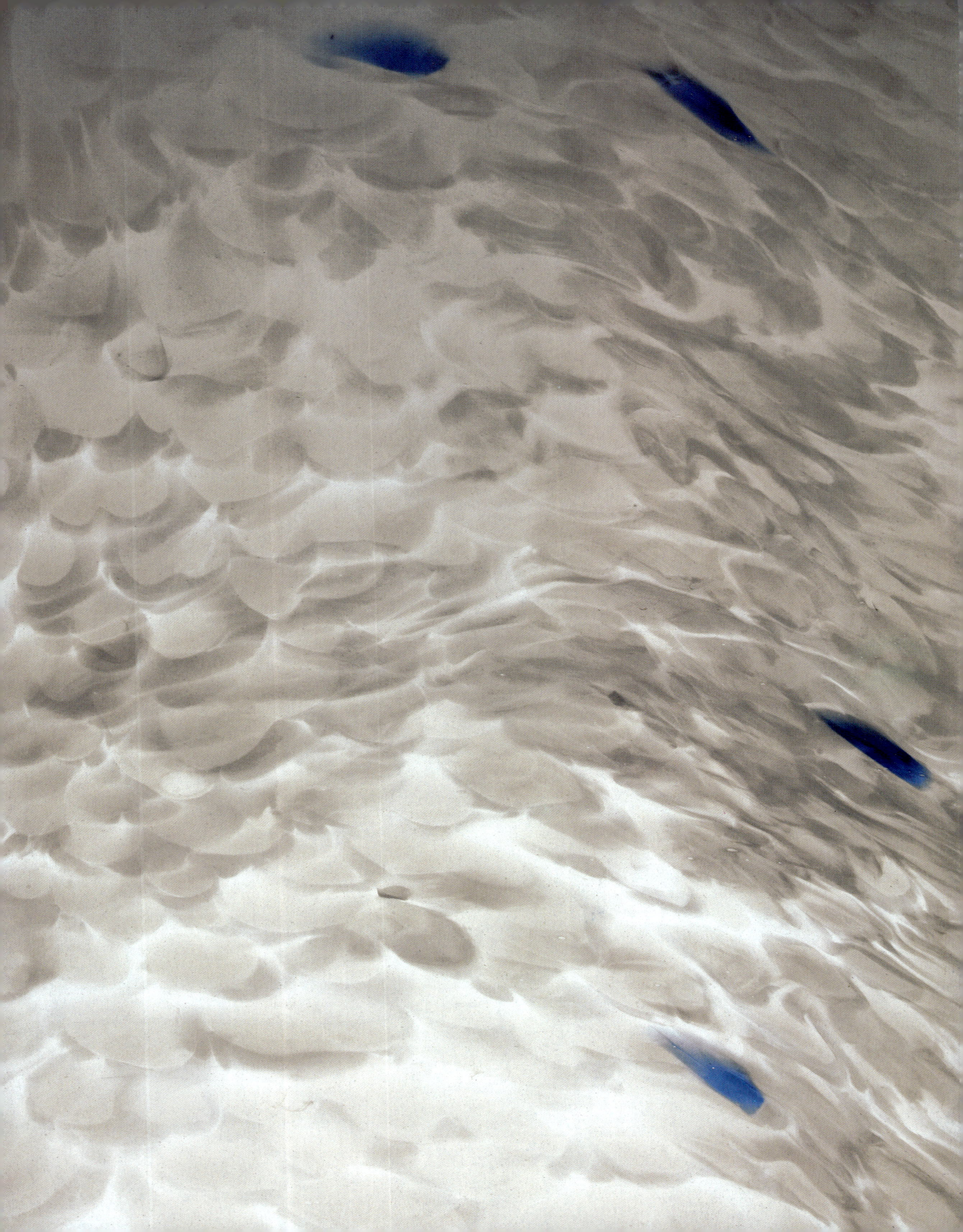

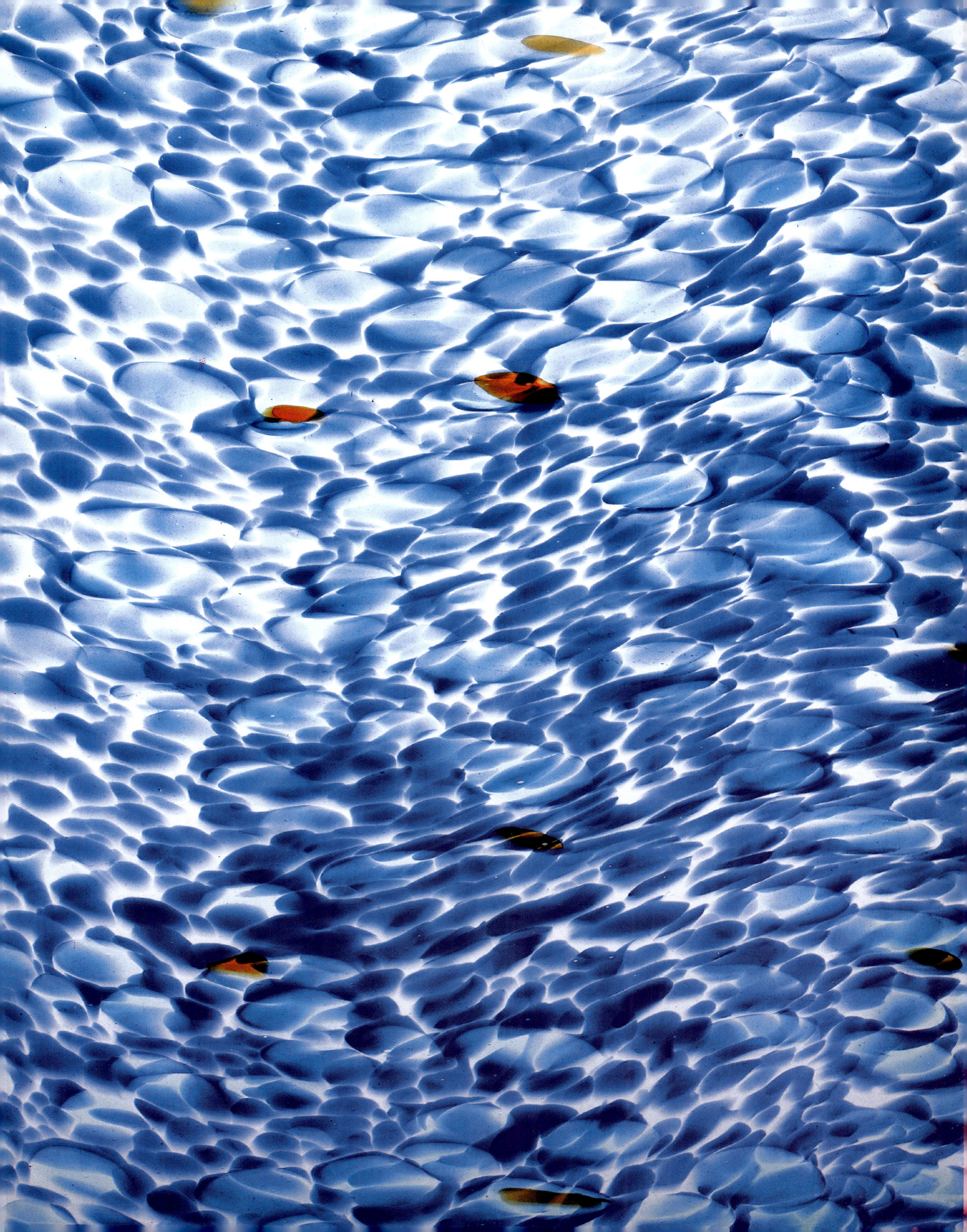

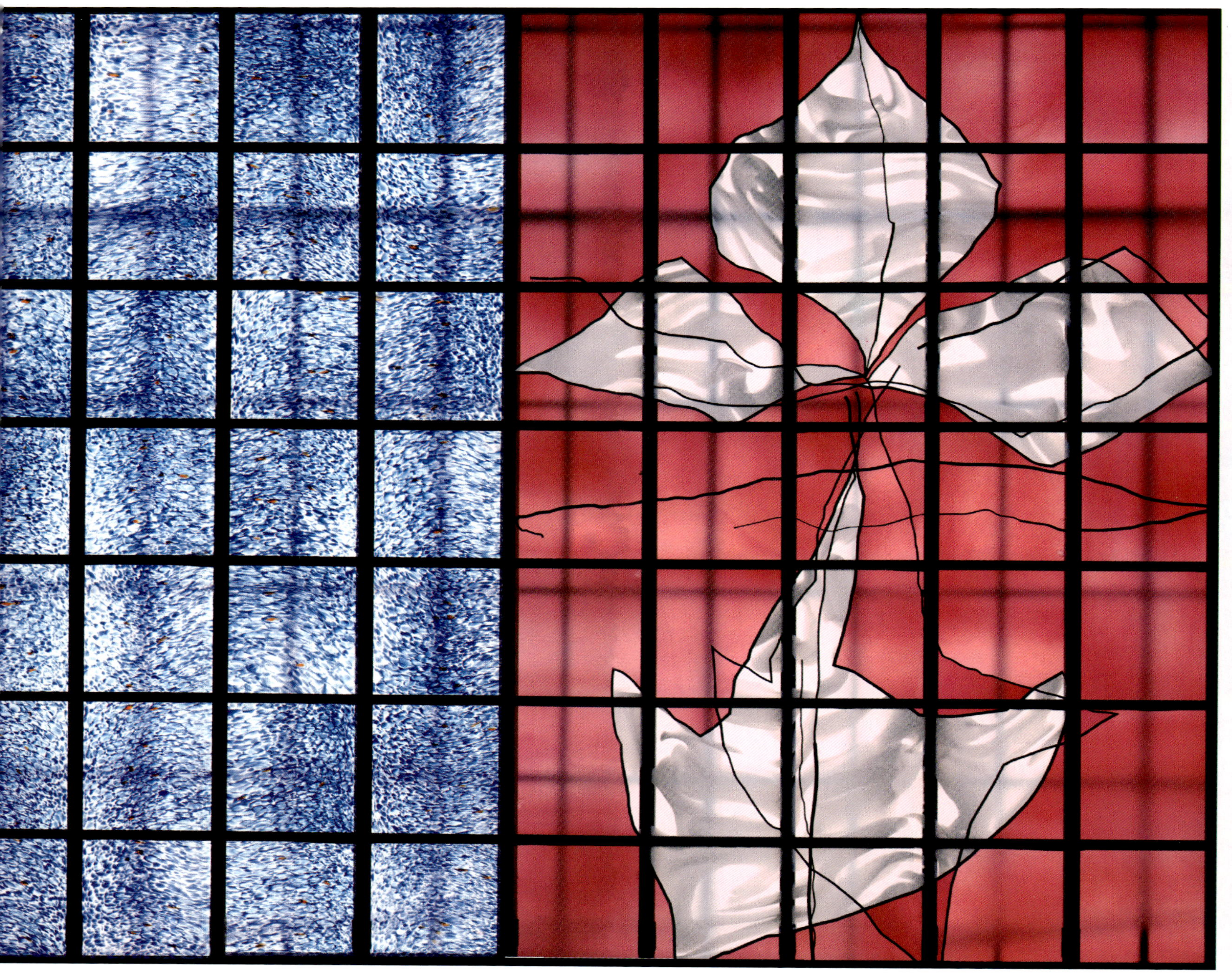

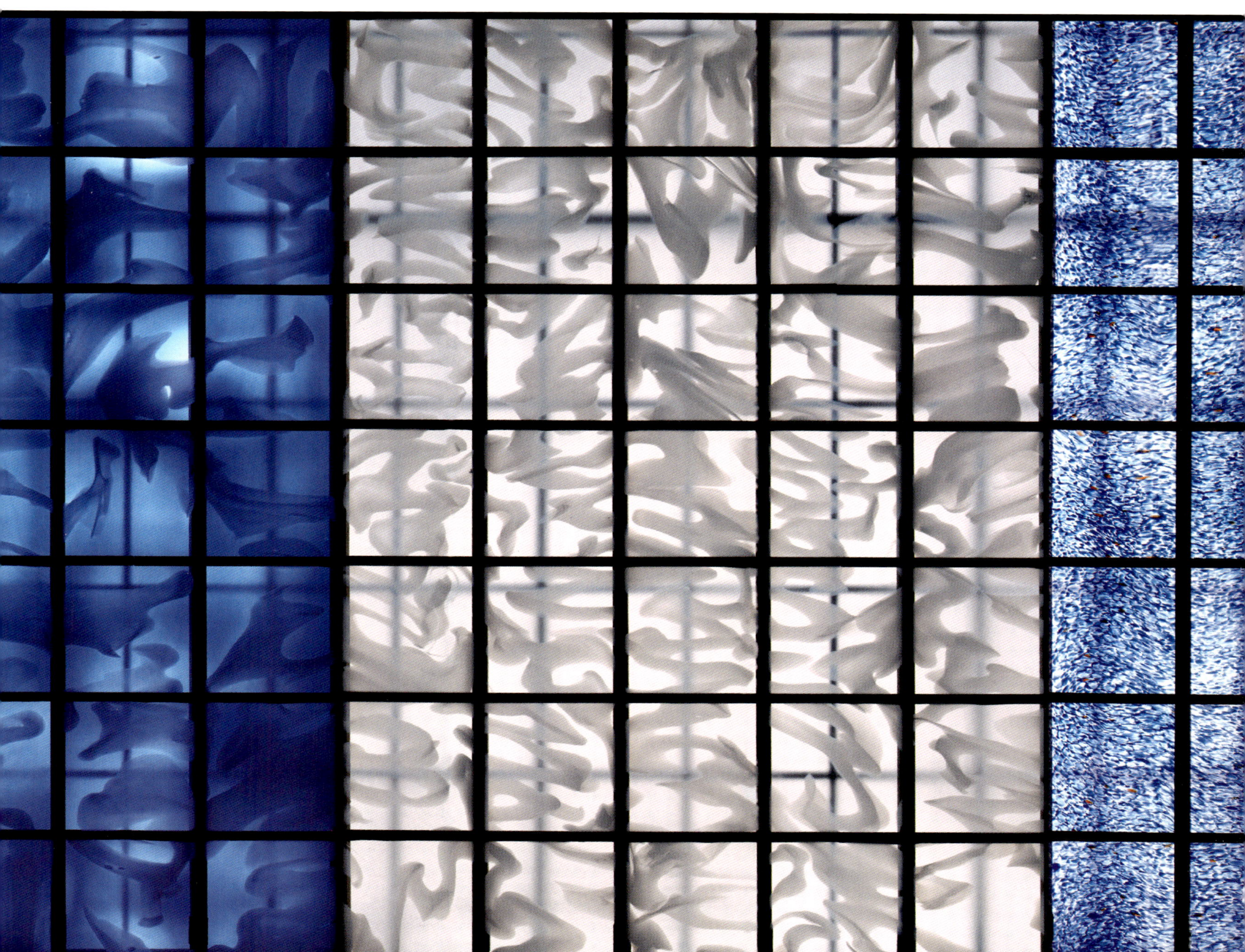

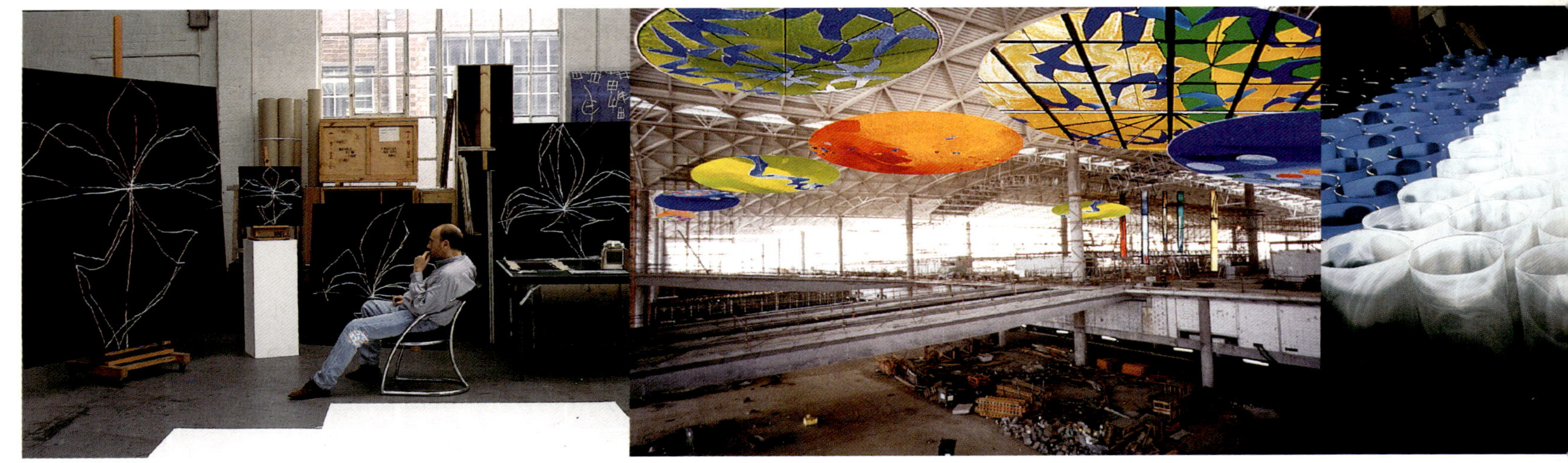

EXHIBITIONS AND PROJECTS

1998   The Glass Wall - An Architectural Installation exhibition at the Tony Shafrazi Gallery,
             New York June 12 - September 12
       New Paintings, exhibition at Faggionato Fine Arts, London (May/ June)
             Brian Clarke - Linda McCartney, exhibition at the German Museum for
             Stained Glass, Linnich (May - September)

1997   Design for RWE Energie AG (backlit stained glass walls)
             refurbishment of headquarter lobby, Essen, Germany
       Cut pile tapestry for Willis Corroon, in company's
             headquarters building by Sir Norman Foster, Ipswich
       Glass wall for the nave of the Synagogue Offenbach, refurbishment and extension, architect: Alfred Jacoby
       Designs for Chep Lap Kok Airport, Hong Kong Architect: Sir Norman Foster & Partners
       Designs for Shopping Center Villa Lobos (stained glass roof lights
             and mosaic for facade), Sao Paulo, Brazil (architect: Julio Neves)
       Design for stained glass windows for Catholic Church Maria Königen in
             Obersalbach near Saarbrücken, Germany (architects: Alt & Britz)
       Stained glass for The Chicago Sinai Synagogue (architect: Lohan Associates)
       Mosaic for Centre NorteShopping, Rio de Janeiro, Brazil
       "The Ruins of Time," new production of a stage set for ballet
             by Wayne Eagling, Het National Ballet, Amsterdam, Netherlands
       Competition designs for windows of Catholic Church (Heiliggeist-Kirche), Heidelberg, Germany
       Exhibition: Brian Clarke - Linda McCartney
             30th August 1997 to 28th April 1998, Musée Suisse du Vitrail, Romont, Switzerland

1996   Stained glass wall / facade
             Valentino Village, Noci, Bari, Italy (architect: Emilio Ambasz & Angelo Rocco Don Giovanni)
       Stained glass and mosaic ceiling
       Pfizer World Headquarters Building, New York, USA (architect: Hixon Design) .
       Design for stained glass cone, Swiss Bank Corporation, Stamford, CT, USA.

Brian Clarke in London studio 1998 • Designed for Chep Lap Kok Airport Hong Kong • Glass for Pfizer in factory

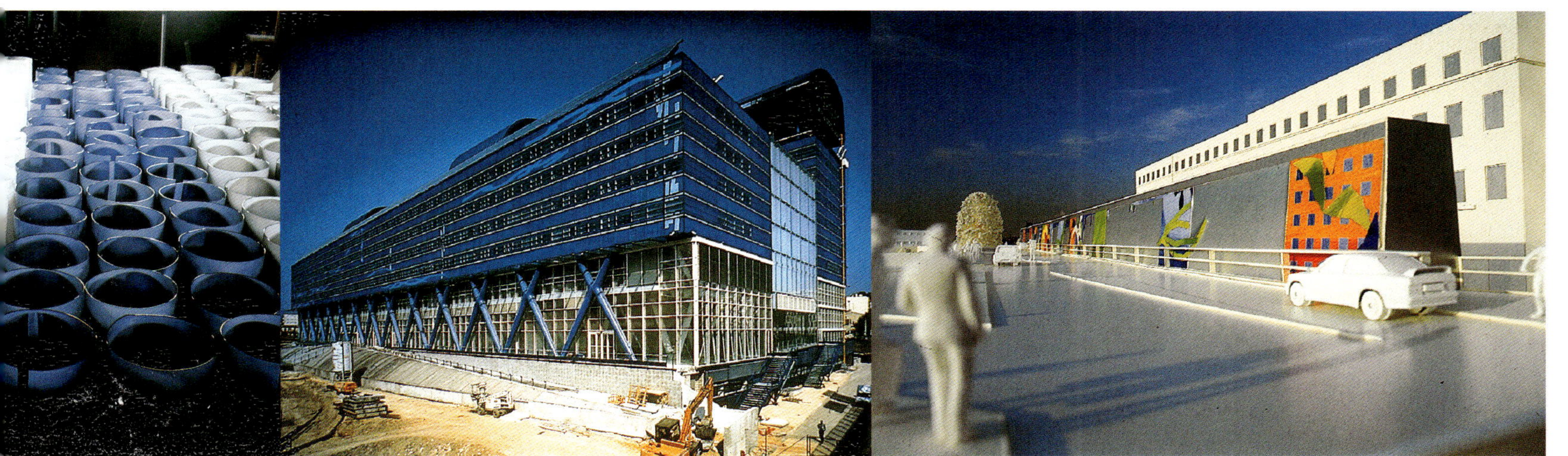

to be completed fall 1998 (engineers: Dewhurst Macfarlane & Partners)
Proposal for the ceiling of the Great Auditorium, Paris Opera (Bastille).
Joint competition entry with architects Alsop & Störmer architects for Hungerford Bridge, London, England.
Stained glass entrance Kinderhaus, Regensburg, Germany. (architect: A2)

1995   Exhibition: Fazit '95 Die Sammlung des Museums für Zeitgenössische
       Glasmalerei Langen.(10/03/1995 - 29/10/1995), Altes Rathaus Langen, Germany.
Exhibition: Exempla '95, Handwerkskammer für München und Oberbayern.
       11/03/95 - 19/03/95, München, Germany.
Lecture at the National Exhibition Centre, England. 21/03/95, RIBA (Royal Institute of British Architects),
Stained glass and mosaic ceilings for Centre NorteShopping
       (Completed 1996)
       Rio de Janeiro, Brazil. 1055 square metres of glass and 150 square metres of mosaic
       (architect: Design Corp, Toronto).
Stained glass windows for the Abbaye de la Fille Dieu, (Completed 1996), Romont, Switzerland
(architect Tomas Mikulas).

1994   Exhibition: "Brian Clarke: Paintings and Stained Glass," Tony Shafrazi Gallery,
      New York, NY, December 10, 1994 - February 4, 1995.
Mosaic and stained glass windows and walls for Lowe SMS & Partners, The Grace Building, New York, USA.
Stained glass window for Clinical Research Building and Hammersmith Hospital Cancer Centre, London.
Stained glass design for Brent Cross Shopping Centre, London, England.
Stained glass dome, design for the Frankfurter Allee Plaza, Berlin, Germany.
      Stained glass cupola and mosaic ceiling for the Schadow Arkaden, Düsseldorf, Germany
      (architect: Brune Cosulting).
      Stained glass design for Crossrail Terminal, Paddington Station, London (architects: Alsop & Störmer).
Designs for stained glass ceiling and mosaic floor for Friedrichstadt Passagen,
      Quartier 206, Berlin (architect: I.M. Pei, Cobb, Freed and Partner).
Mosaic for W.H.Smith & Sons Ltd. Training Office, Abingdon, Oxon, England.
Collaborative proposal, with Zaha Hadid for stained glass and mosaic at Spittelau, Vienna, Austria.
Designs for the compact disc covers of the Sir William Walton classical music catalogue for EMI Records, London.
Designs for stained glass for the Aachen Synagogue, Aachen, Germany (architect: Alfred Jacoby).

Le Grand Bleu, Marseilles • Model for Crossrail Terminal, London

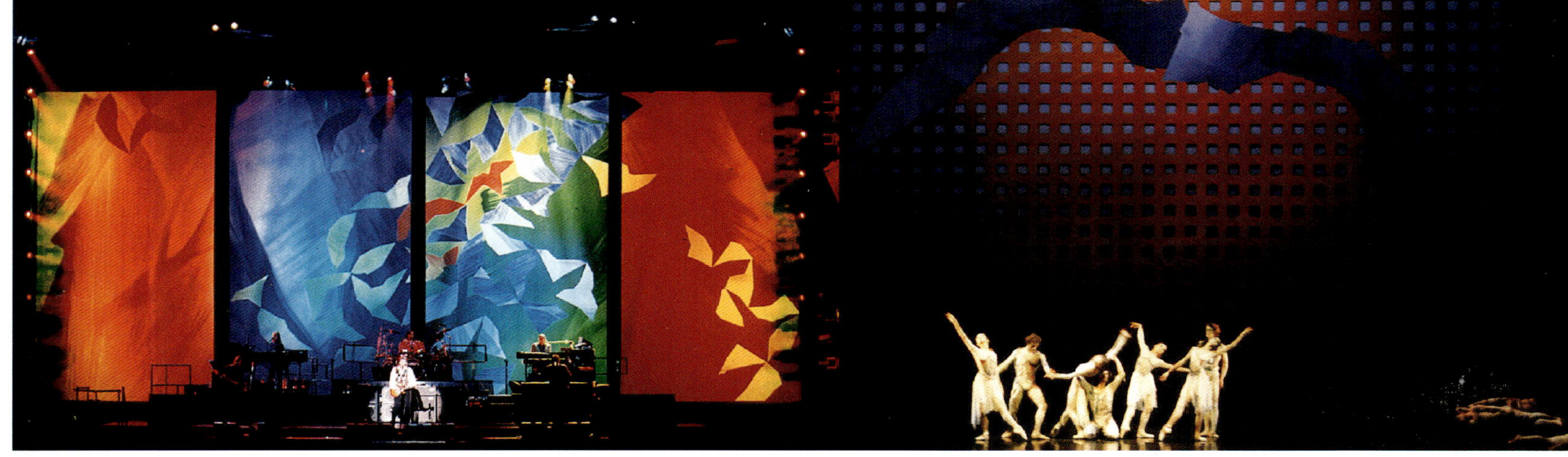

Proposal for a glass tower at Willis Faber Building, Ipswich, England. (Arch. Sir Norman Foster).
Created Professor of Architectural Art, Bartlett Institute of Architecture, University College, London.

1993   Designed the stadia stage sets for the Paul McCartney 1993 World Tour.
Stained glass for the North wall of the EAM Building, Kassel, Germany
        (architect: von Gerkan, Marg and Partners).
"The Ruins of Time," stage sets for a ballet by Wayne Eagling in tribute to
        Rudolph Nuryev, Het National Ballet, Amsterdam.
 Award: Honorary Fellowship of the Royal Institute of British Architects.
 Exhibition: "Images of Christ," Northampton Museum and St. Paul's Cathedral, London.
 Stained glass roofs for the Spindles, Oldham, Lancashire.
"Brian Clarke, Designs on Architecture," Oldham Art Gallery,
        Oldham, Lancashire, October 2 - November 9, (catalogue).
"Brian Clarke, New Paintings," The Mayor Gallery, London.
 Stained glass windows for the new Heidelberg Synagogue, Heidelberg, Germany.
 Exhibition: "Architecture and the Sacred Space in the Modern Age -
        Venice Biennale," (with architect Alfred Jacoby.)

1992   Exhibition: "Addressing the Forbidden," Brighton Festival, Brighton.
Stills Gallery, Edinburgh Festival, Edinburgh.
Lecture at the University of Seoul, Korea.
Stained glass tower windows for Espana Telefonica, Placa Catalunya, Barcelona for the 1992 Olympiad.
Tapestries and stained glass for the Carmelite, Carmelite Street, London (architect: Trehearne & Norman).
Architectural Competition: The Glass Dune - Ministry of Environmental Building, Hamburg
        (architects: Future Systems).
Glass cladding and colouring to the main facade of the Hotel du Department des Bouches-du Rhone, Marseille,
        France (architect: Alsop & Störmer).
Stained glass screen for Chateau d'Orain, France.
 Exhibition: "Light and Architecture," Ingolstadt, Germany (in collaboration with Future Systems).
 Exhibition: "The Painter in Glass," Glyn Vivian Art Gallery, Swansea, England (catalogue).

Paul McCartney World Tour • The National Ballet, Amsterdam

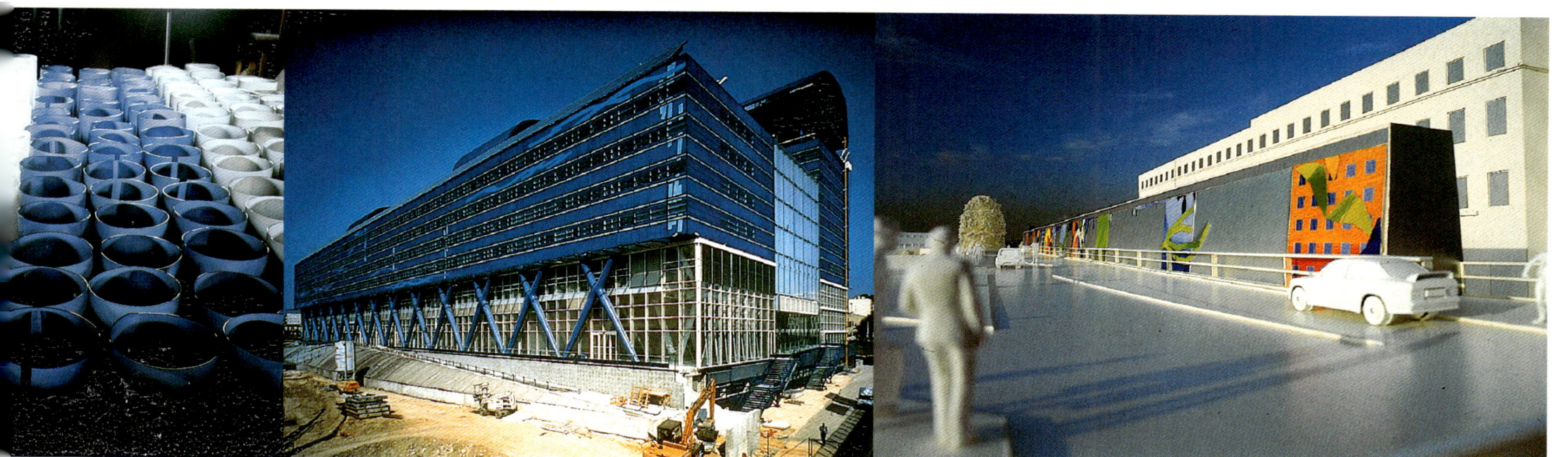

to be completed fall 1998 (engineers: Dewhurst Macfarlane & Partners)
Proposal for the ceiling of the Great Auditorium, Paris Opera (Bastille).
Joint competition entry with architects Alsop & Störmer architects for Hungerford Bridge, London, England.
Stained glass entrance Kinderhaus, Regensburg, Germany. (architect: A2)

1995   Exhibition: Fazit '95 Die Sammlung des Museums für Zeitgenössische
            Glasmalerei Langen.(10/03/1995 - 29/10/1995), Altes Rathaus Langen, Germany.
        Exhibition: Exempla '95, Handwerkskammer für München und Oberbayern.
            11/03/95 - 19/03/95, München, Germany.
        Lecture at the National Exhibition Centre, England. 21/03/95, RIBA (Royal Institute of British Architects),
        Stained glass and mosaic ceilings for Centre NorteShopping
            (Completed 1996)
            Rio de Janeiro, Brazil. 1055 square metres of glass and 150 square metres of mosaic
            (architect: Design Corp, Toronto).
        Stained glass windows for the Abbaye de la Fille Dieu, (Completed 1996), Romont, Switzerland
        (architect Tomas Mikulas).

1994   Exhibition: "Brian Clarke: Paintings and Stained Glass," Tony Shafrazi Gallery,
            New York, NY, December 10, 1994 - February 4, 1995.
        Mosaic and stained glass windows and walls for Lowe SMS & Partners, The Grace Building, New York, USA.
        Stained glass window for Clinical Research Building and Hammersmith Hospital Cancer Centre, London.
        Stained glass design for Brent Cross Shopping Centre, London, England.
        Stained glass dome, design for the Frankfurter Allee Plaza, Berlin, Germany.
            Stained glass cupola and mosaic ceiling for the Schadow Arkaden, Düsseldorf, Germany
            (architect: Brune Cosulting).
            Stained glass design for Crossrail Terminal, Paddington Station, London (architects: Alsop & Störmer).
        Designs for stained glass ceiling and mosaic floor for Friedrichstadt Passagen,
            Quartier 206, Berlin (architect: I.M. Pei, Cobb, Freed and Partner).
        Mosaic for W.H.Smith & Sons Ltd. Training Office, Abingdon, Oxon, England.
        Collaborative proposal, with Zaha Hadid for stained glass and mosaic at Spittelau, Vienna, Austria.
        Designs for the compact disc covers of the Sir William Walton classical music catalogue for EMI Records, London.
        Designs for stained glass for the Aachen Synagogue, Aachen, Germany (architect: Alfred Jacoby).

Le Grand Bleu, Marseilles • Model for Crossrail Terminal, London

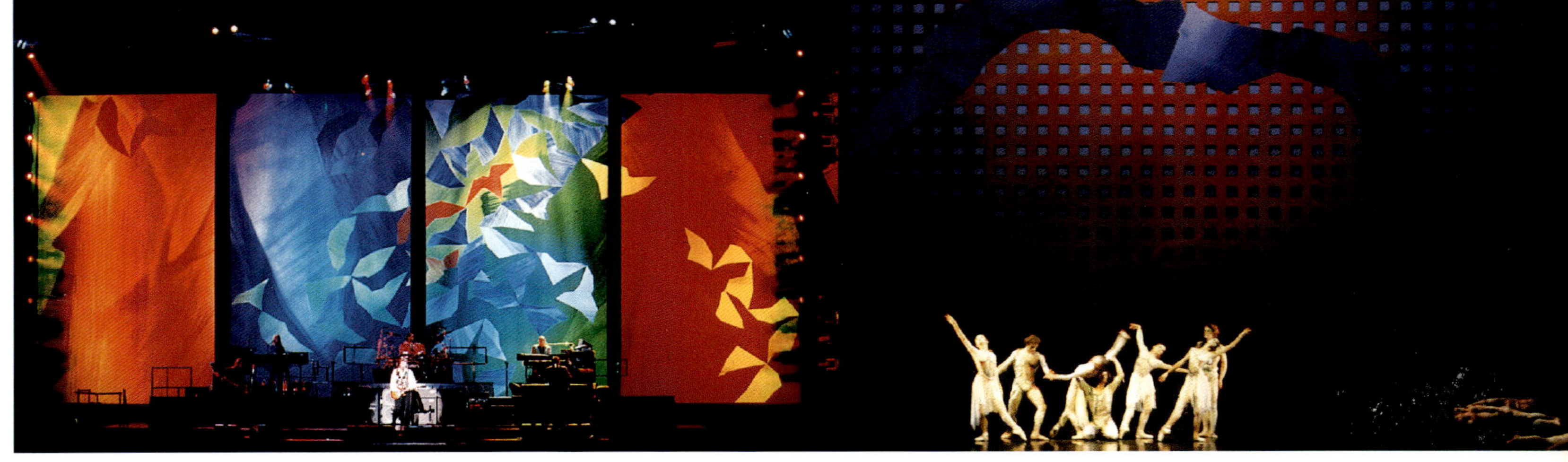

Proposal for a glass tower at Willis Faber Building, Ipswich, England. (Arch. Sir Norman Foster).
Created Professor of Architectural Art, Bartlett Institute of Architecture, University College, London.

1993   Designed the stadia stage sets for the Paul McCartney 1993 World Tour.
Stained glass for the North wall of the EAM Building, Kassel, Germany
        (architect: von Gerkan, Marg and Partners).
"The Ruins of Time," stage sets for a ballet by Wayne Eagling in tribute to
        Rudolph Nuryev, Het National Ballet, Amsterdam.
 Award: Honorary Fellowship of the Royal Institute of British Architects.
 Exhibition: "Images of Christ," Northampton Museum and St. Paul's Cathedral, London.
 Stained glass roofs for the Spindles, Oldham, Lancashire.
"Brian Clarke, Designs on Architecture," Oldham Art Gallery,
        Oldham, Lancashire, October 2 - November 9, (catalogue).
"Brian Clarke, New Paintings," The Mayor Gallery, London.
 Stained glass windows for the new Heidelberg Synagogue, Heidelberg, Germany.
 Exhibition: "Architecture and the Sacred Space in the Modern Age -
        Venice Biennale," (with architect Alfred Jacoby.)

1992   Exhibition: "Addressing the Forbidden," Brighton Festival, Brighton.
Stills Gallery, Edinburgh Festival, Edinburgh.
Lecture at the University of Seoul, Korea.
Stained glass tower windows for Espana Telefonica, Placa Catalunya, Barcelona for the 1992 Olympiad.
Tapestries and stained glass for the Carmelite, Carmelite Street, London (architect: Treharne & Norman).
Architectural Competition: The Glass Dune - Ministry of Environmental Building, Hamburg
        (architects: Future Systems).
Glass cladding and colouring to the main facade of the Hotel du Department des Bouches-du Rhone, Marseille,
        France (architect: Alsop & Störmer).
Stained glass screen for Chateau d'Orain, France.
Exhibition: "Light and Architecture," Ingolstadt, Germany (in collaboration with Future Systems).
Exhibition: "The Painter in Glass," Glyn Vivian Art Gallery, Swansea, England (catalogue).

Paul McCartney World Tour • The National Ballet, Amsterdam

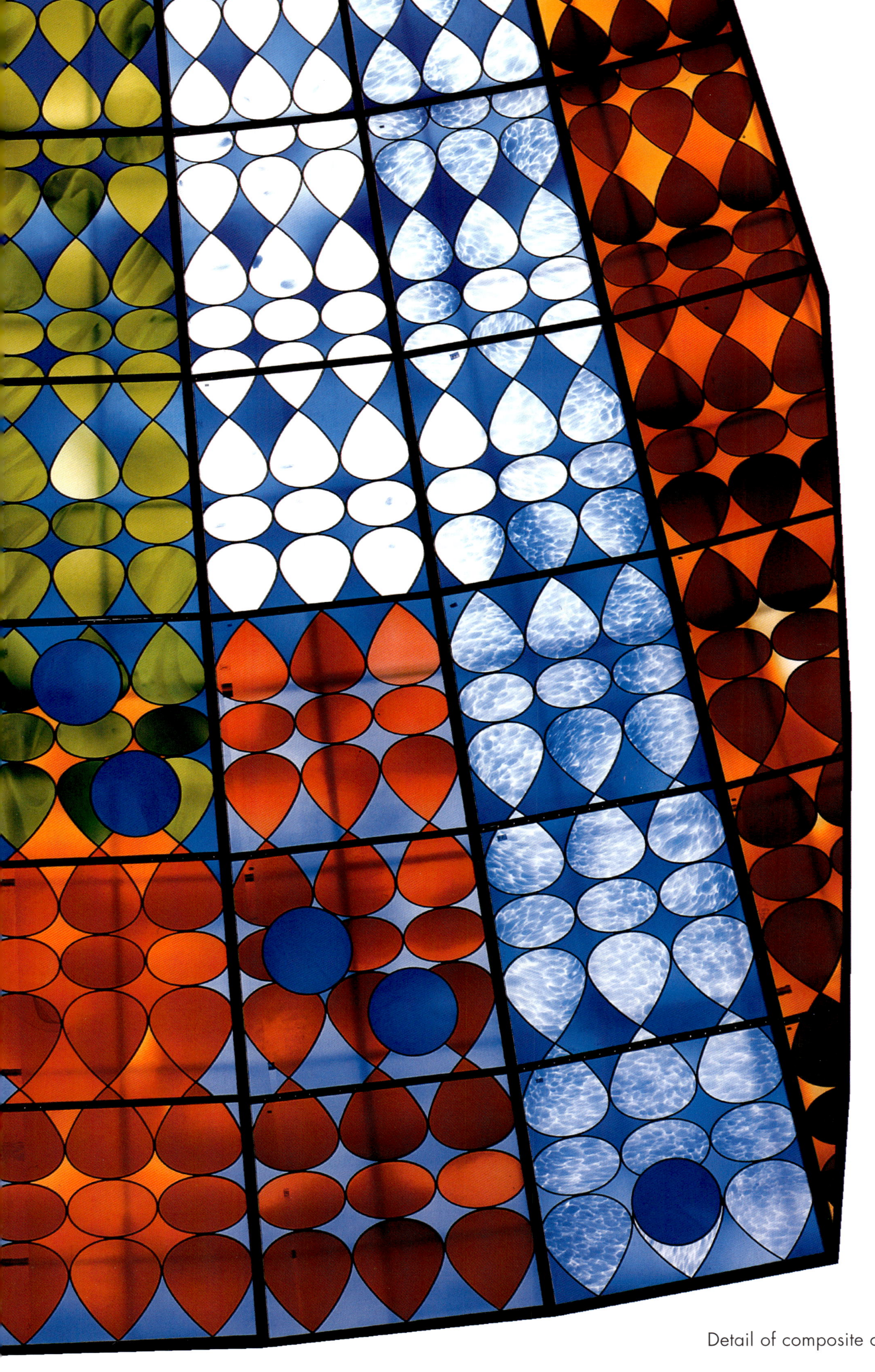

Detail of composite of actual stained glass

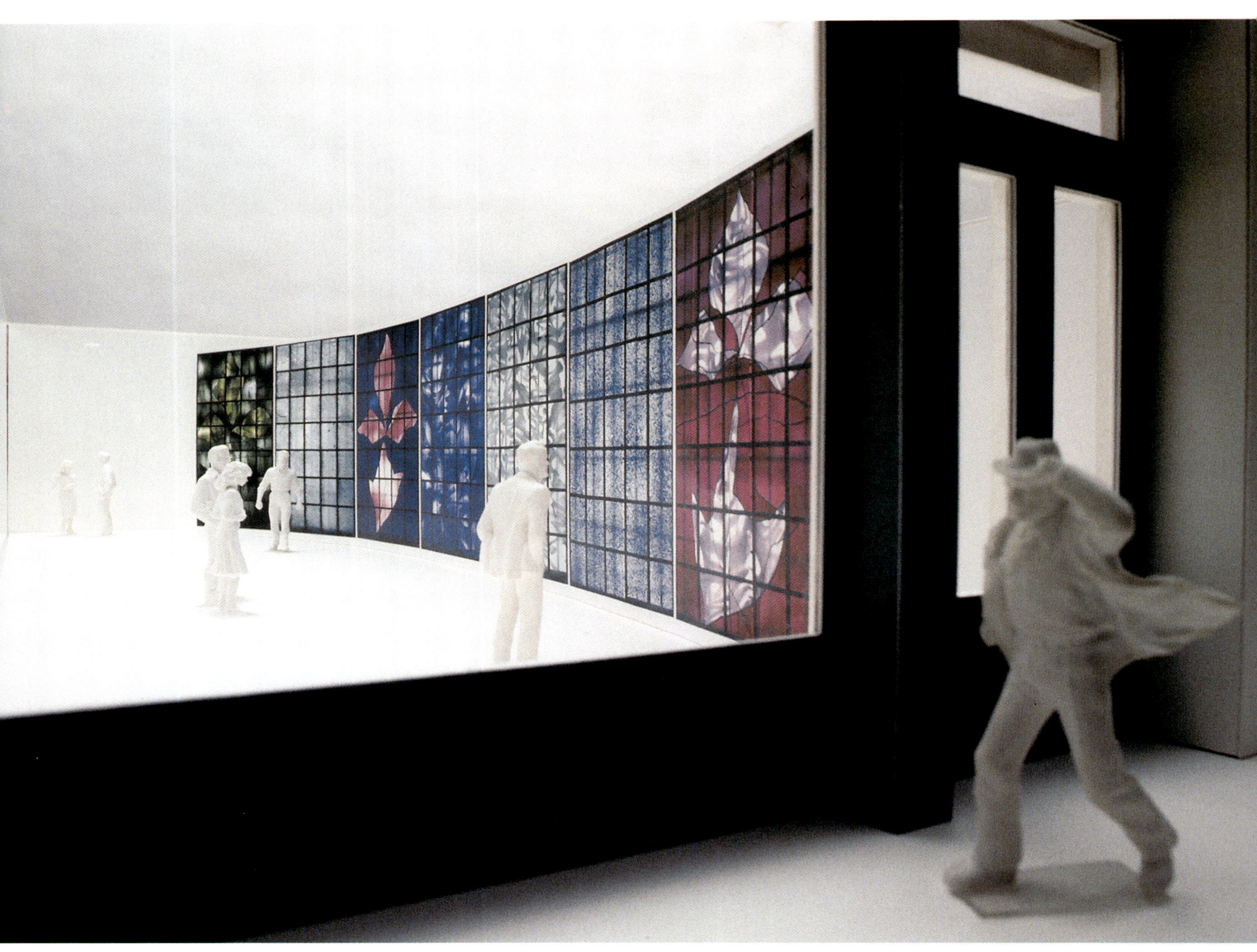

Engineers: Dewhurst Macfarlane & Partners

Stained glass and steel cable framing system
1,012 sq ft

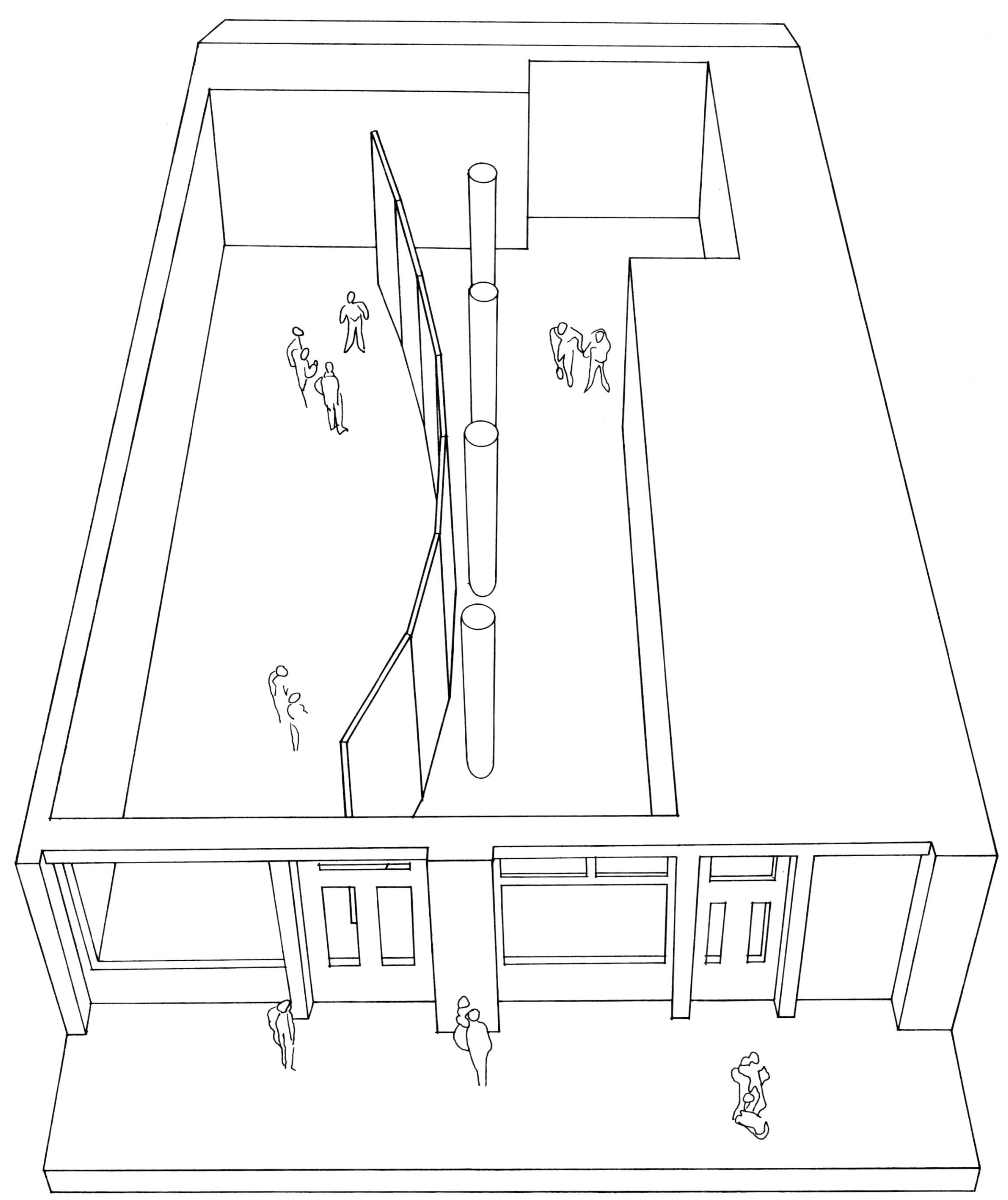

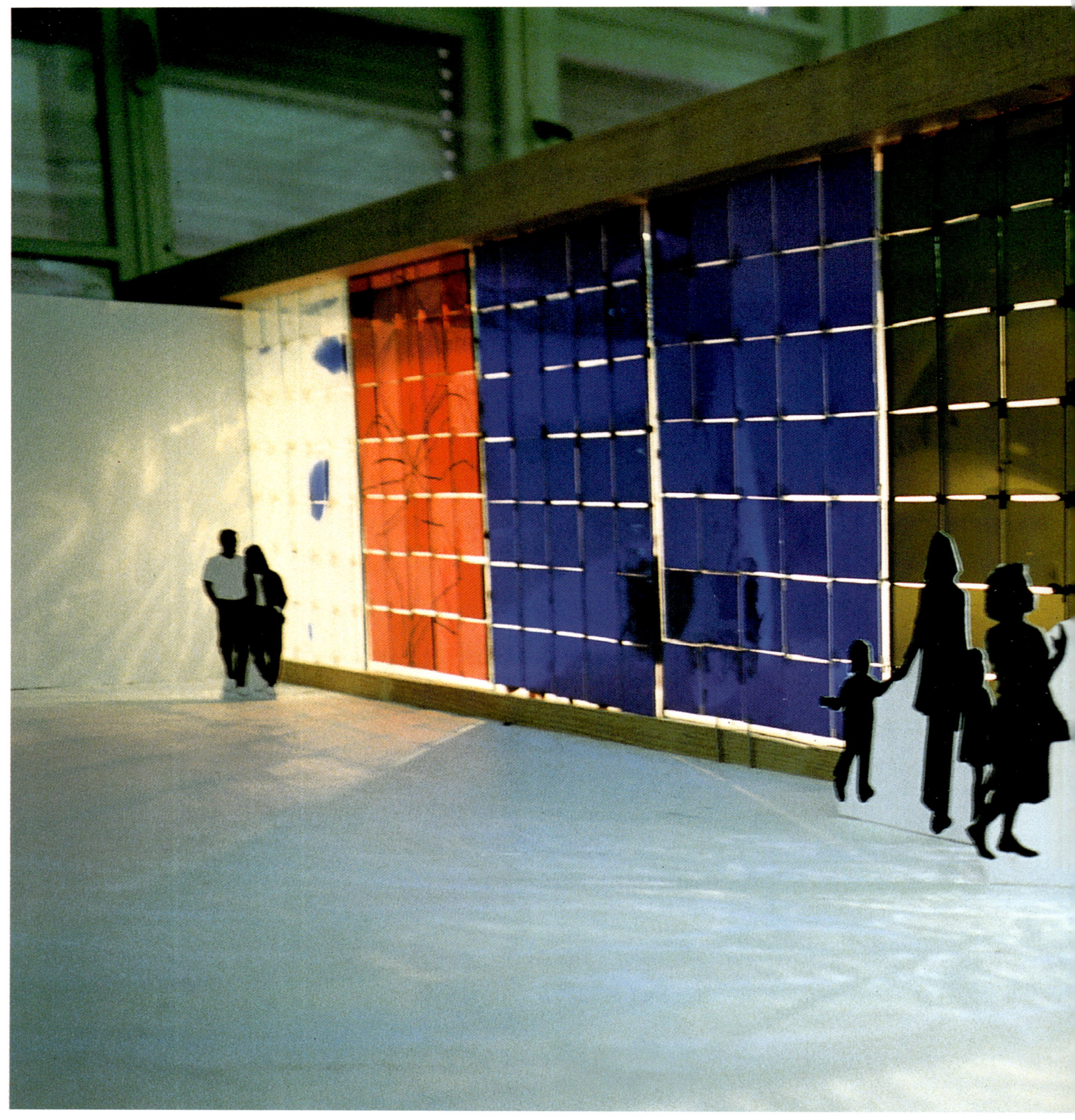

This "wall of glass", this membrane of fluid forms and liquid colour is derived from my fascination and love for heraldry and in particular the Fleur de Lys [*flower of lily*] . It is dedicated to my beautiful friend Linda McCartney.

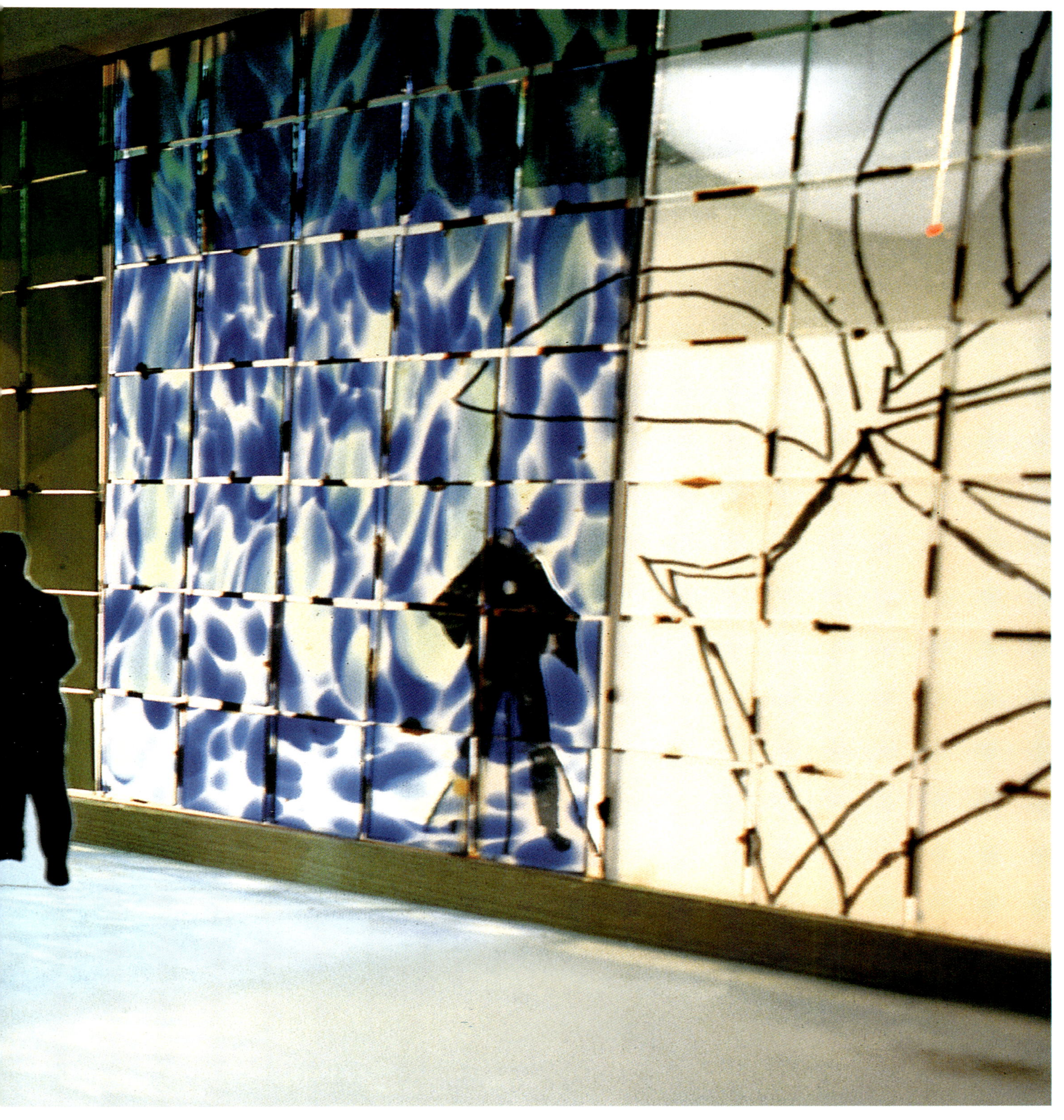

Scale model of installation using actual materials

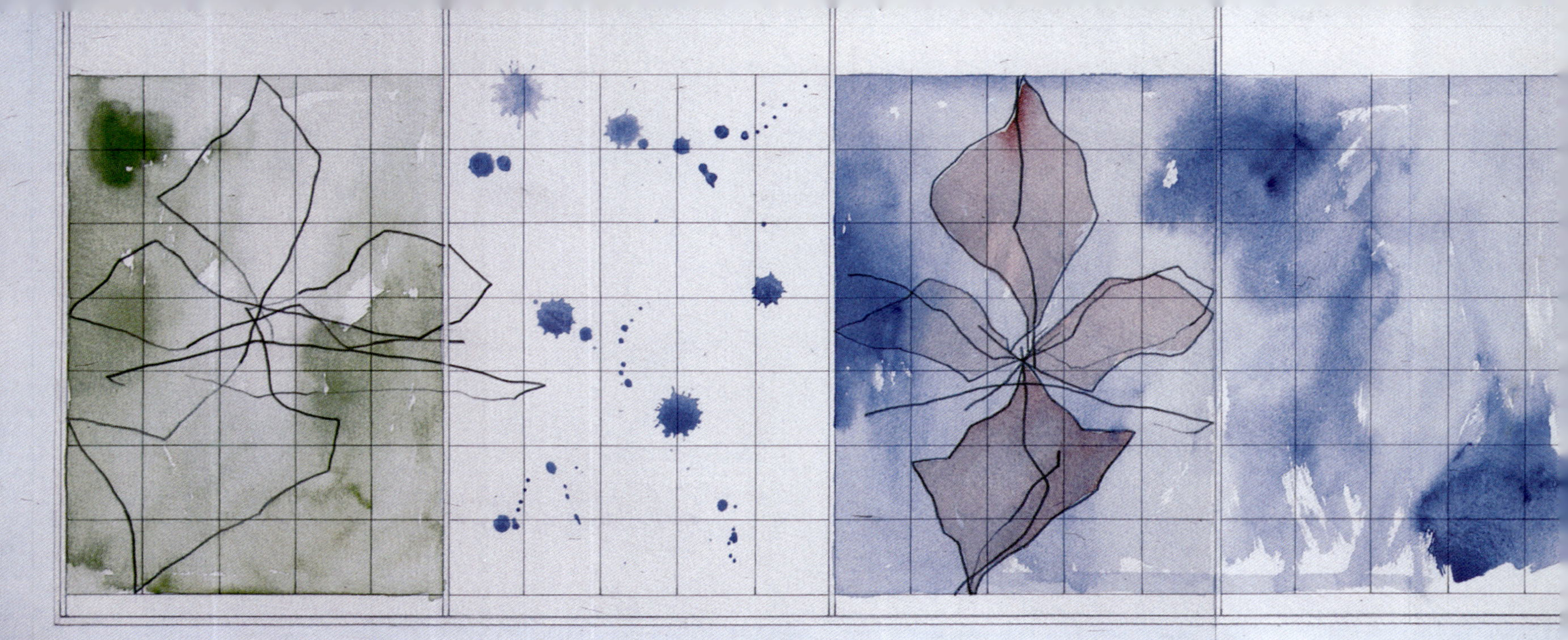

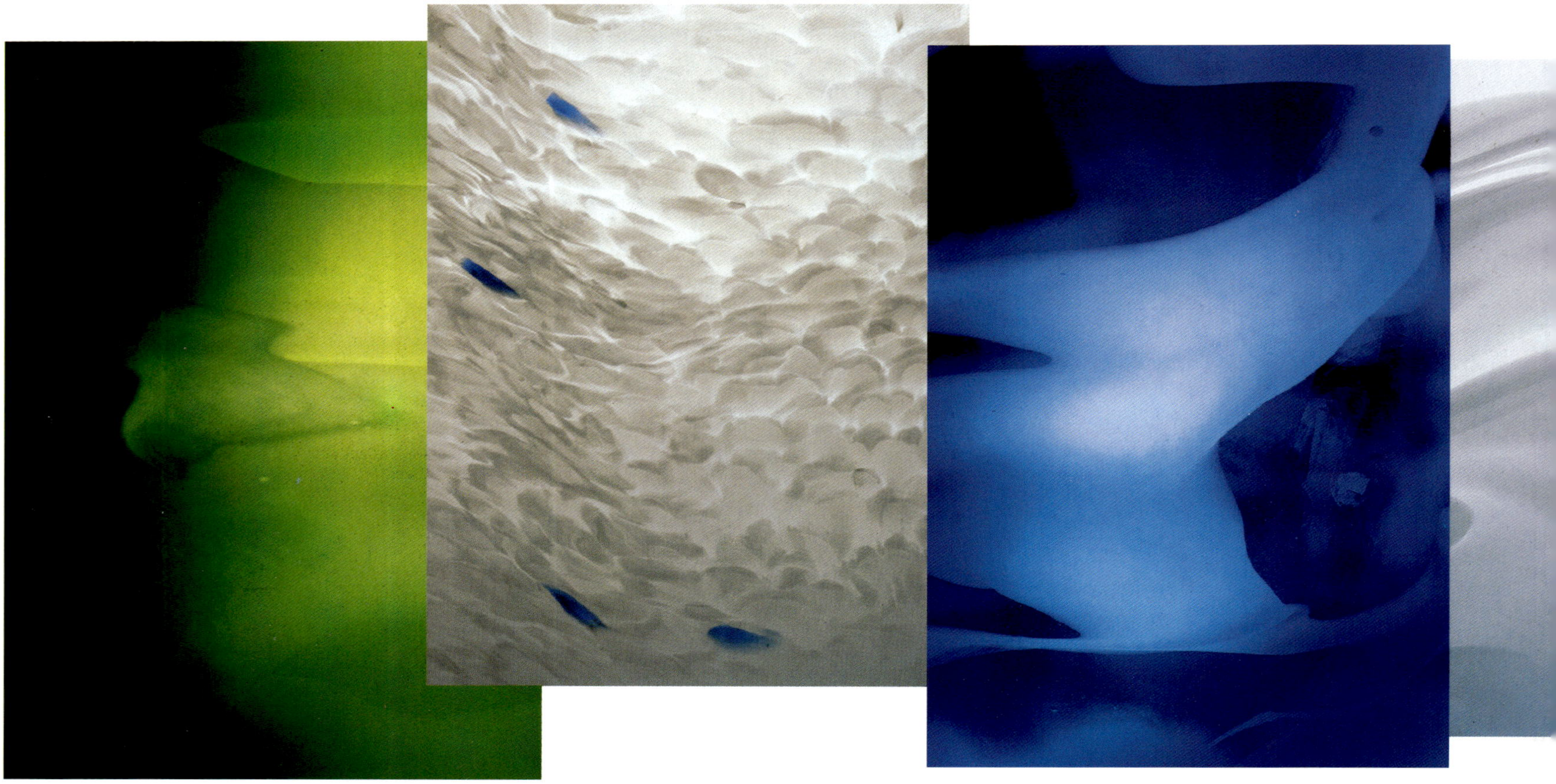

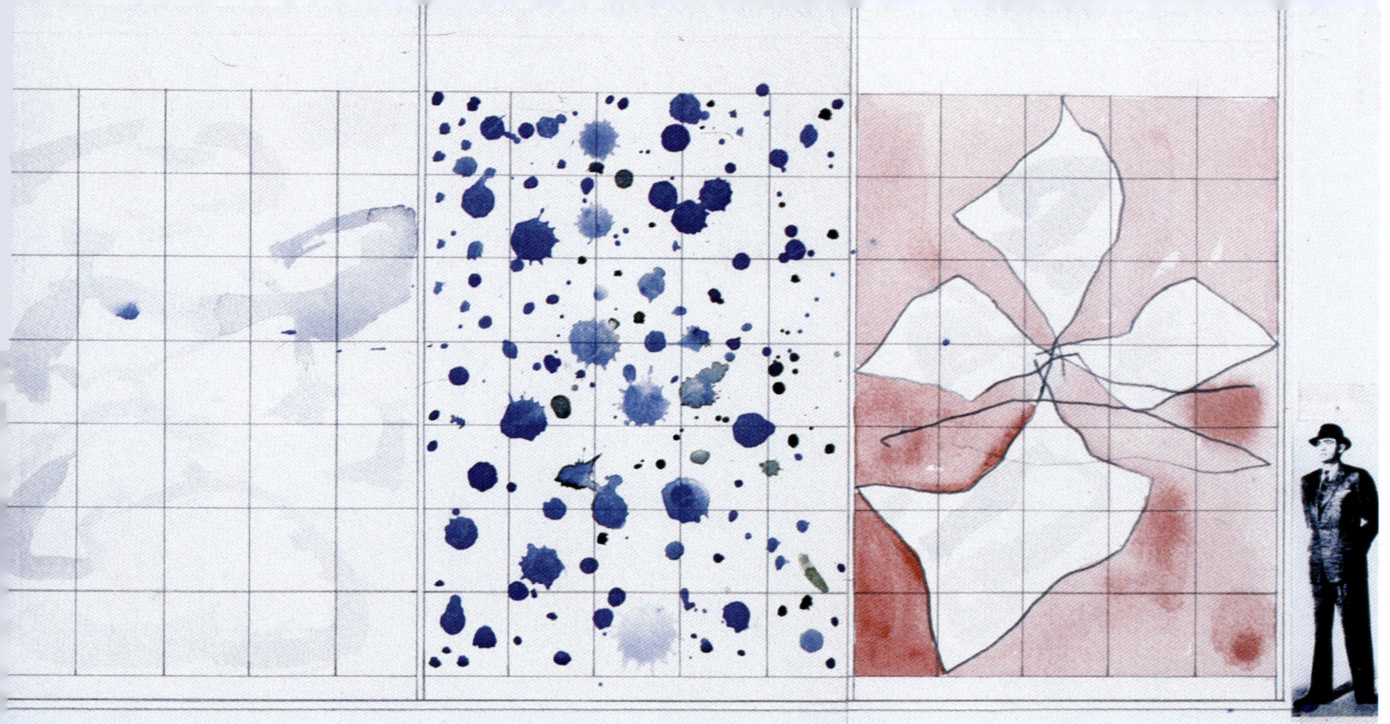

Scale design

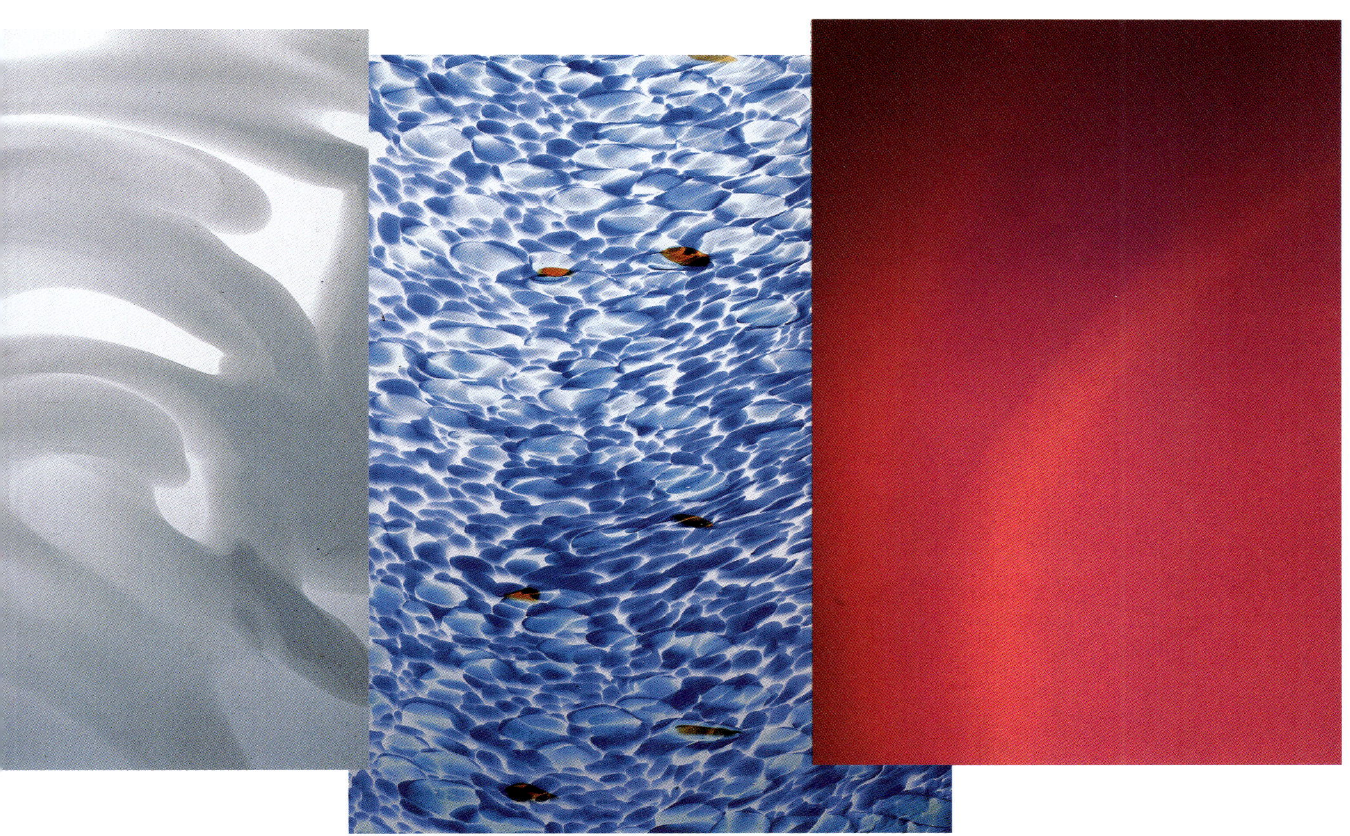

Glass samples corresponding left-to-right with the above design

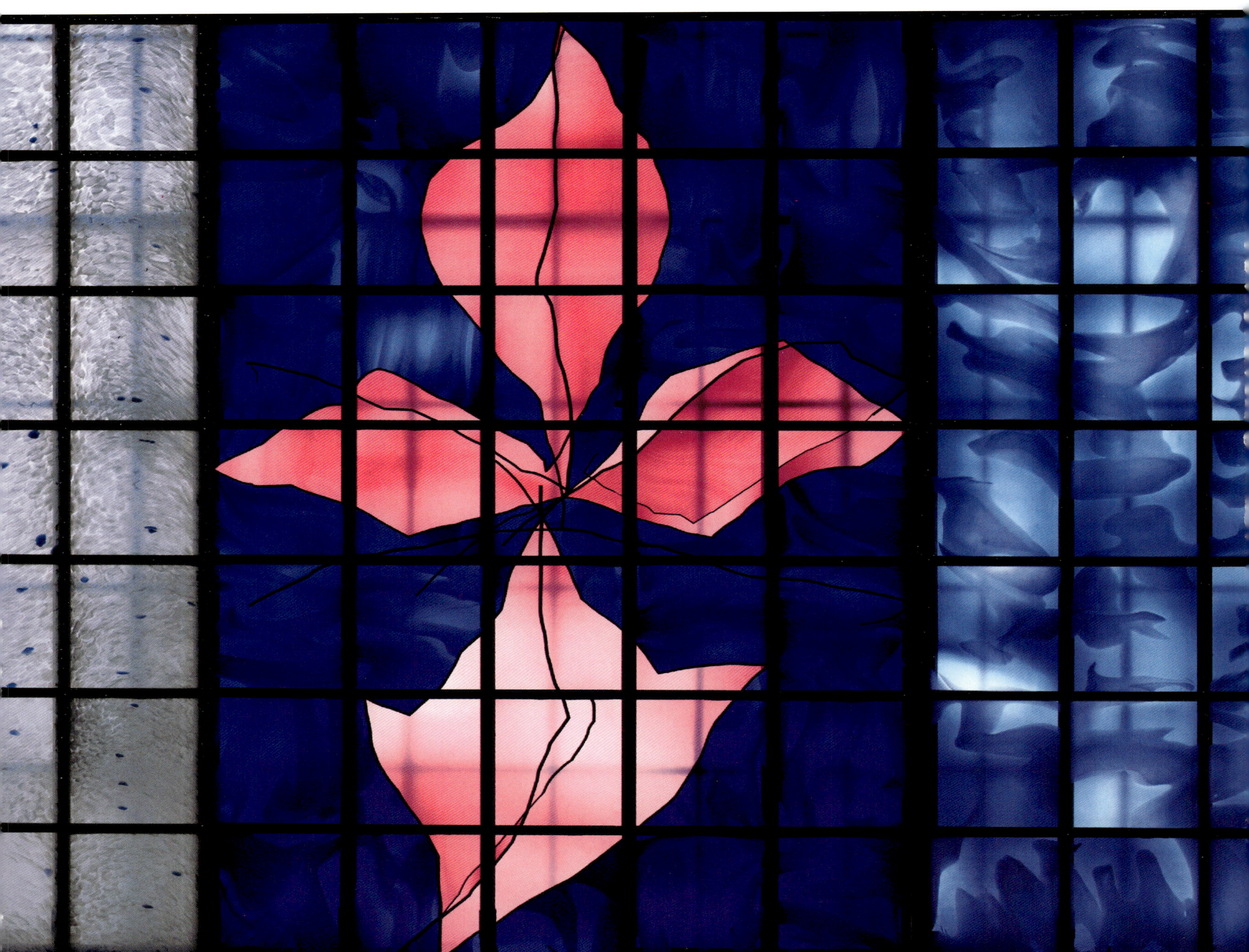

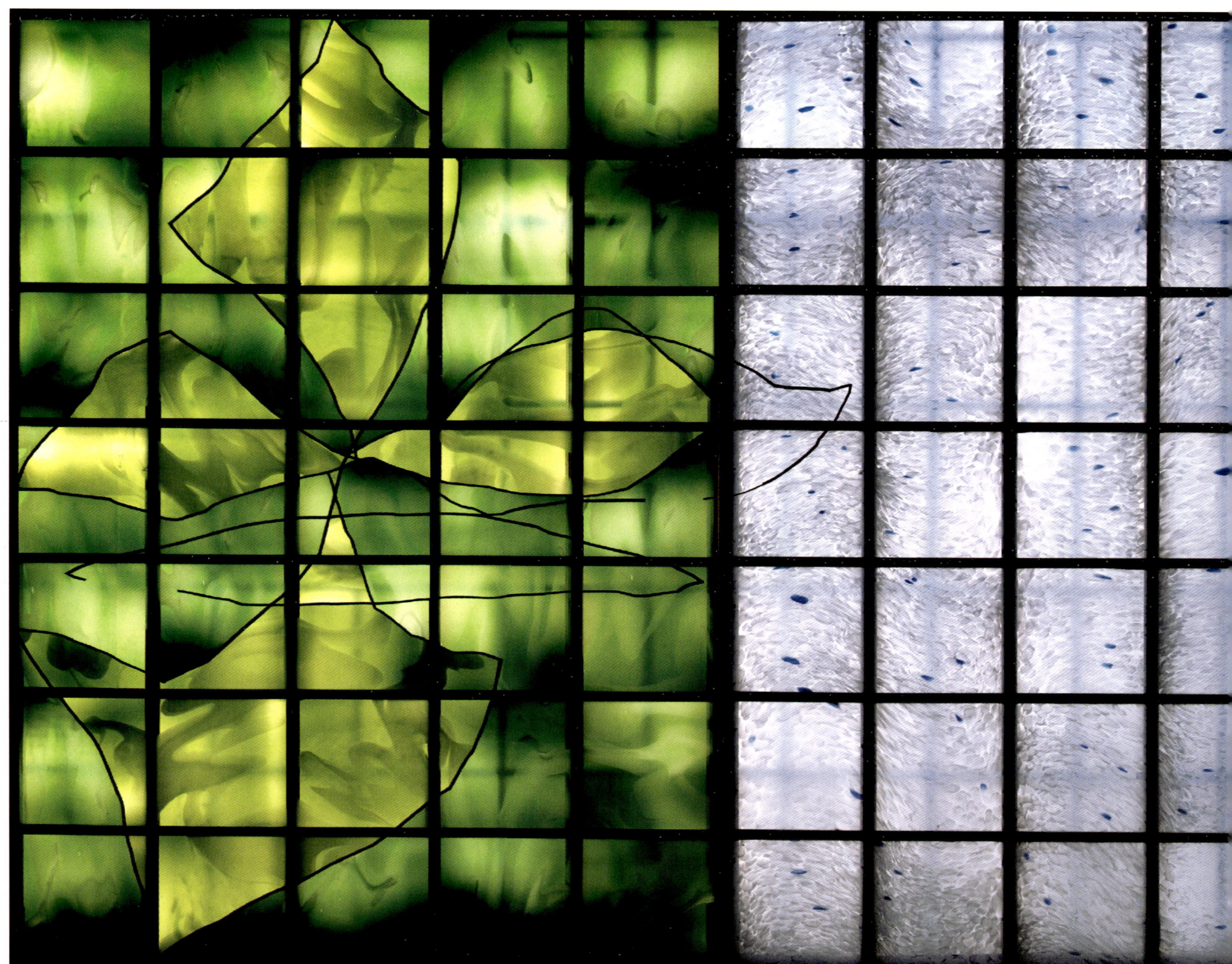

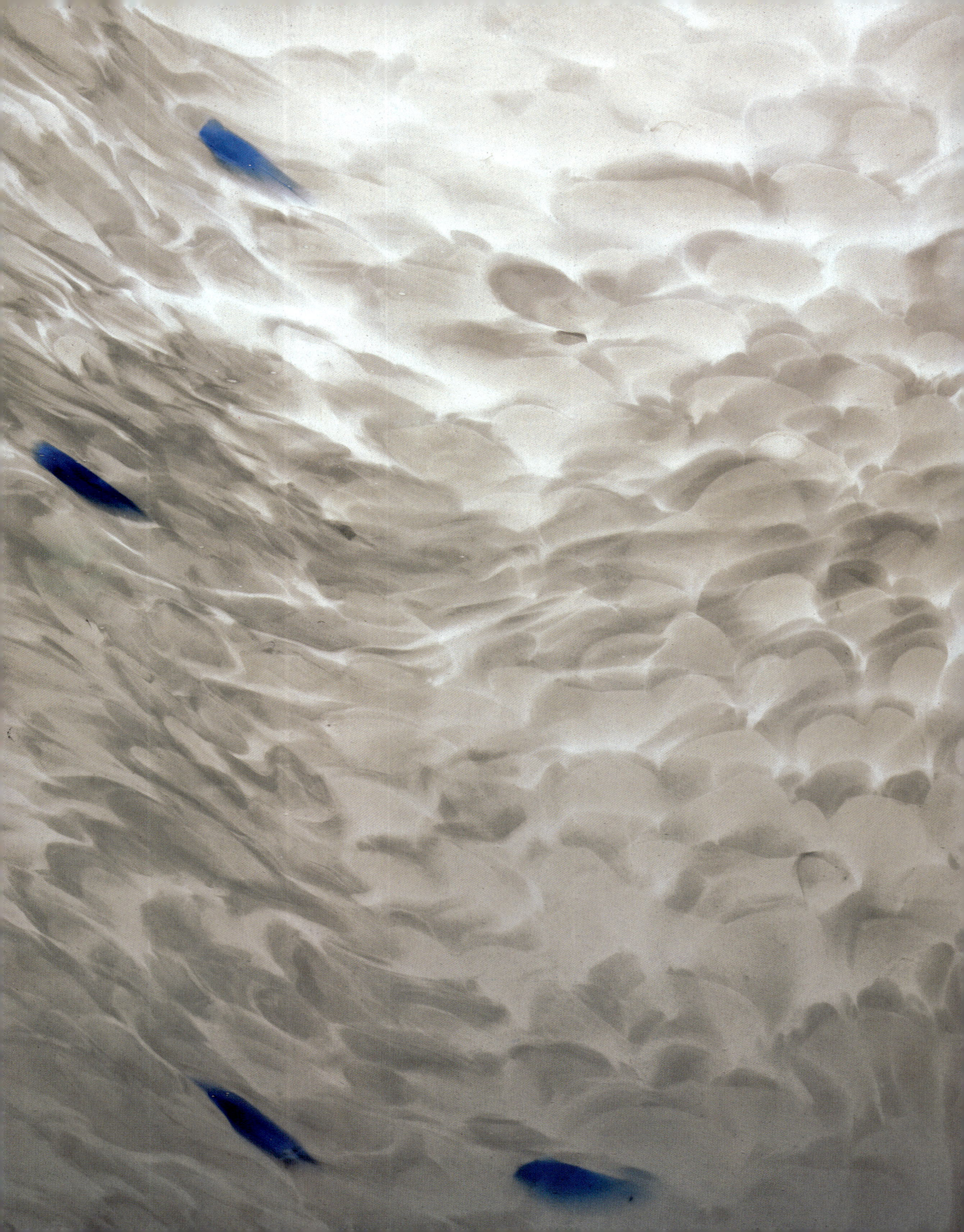

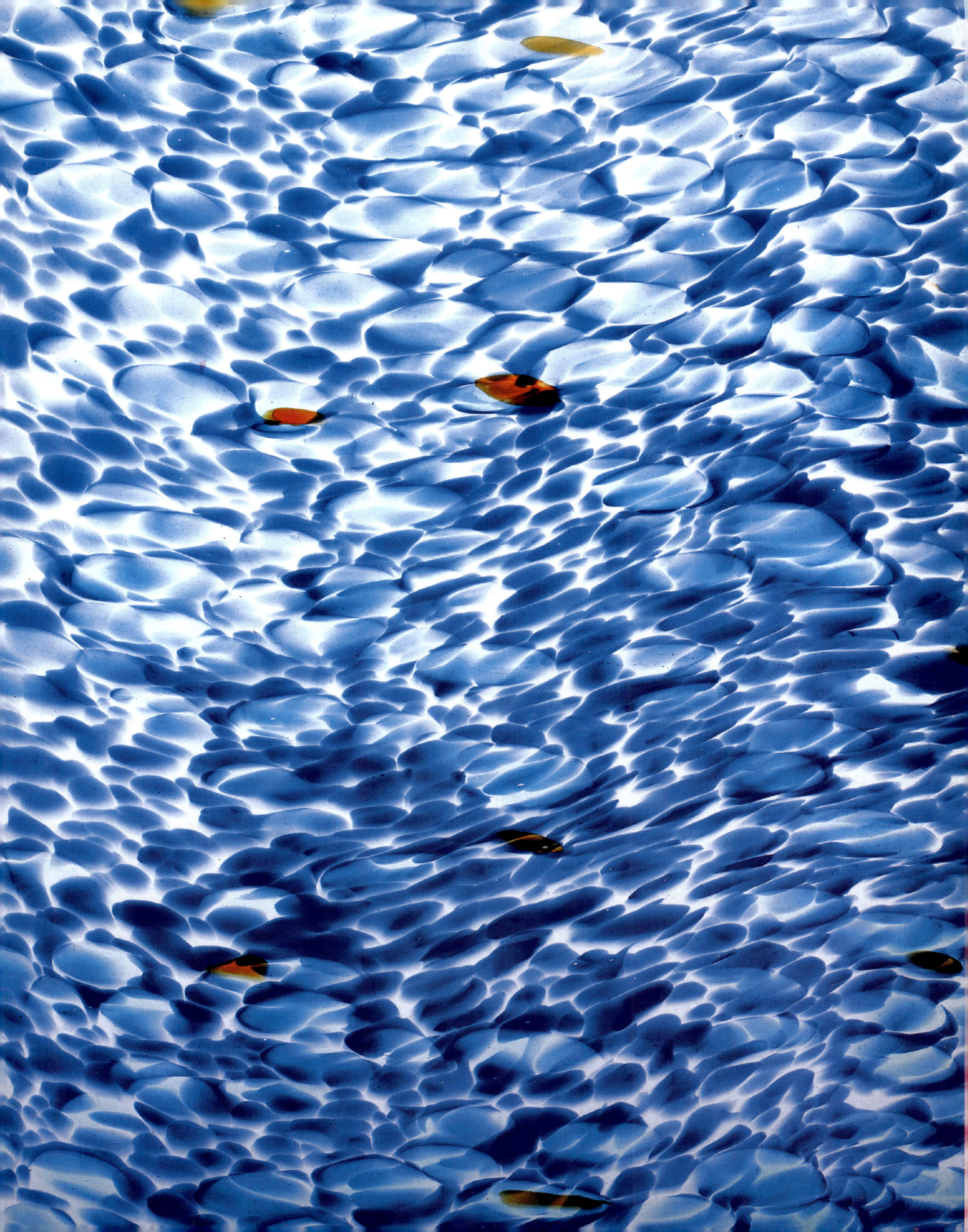

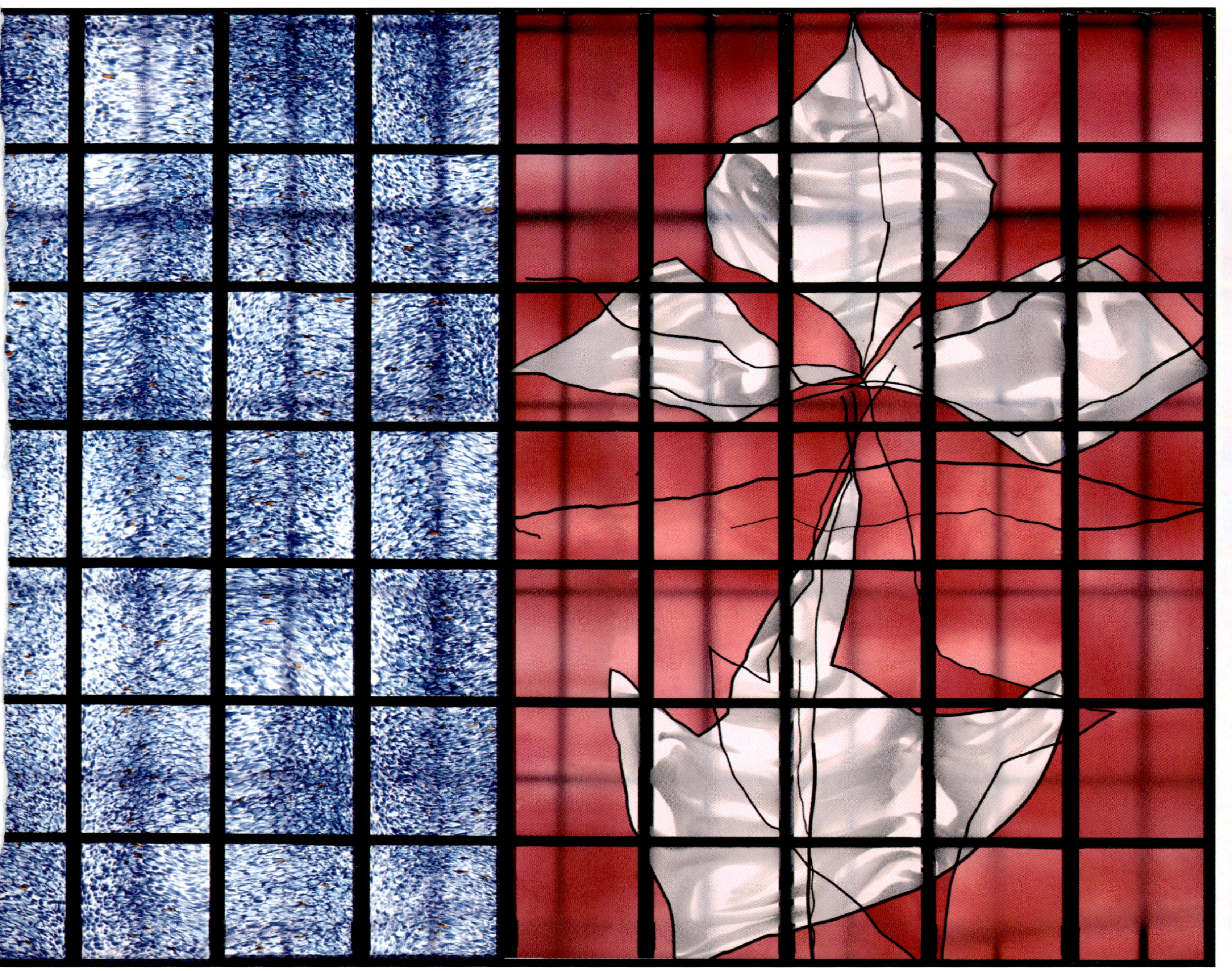

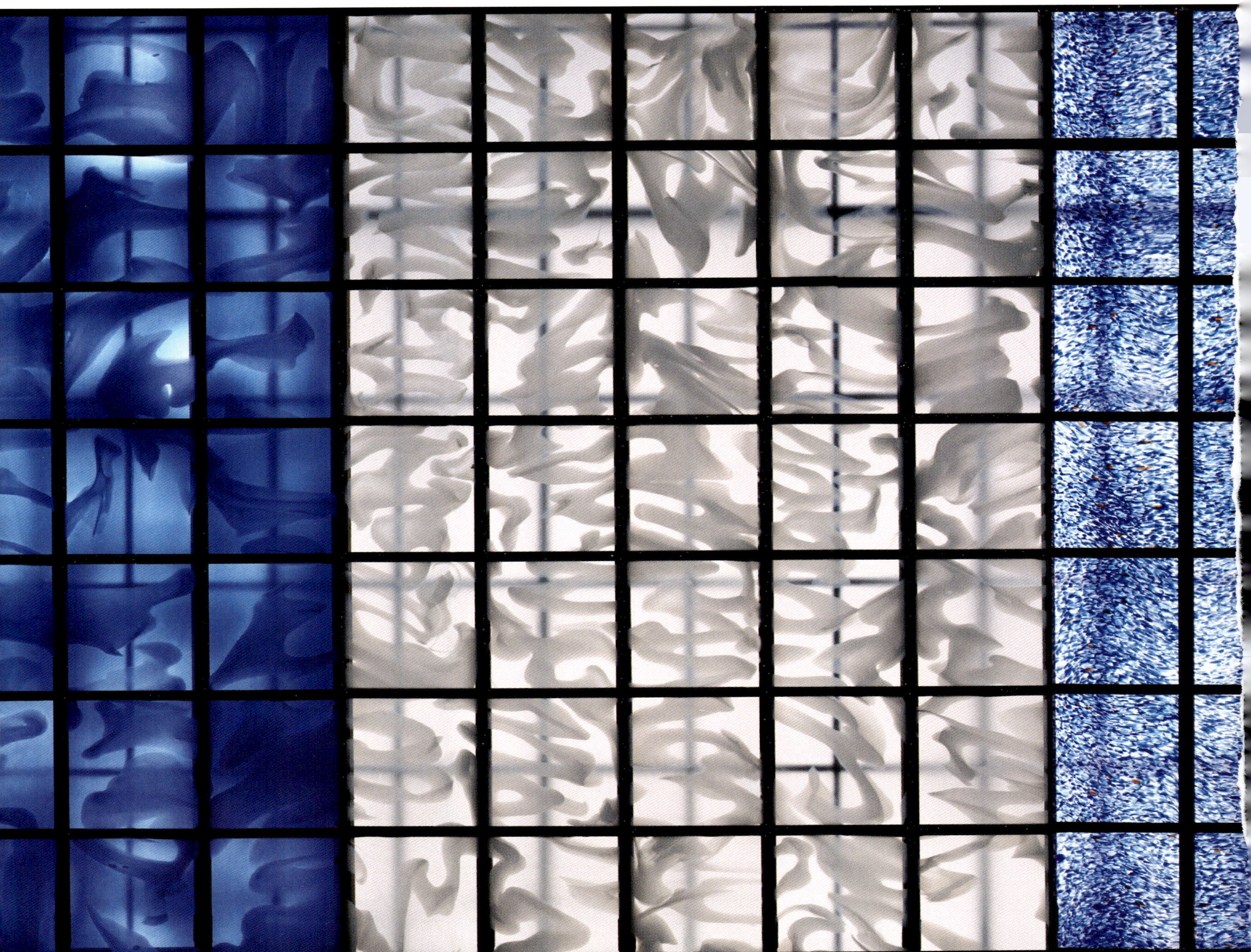

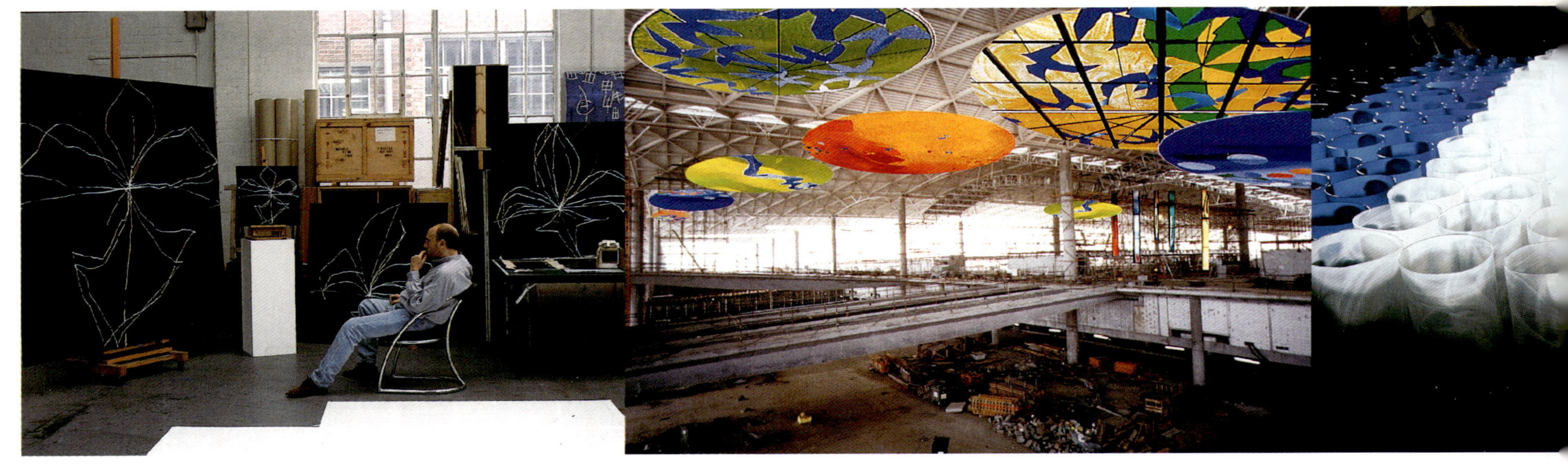

EXHIBITIONS AND PROJECTS

1998   The Glass Wall - An Architectural Installation exhibition at the Tony Shafrazi Gallery,
            New York June 12 - September 12
       New Paintings, exhibition at Faggionato Fine Arts, London (May/ June)
            Brian Clarke - Linda McCartney, exhibition at the German Museum for
            Stained Glass, Linnich (May - September)

1997   Design for RWE Energie AG (backlit stained glass walls)
            refurbishment of headquarter lobby, Essen, Germany
       Cut pile tapestry for Willis Corroon, in company's
            headquarters building by Sir Norman Foster, Ipswich
       Glass wall for the nave of the Synagogue Offenbach, refurbishment and extension, architect: Alfred Jacoby
       Designs for Chep Lap Kok Airport, Hong Kong Architect: Sir Norman Foster & Partners
       Designs for Shopping Center Villa Lobos (stained glass roof lights
            and mosaic for facade), Sao Paulo, Brazil (architect: Julio Neves)
       Design for stained glass windows for Catholic Church Maria Königen in
            Obersalbach near Saarbrücken, Germany (architects: Alt & Britz)
       Stained glass for The Chicago Sinai Synagogue (architect: Lohan Associates)
       Mosaic for Centre NorteShopping, Rio de Janeiro, Brazil
       "The Ruins of Time," new production of a stage set for ballet
            by Wayne Eagling, Het National Ballet, Amsterdam, Netherlands
       Competition designs for windows of Catholic Church (Heiliggeist-Kirche), Heidelberg, Germany
       Exhibition: Brian Clarke - Linda McCartney
            30th August 1997 to 28th April 1998, Musée Suisse du Vitrail, Romont, Switzerland

1996   Stained glass wall / facade
            Valentino Village, Noci, Bari, Italy (architect: Emilio Ambasz & Angelo Rocco Don Giovanni)
       Stained glass and mosaic ceiling
       Pfizer World Headquarters Building, New York, USA (architect: Hixon Design) .
       Design for stained glass cone, Swiss Bank Corporation, Stamford, CT, USA.

Brian Clarke in London studio 1998 • Designed for Chep Lap Kok Airport Hong Kong • Glass for Pfizer in factory

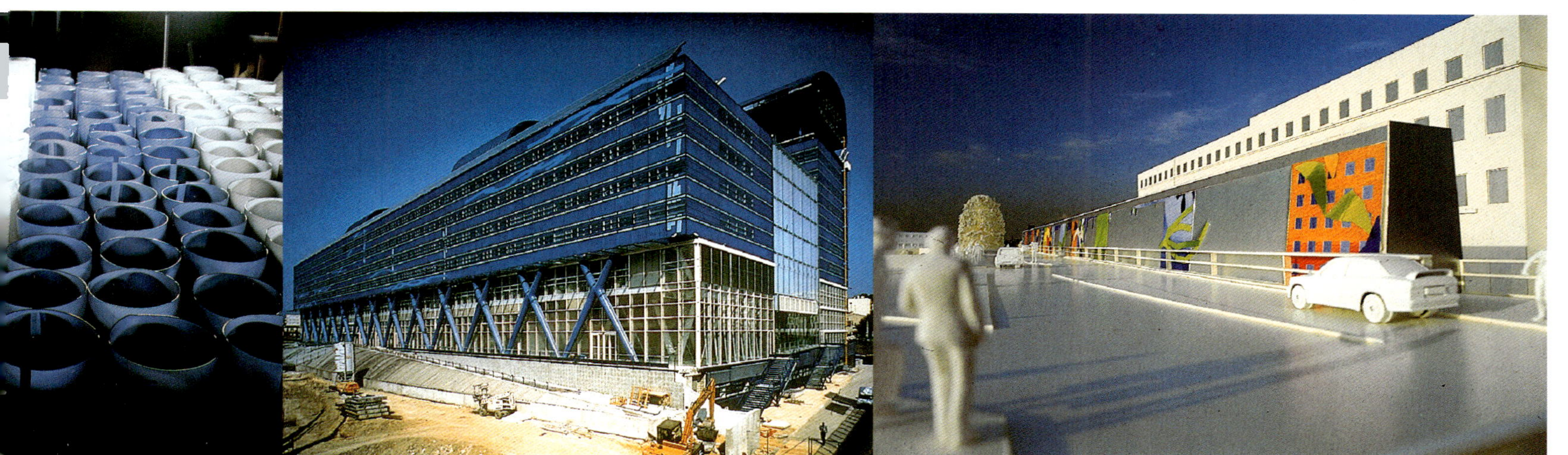

to be completed fall 1998 (engineers: Dewhurst Macfarlane & Partners)
Proposal for the ceiling of the Great Auditorium, Paris Opera (Bastille).
Joint competition entry with architects Alsop & Störmer architects for Hungerford Bridge, London, England.
Stained glass entrance Kinderhaus, Regensburg, Germany. (architect: A2)

1995   Exhibition: Fazit '95 Die Sammlung des Museums für Zeitgenössische
       Glasmalerei Langen.(10/03/1995 - 29/10/1995), Altes Rathaus Langen, Germany.
Exhibition: Exempla '95, Handwerkskammer für München und Oberbayern.
       11/03/95 - 19/03/95, München, Germany.
Lecture at the National Exhibition Centre, England. 21/03/95, RIBA (Royal Institute of British Architects),
Stained glass and mosaic ceilings for Centre NorteShopping
       (Completed 1996)
       Rio de Janeiro, Brazil. 1055 square metres of glass and 150 square metres of mosaic
       (architect: Design Corp, Toronto).
Stained glass windows for the Abbaye de la Fille Dieu, (Completed 1996), Romont, Switzerland
(architect Tomas Mikulas).

1994   Exhibition: "Brian Clarke: Paintings and Stained Glass," Tony Shafrazi Gallery,
       New York, NY, December 10, 1994 - February 4, 1995.
Mosaic and stained glass windows and walls for Lowe SMS & Partners, The Grace Building, New York, USA.
Stained glass window for Clinical Research Building and Hammersmith Hospital Cancer Centre, London.
Stained glass design for Brent Cross Shopping Centre, London, England.
Stained glass dome, design for the Frankfurter Allee Plaza, Berlin, Germany.
       Stained glass cupola and mosaic ceiling for the Schadow Arkaden, Düsseldorf, Germany
       (architect: Brune Cosulting).
       Stained glass design for Crossrail Terminal, Paddington Station, London (architects: Alsop & Störmer).
Designs for stained glass ceiling and mosaic floor for Friedrichstadt Passagen,
       Quartier 206, Berlin (architect: I.M. Pei, Cobb, Freed and Partner).
Mosaic for W.H.Smith & Sons Ltd. Training Office, Abingdon, Oxon, England.
Collaborative proposal, with Zaha Hadid for stained glass and mosaic at Spittelau, Vienna, Austria.
Designs for the compact disc covers of the Sir William Walton classical music catalogue for EMI Records, London.
Designs for stained glass for the Aachen Synagogue, Aachen, Germany (architect: Alfred Jacoby).

Le Grand Bleu, Marseilles • Model for Crossrail Terminal, London

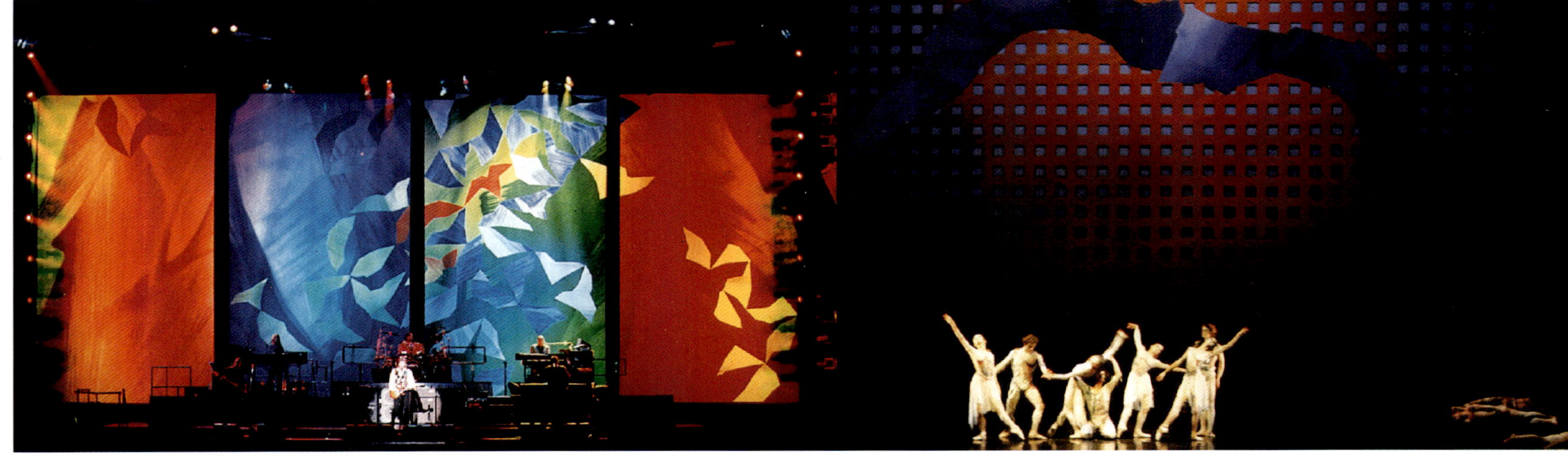

Proposal for a glass tower at Willis Faber Building, Ipswich, England. (Arch. Sir Norman Foster).
Created Professor of Architectural Art, Bartlett Institute of Architecture, University College, London.

1993   Designed the stadia stage sets for the Paul McCartney 1993 World Tour.
Stained glass for the North wall of the EAM Building, Kassel, Germany
  (architect: von Gerkan, Marg and Partners).
"The Ruins of Time," stage sets for a ballet by Wayne Eagling in tribute to
  Rudolph Nuryev, Het National Ballet, Amsterdam.
Award: Honorary Fellowship of the Royal Institute of British Architects.
Exhibition: "Images of Christ," Northampton Museum and St. Paul's Cathedral, London.
Stained glass roofs for the Spindles, Oldham, Lancashire.
"Brian Clarke, Designs on Architecture," Oldham Art Gallery,
  Oldham, Lancashire, October 2 - November 9, (catalogue).
"Brian Clarke, New Paintings," The Mayor Gallery, London.
Stained glass windows for the new Heidelberg Synagogue, Heidelberg, Germany.
Exhibition: "Architecture and the Sacred Space in the Modern Age -
  Venice Biennale," (with architect Alfred Jacoby.)

1992   Exhibition: "Addressing the Forbidden," Brighton Festival, Brighton.
Stills Gallery, Edinburgh Festival, Edinburgh.
Lecture at the University of Seoul, Korea.
Stained glass tower windows for Espana Telefonica, Placa Catalunya, Barcelona for the 1992 Olympiad.
Tapestries and stained glass for the Carmelite, Carmelite Street, London (architect: Trehearne & Norman).
Architectural Competition: The Glass Dune - Ministry of Environmental Building, Hamburg
  (architects: Future Systems).
Glass cladding and colouring to the main facade of the Hotel du Department des Bouches-du Rhone, Marseille,
  France (architect: Alsop & Störmer).
Stained glass screen for Chateau d'Orain, France.
Exhibition: "Light and Architecture," Ingolstadt, Germany (in collaboration with Future Systems).
Exhibition: "The Painter in Glass," Glyn Vivian Art Gallery, Swansea, England (catalogue).

Paul McCartney World Tour • The National Ballet, Amsterdam

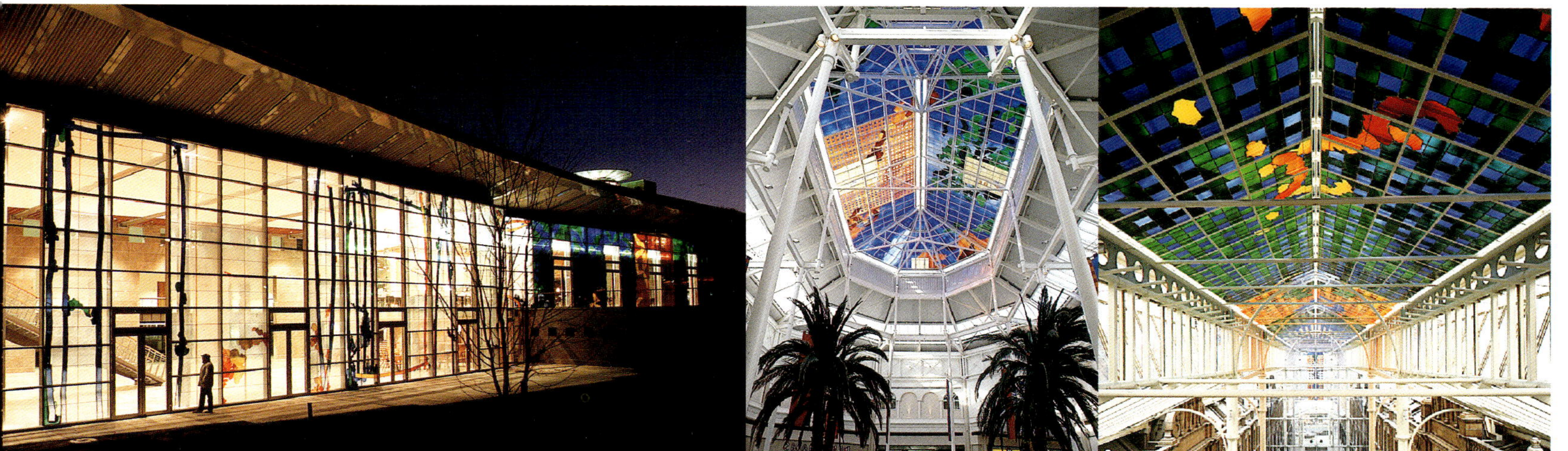

1991   Stained glass screen for Glaxo Pharmaceuticals, London (architect: Skidmore, Owings & Merrill).
The BBC Design Awards (juror).
Stained glass screens and tower for Stansted Airport, Stansted, Essex, England (architect: Sir Norman Foster).
Stained glass roofs for the Spindles Shopping Centre, Oldham, Lancashire (architect: Bernard Engle).
Stained glass entrance hall and canopies for 100 New Bridge Street, London
      (architect: Renton Howard Wood and Levin).
Stained glass skylights for Aram Designs, Heath Street, Hampstead, London.
Stained glass entrance for stairwell windows for 35-38 Chancery Lane,
      in collaboration with sculptor Ivor Abrahams
London, (architect: Building Design Partnership).
      Entrance wall with onyx, mosaic and stained glass for America House,
      1 America Square, London (architect: Renton Howard Wood & Levin).

1990   Painting and stained glass for Cibreo Restaurant,
      Tokyo, Japan, (architect for the interior: Naoki Iijima, building architect: Nigel Coates).
Exhibition: "Brian Clarke - Into and Out of Architecture,"
      The Mayor Gallery, London, April 26 - June 9, (catalogue).
"Brian Clarke," by Paul Beldock, Art Random book published by Kyoto Shoin, Japan.
Exhibition: °"Rockens Billeder - Images of Rock," Kunsthallen Brandts Klaedefabrik, Odense, Denmark.
Exhibition: "Brian Clarke - Architecture and Stained Glass, "The Sezon Museum of Art, Annex Tokyo, Tokyo.

1989   Fellow of the Royal Society of Arts.
Exhibition: "Brian Clarke - Paintings," The Indar Pasricha Gallery, Hauz Khas, New Delhi, India.
Exhibition: The Pyrri Art Centre, Savolinna, Finland.
Stained glass for the skylight of the Victoria Quarter, (the world's largest stained glass window) Leeds, England.
Award: Leeds Award for Architecture, Civic Trust Award, 1991.
Arts Council, British Gas, Working for Cities, 1992 (special commendation).
Designed the Arena and Stadia stage sets for the Paul McCartney World Tour.

1988   Stained glass for the central lantern tower and skylights of the Lake Sagami Country Club,
      Yamanishi, Japan (architect: Arata Isozaki).
Stained glass and Torah shrine for the New Synagogue, Darmstadt, Germany (architect: Alfred Jacoby).

EAM, Kassel, Germany • The Spindles, Oldham, England • Victoria Quarter, Leeds, England

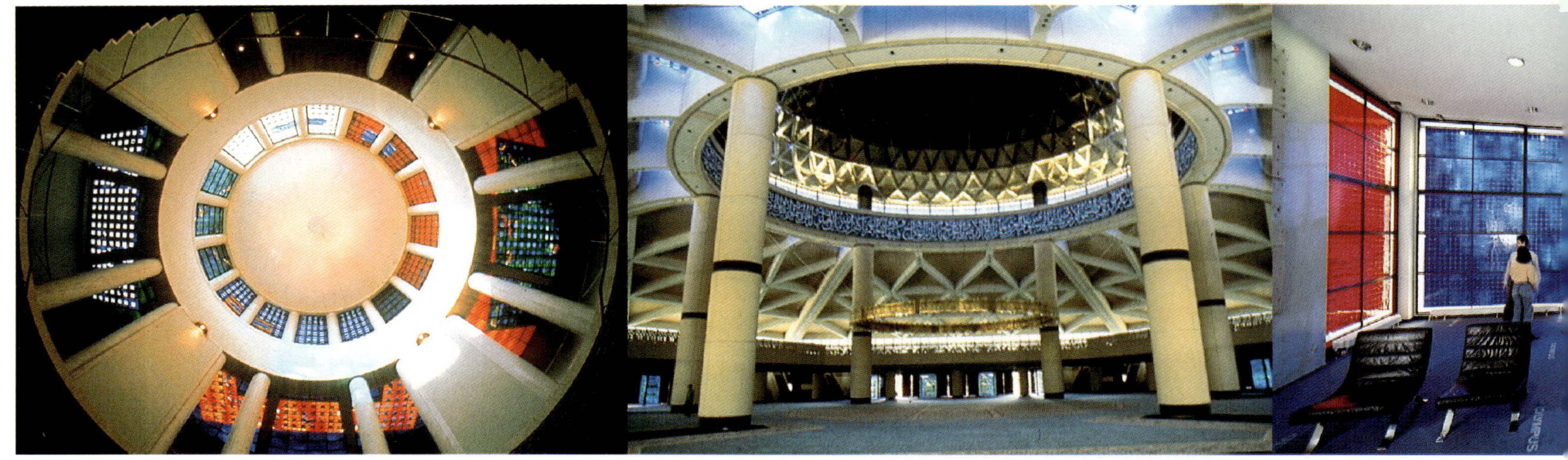

Lecture at the University of Edinburgh, Acanthus.
Exhibition: "British Art," The Mayor Gallery, London.
Exhibition: "Die Architektur der Synagoge" Deutsches Architekturmuseum, Frankfurt.
Exhibition: "Brian Clarke, Malerei und Farbfenster 1977 - 1988", Hessisches Landesmuseum, Darmstadt
Exhibition: "Brian Clarke - Intimations of Mortality," Galerie Karsten Greve, Cologne.

1987   "Brian Clarke, Paintings - 1976 - 1986," Seibu Museum of Art, Ikebukuro,
          Tokyo, travelled to Yao Seibu Exhibition Hall, Yao, Osaka, Japan (catalogue).
Elan Vital by Junji Ito, published by Sezon Museum of Art, Tokyo, Japan.
Stained glass for the barrel vaulted roof of the Cavendish Arcade, Derbyshire, England.
          Europa Nostra Award. (architect: Sir Joseph Paxton, restoration: Derek Latham).
Installation of two opal screen windows in Tokyo for the Sezon Museum of Art, Tokyo, Japan.

1986   Lived in Rome, Italy.
Exhibition: "Brian Clarke - Stained Glass" Seibu Museum of Art, Yurakacho, Tokyo.
Installation of "Modular Assemblage" for Texas Instruments, Texas, USA

1984   Lived and worked in New York City.
Exhibition: "Brian Clarke - Works on Paper, 1976 - 1984," with Ellsworth Kelly, Robert Fraser Gallery, London.
Doha Palace, designed a series of sculptural stained glass and windows for the new Government Building
          Doha, Qatar.
Lectures in New York and Rome, and at the Royal College of Art, London.
Council member of the Winston Churchill Memorial Trust.
BBC2 Saturday Review, 6/16/84.

1983   Exhibition: "Brian Clarke - Paintings," opening exhibition of
          Robert Fraser Gallery, London, June 14 - July 15, 1983.
Exhibition: "Black/White," exhibition with Jean-Michel Basquiat, Robert Fraser Gallery, London.

1982   Lived and worked in Düsseldorf, Germany.
Exhibition: "Brian Clarke - Serigraphien und Mosaik," Franz Mayer'sche Hofkunstanstalt, München.
Stained glass for the skylight and clerestory, main hall, library and office of

Lake Sagami Country Club, Japan • The Royal Mosque at K.K.I.A. Riyadh, Saudi Arabia • Olympus Europa GmbH, Hamburg, Germany

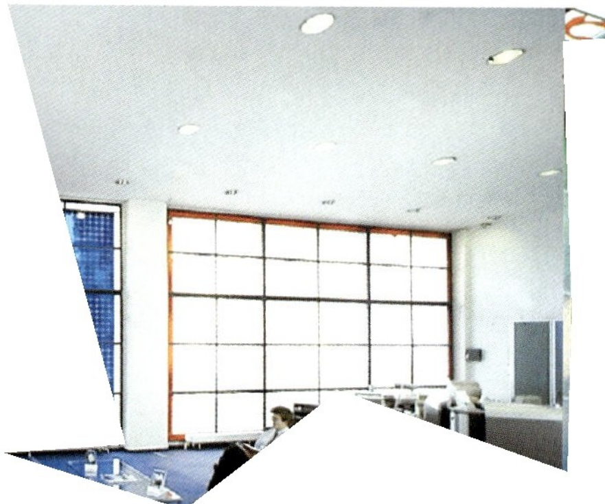

the King Khaled International Airport, Riyadh, Saudi Arabia (architect: Hellmuth, Obata & Kassabaum).
Exhibition: "British Stained Glass," Centre International de Vitrail, Chartres, France
Lived and worked in Rome, Italy.

1981   Stained glass for the Laver's & Barraud Building, Endell Street, London.
Paintings and stained glass for the lobby of Olympus Optical Europa GmbH, Headquarters Building, Hamburg.

Exhibition: "Brian Clarke - New Paintings, Constructions and Prints, "The Royal Institute of British Architects, London
          (in association with Robert Fraser Gallery, London).
Lecture tour of Edinburgh, Preston, London and Manchester Polytechnics
Exhibition: "Brian Clarke - Prints," Vernon Gallery, Preston.
Publication of a series of prints dedicated to C.P. Snow, "The Two Cultures,"
          published in association with the Robert Fraser Gallery, London.

1980   Exhibition: "Brian Clarke - Paintings," Mappin Art Gallery and Museum, City of Sheffield, England.
Exhibition: "Art in Education," Whitechapel Art Gallery, London.
Granada TV documentary "Celebration: Brian Clarke."

1979   Exhibition: "Brian Clarke Drawings," St. Edmunds Art Centre, Salisbury, England.
Exhibition: "Glass/Light Exhibition," Festival of the City of London, with John Piper and Marc Chagall.
BBC1/Omnibus TV documentary "Brian Clarke - The Story So Far".

1978   Lecture tour of the Universities of Kent, Manchester, Swansea and Whitechapel Art Gallery.

1977   Paintings and stained glass of the Queen's Medical Centre Chapel, University of Nottingham, England.

1976   Stained glass for the Baptistery windows at St. Gabriel's Church, Blackburn, England
          (architect: F.X. Verlarde).
Stained glass for the East window of All Saints Church, Habergham, England.

1975   Exhibition: "Brian Clarke - Glass Art One," Stained glass, Mid-Pennine Arts
          Association, Arts Council of Great Britain.

Cavendish Arcade, Buxton, England • Habergham All Saints Church, England • St. Gabriel's Church, Blackburn, England

This catalogue has been published to coincide with the occasion of the Exhibition,
Brian Clarke — The Glass Wall from June 12 through September 12, 1998 at Tony Shafrazi Gallery.

Copyright © 1998

Tony Shafrazi Gallery

119 Wooster Street

New York, NY 10012

tel 212 274 9300

fax 212 334 9499

Introduction © Sir Norman Foster 1998

The Personal Story of a Gothic Modernist © Brian Clarke 1998

Brian Clarke and the Medium of Stained Glass © Susanne K. Frantz 1998

Project texts © Brian Clarke 1998

Catalogue production

Martin Booth

Ben A. J. Harrison

Paul Laster

Joachim Mannebach

Hiroko Onoda

Mark Thaler

Editing and design supervisor: Tony Shafrazi

Design consultant: Martin Harrison

Production assistance: Paola Gribaudo

Color Separations: Fotolito Garbero, Turin

Printed by: Pozzo Gros Monti, Italy

Photography

Martin Booth, Ian Bruce (Arcaid), Barry Clarke, Brian Clarke, Jeremy Cockayne (Arcaid), Peter Cook,

Prudence Cuming Associates, Mark Feinnes (Arcaid), Abbaye de la Fille-Dieu, Flash Photographic,

Sir Norman Foster & Partners, Richard Glover (Arcaid), Hixon Design Consultants, Glashütte Lamberts,

Franz Mayer of Munich [Inc.], Tomas Mikulas, Jean Mülhauser, Photodisc [Inc.], Nicola Putignano, Fred Scruton,

Tony Shafrazi, Swiss Bank Corporation, Mohammed Rana, Paul Warchol.

Edition of 2,000

ISBN: 1-891475-13-4

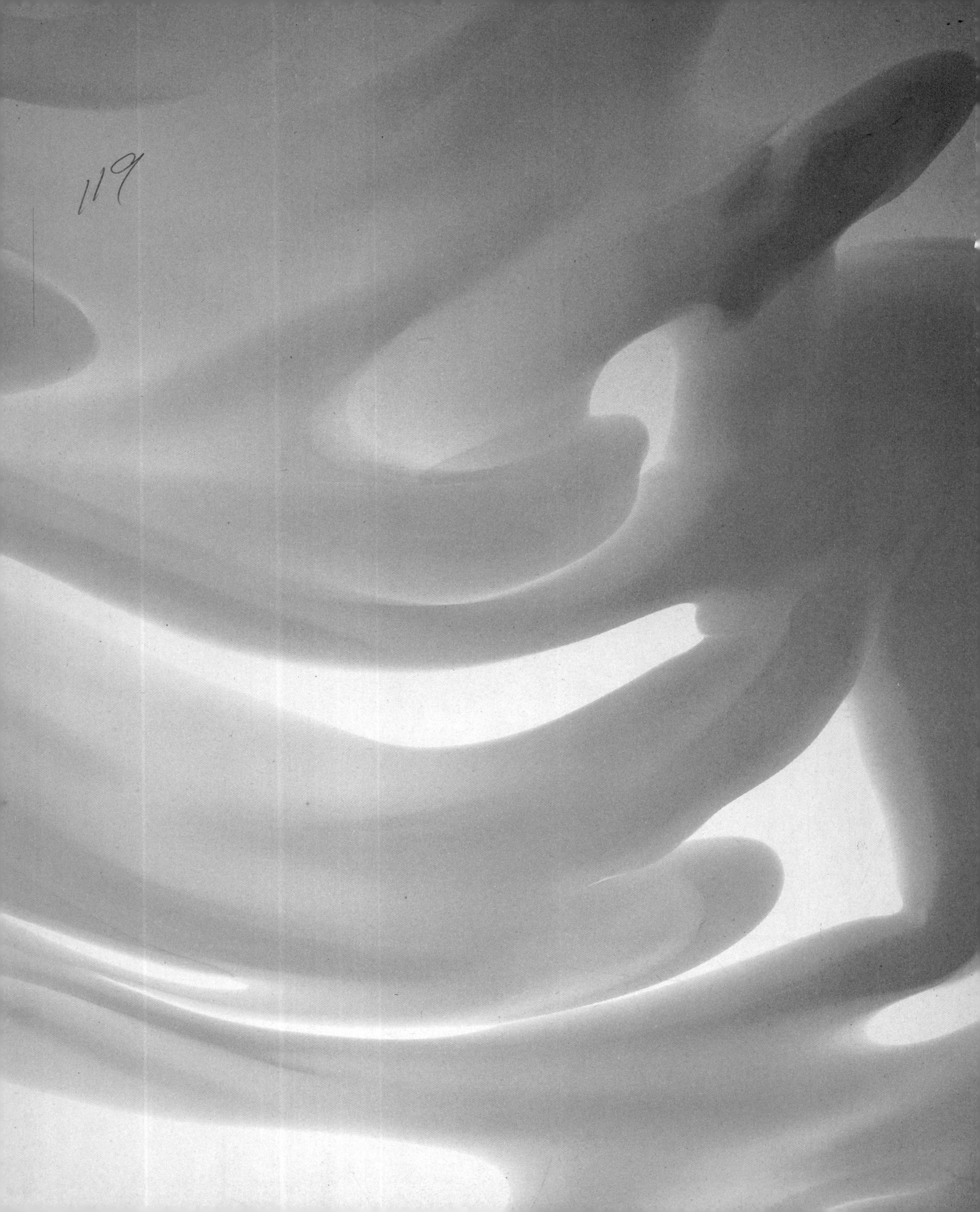